THE KENTUCKY
ADVENTURE

Tracy Campbell

Gibbs Smith, Publisher
Salt Lake City

For Alex and Drew

Published by
Gibbs Smith, Publisher
P.O. Box 667
Layton, UT 84041
800-748-5439
www.gibbs-smith.com/textbooks

Managing Editor: Valerie Thursby Hatch
Editorial Assistants: Jennifer Petersen, Courtney Thomas, Carrie Gibson
Education Editor: Rachel Pike
Photo Editor: Janis Hansen
Cover and Book Design: Alan Connell
Maps and Graphs: Alan Connell

Cover Photo Credit: Adam Jones/www.adamjonesphoto.com

Cover Image: Millcreek Lake, Natural Bridge State Park, Daniel Boone National Forest

Printed and bound in China.
ISBN 10: 1-58685-427-5
ISBN 13: 978-1-58685-427-0

13 12 11 10 09 08 07   10 9 8 7 6 5 4 3 2

ABOUT THE AUTHOR

Tracy Campbell is a professor of history at the University of Kentucky, where he also is Co-Director of the Wendell H. Ford Public Policy Research Center. He is a native Kentuckian who graduated from the University of Kentucky and received his Ph.D. from Duke University. He has written three books that concern Kentucky history, including *Short of the Glory: The Fall and Redemption of Edward F. Prichard, Jr.* (Lexington, 1998), which was nominated for a Pulitzer Prize and was featured on NPR's *Morning Edition*. His latest book is *Deliver the Vote: A History of Election Fraud, an American Political Tradition, 1742-2004* (New York, 2005).

CONTRIBUTORS & REVIEWERS

Thomas Kiffmeyer earned a Ph.D. in American History from the University of Kentucky in 1998 and currently is an associate professor of history at Morehead State University. In 1998, he published "From Self-Help to Sedition: The Appalachian Volunteers in Eastern Kentucky, 1964-1970" in *The Journal of Southern History*. His essay, "Ideology Portrayed in Jacksonian Lexington: Politics, Popular Culture, and Conscious Language," appeared in *The Register of the Kentucky Historical Society* in 2002. Though currently he is completing a book on the War on Poverty in Appalachian Kentucky, he was last seen rummaging around in early nineteenth century Kentucky.

James Duane Bolin is a professor of history at Murray State University. Bolin's publications include *Bossism and Reform in a Southern City: Lexington, Kentucky, 1880-1940* (Lexington, 2000) and *Kentucky Baptists, 1925-2000: A Story of Cooperation* (Brentwood and Nashville, 2000). Bolin graduated from Belmont University with a B.A. in History. He completed M.A. (1982) and Ph.D. (1988) degrees in History from the University of Kentucky. Bolin has won teaching awards at each of the institutions where he has taught, including the Board of Regents Award for Teaching Excellence at Murray State University.

Richard E. Holl is professor of history at Hazard Community and Technical College. Holl earned his Ph.D. at the University of Kentucky. He is a co-author of *Kentucky Through the Centuries*, a book of readings on Kentucky's past. In 2002, he won the Collins Award for best article appearing in *The Register of the Kentucky Historical Society*. Holl has taught Kentucky History for many years.

Dwight "Doc" Holliday is a professor of education at Murray State University. Holliday earned a Ph.D. at University of Southern Mississippi in 1995. He has presented and published several articles on Cooperative Learning and the teaching of social studies in the elementary and middle schools. Holliday has reviewed several books and chapters for publishers on the subject of Introduction to Education.

Contents

Maps & Charts

Portraits

Activities

Becoming Better Readers

Our Amazing Geography

What Do You Think?

Linking the Past to the Present

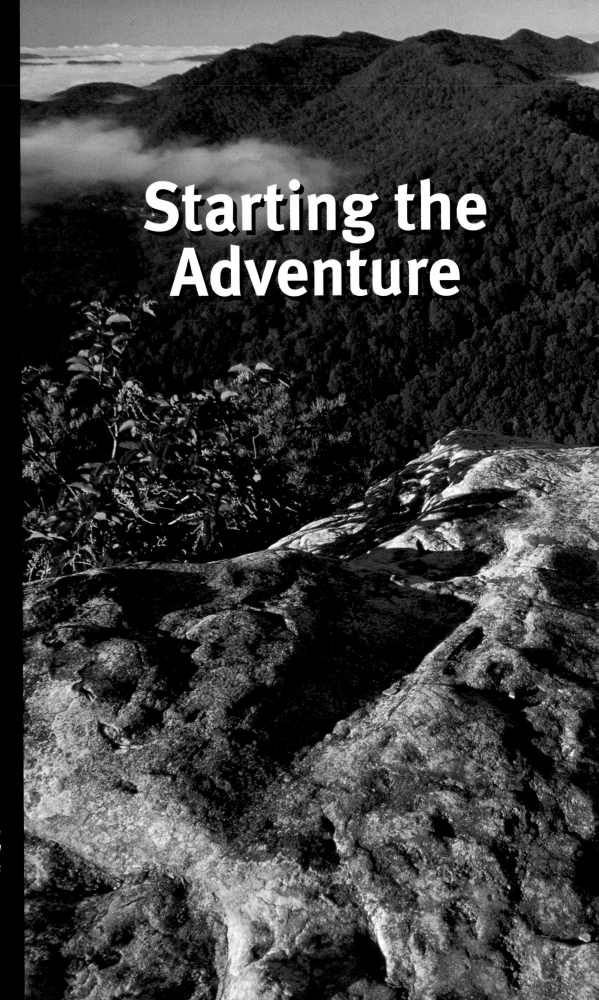

"**U**nited We Stand;
Divided We Fall"
—Kentucky state motto

Starting the Adventure

*Have you ever looked out from
Pinnacle Overlook at Cumberland
Gap National Historic Park? This
is the view from there.*

Chapter 1

Today, you are beginning a journey into Kentucky's past. Learning about history is like a treasure hunt. As you read this book, you will study clues that tell you about the past.

3

Introducing Kentucky

Welcome to *The Kentucky Adventure*! The story of Kentucky is a great one. It is the story of people who lived on the land for thousands of years. It is also the story of people who built a state. They crossed mountains, settled villages and towns, and formed communities and governments. This is their story. It is also your story.

As you read this book, you will learn about your home. You will learn about the ways people have lived here. You will see how our state has changed over time.

These children are playing in the fountains at the riverfront in Henderson.

Our State Symbols

Studying our state symbols is a good way to start learning about our state. A  is something that represents something else. Kentucky has a lot of symbols that help us remember what makes our state special.

Our State Flag

You have probably seen the Kentucky state flag many times. In fact, you may have seen it as you walked into your school building this morning. No other state has a flag like ours. Our flag tells people something about Kentucky. Do you remember what our flag looks like?

The Kentucky state flag is dark blue with the state seal in the middle. The state seal shows two men shaking hands. One is a frontiersman, and one is a statesman. Do you think they are friends?

The words "Commonwealth of Kentucky" also appear on our flag. That is the official name of our state. A *commonwealth* is a state set up "for the common good of all people." Our state motto, "United We Stand; Divided We Fall," also appears on our state flag.

What Do You Think?

Why do you think the state seal shows the men shaking hands? What do you think "the common good" means?

The Kentucky State Seal

Our State Tree

Did you know Kentucky has a state tree? It is the Tulip Poplar. It is also called the Yellow Poplar. The "tulip" name comes from the tree's tulip-shaped blossoms. Tulip Poplars can live for 200 years. Some grow to almost 150 feet high! Do you have a Tulip Poplar in your yard?

Our State Flower

The Kentucky state flower is goldenrod. It is a wildflower that grows in every part of the state. When goldenrod blooms, it turns a bright yellow-gold color. You can see it in the fall along many Kentucky roads. Have you noticed goldenrod growing in your neighborhood?

Our State Bird

The cardinal is the Kentucky state bird. The male is a deep red color with a few touches of black. The female is grayish-brown with streaks of red. Cardinals love to sing. Can you think of any sports teams or businesses named after the cardinal?

Years ago, mansion homes were given names. The mansion Stephen Foster called "My Old Kentucky Home" is actually named Federal Hill.

Our State Song

Kentucky's state song is called "My Old Kentucky Home." There is also a house called "My Old Kentucky Home." John Rowan built it almost 200 years ago. Today, this home is part of a state park in Bardstown.

Our state song was written by a famous songwriter named Stephen Collins Foster. Have you ever heard the song? It is about a slave who has been sold away from Kentucky. The slave longs for his home and family. Here are some of the words:

What do you notice at the bottom of this drawing of Stephen Foster?

The sun shines bright in the old Kentucky home
'Tis summer, the people are gay;
The corn top's ripe and the meadow's in the bloom,
While the birds make music all the day;
The young folks roll on the little cabin floor,
All merry, all happy, and bright,
By'n by hard times comes a-knocking at the door,
Then my old Kentucky home, good night!
Weep no more, my lady,
Oh weep no more today!
We will sing one song for the old Kentucky home,
For my old Kentucky home far away.

What Do You Think

The words to our state song show a change in mood. Can you name the two feelings? Where does the change occur?

● Bardstown

More State Symbols

Did you know Kentucky has a state fish? It is the Kentucky spotted bass. That is a good name for it because it has lots of very dark spots. Even though it isn't very big, the Kentucky spotted bass is strong and tough. It is an excellent fighter.

The state butterfly is the viceroy butterfly. It is dark orange with black veins and white spots. It likes to eat the leaves of our state tree. Do you remember what our state tree is?

The gray squirrel is our state's wild-game animal. Gray squirrels aren't really gray. They are brown, black, and white with a light gray or white belly. Gray squirrels like to eat acorns and walnuts, and they often build their nests in old woodpecker holes. Their bushy tails are very useful. A gray squirrel can use its tail as a blanket, an umbrella, or even as a parachute!

What Do You Think **?**

Why do states choose state symbols? Why do they change?

Viceroy Butterfly

Activity

A New State Flag

Imagine you have been asked to create a new Kentucky state flag. This is a very important job. The new design must represent our state. It should be colorful and have at least three different objects on it.

What do you think Kentuckians would want the rest of the world to know about Kentucky? What do YOU want the rest of the world to know about Kentucky? Draw a new state flag, and then color it.

① MEMORY MASTER

1. Name two things that appear on our state flag.
2. What is the Kentucky state motto?
3. Why is the Yellow Poplar sometimes called the Tulip Poplar?
4. What is the title of our state song?

What Is History?

History is the story of the past. Have you ever read a story about someone who lived long ago? Have you seen old clothes or tools in a museum? Learning about the past is fun—and important. It helps us understand why things are the way they are.

Kentucky has an exciting history, but sometimes it is sad, too. As we learn about our state, we will study events and people from long ago. We will learn how choices made in the past affect our lives today. History is not just the story of "other" people. It is *our* story, and we are still writing it. One day, you may make a choice that a child of the future will read about in a history book!

What Do Historians Do?

Have you ever watched a detective show or played a game with clues? Did you try to solve the mystery before anyone else did? Detectives solve mysteries by studying clues. **Historians** are like detectives, but they study different types of clues. The clues historians study are called **evidence.**

PEOPLE TO KNOW

Thomas D. Clark

WORDS TO UNDERSTAND

artifact
culture
document preservation
evidence
historian
oral history
point of view
primary source
secondary source

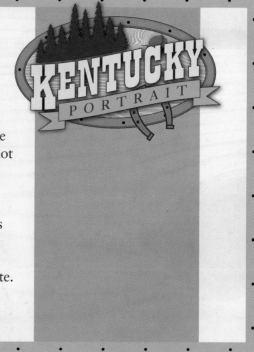

Thomas D. Clark
1903–2005

Have you ever heard of Thomas D. Clark? He was our state historian and wrote more than 30 books about Kentucky.

Clark grew up and went to school in east-central Mississippi. Then he won a scholarship to the University of Kentucky. While in school, he noticed that Kentucky's important records were not being protected properly. He grew very worried.

After finishing his education, Thomas began teaching at the University of Kentucky. He learned that many of Kentucky's historical records had been burned in fires. In the past, soldiers had even used them to light their pipes! Thomas made *document preservation* his life's work.

Thomas lived through almost half of Kentucky's history as a state. He helped protect our important records of the past. In June of 2005, Thomas passed away. He was almost 102 years old.

KENTUCKY PORTRAIT

Primary Sources

One kind of evidence historians study is called a primary source. A *primary source* is something that was made, said, written, or used by someone who was at an event when it happened. Sometimes, it is an eye-witness account.

Diaries and Letters

Have you ever written in a diary? A diary is a book people use to write about things that happen. Historians often read the diaries of people who lived in the past. They also read letters people sent to one another. Letters offer clues about the past. Have you ever written a letter or an email? What would a future historian learn by reading it?

Newspapers

A newspaper is a primary source because it is written and printed during the time the event took place. Historians read old newspapers to learn what was important to people long ago. Today's newspaper tells us what is going on in the world right now. Newspapers did the same thing in the past. Have you ever wondered what happened on the day you were born? You can go to the library and look at a copy of a newspaper printed on or just after the day you were born. If you do that, you will be working like a historian.

Oral History

Have you ever asked anyone, like your parents or grandparents, a question about the past? Did they tell you a story or describe something that happened in their lifetime? The story they told you is called an *oral history*. Oral means it comes from someone's mouth. Historians like to record oral histories so they can listen to them again and again.

18

Artifacts

Lots of things happened before tape recorders or newspapers were invented. Historians want to learn about those things, too, but how can they do it? They can study artifacts! *Artifacts* are things people made or used in the past.

Artifacts can be clothing, cooking utensils, weapons, tools, toys, even garbage. Imagine what a historian of the future might guess about you if he or she found your backpack. What if someone of the future found a CD case or a video game? The historian might learn that we use electricity, listen to music, or have enough free time to play games. Today, we learn about people of the past by studying the artifacts they left behind.

Photographs

A photograph is a primary source because it records what happened at a certain moment in time. To see how things have changed, we can compare old photographs to new photographs. Old photographs tell us about how things used to be.

Things you use every day, like backpacks and CDs, are artifacts.

Activity

Old and New

Look at the two photographs of the racetrack at Churchill Downs below. When do you think they were taken? What do they tell you about the past? How have things changed?

Secondary Sources

Have you or your parents ever bought something at a garage sale? If so, the item was "second hand". That means someone owned it or used it before you did. Now that you know what "second hand" means, can you guess what a *secondary source* is? It is something made, written, said, or used by someone who was not at an event when it happened.

Books and articles that were written by people who were not at the event are secondary sources. This textbook tells about things that happened hundreds or even thousands of years ago. Is it a secondary source?

This drawing shows a covered wagon entering Kentucky through the Cumberland Gap. Do you think there were grocery stores when the settlers first arrived? Can you see why secondary sources are not as correct as primary sources?

Point of View

Different people have different opinions. An opinion is sometimes called a *point of view.*

Point of view has an effect on how history is recorded. Most people form opinions about events. They think the events are right, wrong, or in between. When someone records something about history, his or her opinion affects the record.

To understand point of view, pretend you and your best friend have a fight. When you tell your mom about it, you might not tell it exactly as it happened. You might change the story a little so you don't get into trouble. You might even leave something out! The same thing happens when people record history. The way they feel affects what they write and how they write it.

Another thing that changes how events are recorded is memory. If you didn't tell anyone about the fight for a year or two, do you think you would remember things just the way they happened? As time passes, people forget details. If people don't write about something until long after it happens, the story might not be exactly right.

Culture

Some people think history is only about presidents and wars, but that is not true. History is about all people. To understand our history, we need to learn about **_culture_**. Culture is a word that describes the things that make up our daily lives. The clothes you wear, the foods you eat, the words you use, and the stories you tell are all part of your culture. Culture is everywhere, and it often changes.

Throughout history, Kentucky has been home to many very different cultures. Learning about these cultures is a lot of fun. You will find out that people you thought were very different from you are really a lot like you.

Activity

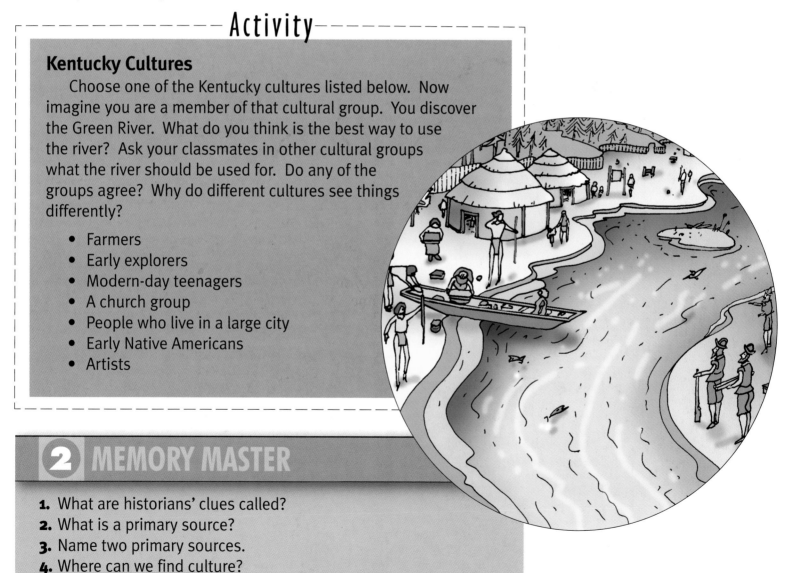

Kentucky Cultures

Choose one of the Kentucky cultures listed below. Now imagine you are a member of that cultural group. You discover the Green River. What do you think is the best way to use the river? Ask your classmates in other cultural groups what the river should be used for. Do any of the groups agree? Why do different cultures see things differently?

- Farmers
- Early explorers
- Modern-day teenagers
- A church group
- People who live in a large city
- Early Native Americans
- Artists

② MEMORY MASTER

1. What are historians' clues called?
2. What is a primary source?
3. Name two primary sources.
4. Where can we find culture?

WORDS TO UNDERSTAND

character
prejudice
stereotype

Character in History

You have read that history is about people and how their choices have shaped our lives. Some people in Kentucky history made good choices and did good things. Some made bad choices and did bad things.

All people have **character.** When we are honest, respectful, or kind, we have good character. When we are dishonest, disrespectful, or rude, we have bad character. In this textbook, we will learn how character shapes who we are and the decisions we make. We will also learn how character—both good and bad—has shaped our state.

Settling in a new place and organizing a new state is a big job. People had to have good character. They had to be responsible and courageous.

Some people in our past did not have good character. They did not show respect for one another. Some were dishonest and did not keep their promises. When that happened, people became angry with one another and argued or fought.

Stereotypes and Prejudice

This textbook is going to tell you how some of the arguments in Kentucky's past first began. You will also learn how stereotypes and prejudices grew. A *stereotype* is a label used to unfairly describe people. *Prejudice* is judging people before you know very much about them.

When you think of Native Americans, do you think of feathers, war cries, and violence? These things are parts of the Native American story, but they are not the most important parts. Most of the time, Native Americans were peaceful. They farmed, raised families, and traded with trappers and explorers. If people believe Native Americans only rode horses and shot arrows, they are wrong. They are stereotyping Native Americans.

When people believe stereotypes, it is often because they are prejudiced. Sometimes, people judge one another by the clothes they wear, the way they talk, or the place they live. This is prejudice. For people to work together successfully, they should not stereotype or be prejudiced. They should try to cooperate and be accepting of different cultures.

What Do You Think ?

Do you think people in other parts of the United States believe stereotypes about Kentuckians? Why? What can be done to change people's opinions?

3 MEMORY MASTER

1. Name three ways to show good character.
2. Name three ways to show bad character.
3. What is a stereotype?
4. What is prejudice?

Chapter 1 Review

What's the Point?

Kentucky's state symbols tell us about our state. History is the story of people of the past. Historians use primary and secondary sources to learn about the past. Kentucky has many cultures. People of character have shaped our state.

Becoming Better Readers: Your Reading Journal

A reading journal is a notebook you can fill with thoughts, ideas, and questions. As you read this textbook, you will often be asked to write in your reading journal. You should use a special notebook that you do not use for other school work. It should only be used for recording your thoughts about Kentucky.

For your first journal entry, write today's date. Then answer this question: Why do you think the author wrote this book? Give three reasons.

Activity

Think Like a Historian

History is not just something that happens in another place. It happens in your life every day. In your home, you are surrounded with artifacts and evidence of your family's, and maybe even Kentucky's, history.

When you go home, begin thinking like a detective. Try to find old photographs, letters, or other things in your closets or basement. Locate three artifacts that tell something about your family's history. When you locate an artifact, ask a parent or grandparent how your family got it. The answer they give you is oral history! See what interesting things you can learn about your family's history.

You Record History

Did you know that what happened ten minutes ago is already part of history? Understanding that, can you remember what happened ten minutes ago in your classroom? What did you see, hear, and feel? Record what you remember, and then share it with the class. What do you notice? Are all the accounts the same? Are they different? Are they correct? Did your location change your point of view?

Comparing Artifacts

Years have passed, and with their grace
Gentler made her gentle face;
Brilliant still the fabrics shine
Of the quilt's antique design,
As she folds it, soft and warm,
Round a fair child's sleeping form.

Lustrous is her lifted gaze
As with half-voice words she prays
That the bright head on that quilt
May not bow in shame or guilt,
And the little feet below
Darksome paths may never know.

—Excerpt from "The Patchwork Quilt"
written by Effie Walker Smith,
an African American woman
from Kentucky who died in 1906

Look at the poem and the quilt. Use your historian skills to answer the following questions about each one:

1. Is each artifact a primary or secondary source? How do you know?
2. How does each show culture?
3. What is each used for?
4. How is each important to Kentucky?

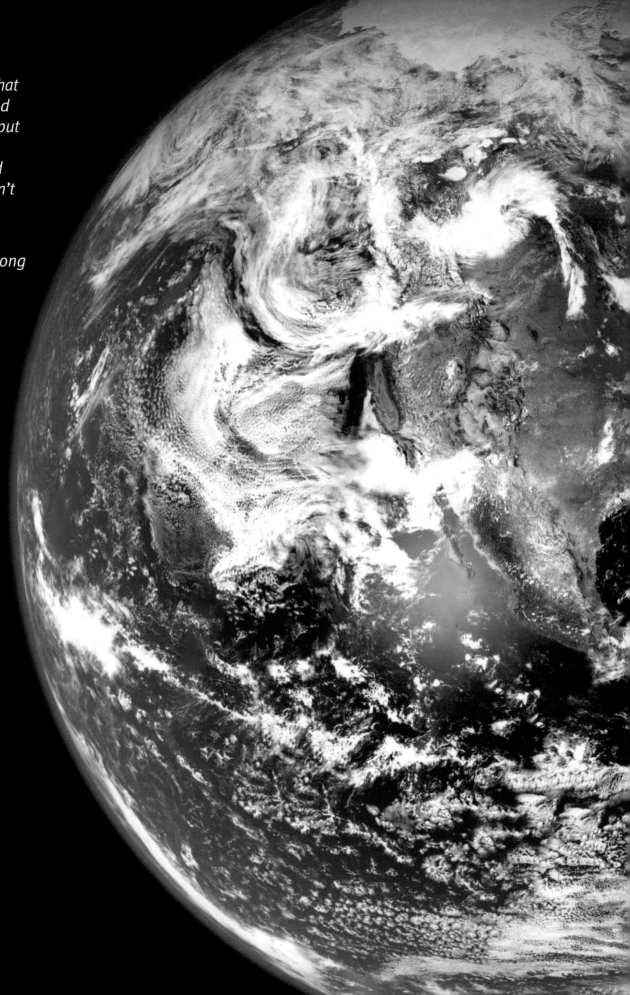

"It suddenly struck me that that tiny pea, pretty and blue, was the Earth. I put up my thumb and shut my eye, and my thumb blotted out the planet Earth. I didn't feel like a giant. I felt very, very small."

—Neil Armstrong

Chapter **2**

As seen from space, Earth looks like a big, blue marble in a black sea of sky. Kentucky is hard to see from so far away. To understand Kentucky, we must look closer. We must find our place in the world and our country.

Kentucky's Place in the World

This is part of the Hensley Settlement in the Cumberland Gap National Historic Park near Middlesboro.

The Kentucky Adventure

The Place We Call Home

Kentucky seems very large to us, but it is only one small part of the world. We live in Kentucky, so it is important to us. It is our home.

In this chapter, we will learn about geography. **Geography** is the study of the land, water, plants, animals, and people of a place. It is also the study of how these things work together. We can study the geography of our state, the United States, or even the world.

People and Places

When we study geography, we begin to see how people and places work together. For example, if you live near water, you could earn a living as a fisherman. But if there is no water near your home, you wouldn't be able to fish. You would have to work in another kind of job.

Weather also affects our lives. Have you ever seen a flood or the damage left by a tornado? If you have, you know how weather affects a place.

Studying geography helps us see why Kentucky is important to people and places across the country and the world. Kentucky has some things other places don't have. That means people in other places depend on our state to supply these special things.

degree
equator
exact location
geography
grid
hemisphere
latitude
longitude
prime meridian
relative location

One of the things that changes people's lives is the place they live.

Locating Places on Earth

On Earth, there are seven very large land masses called continents. They are North America, South America, Europe, Asia, Africa, Australia, and Antarctica. Kentucky is on the continent of North America.

A country is a land region under the control of one government. Our country is called the United States of America. The country of Canada is north of the United States, and the country of Mexico is south of it.

The United States of America has 50 states. Kentucky is one of them. Seven other states touch Kentucky. They are Ohio, West Virginia, Virginia, Tennessee, Missouri, Illinois, and Indiana.

Relative and Exact Location

There are two ways to describe location. One is relative location. *Relative location* tells us where a place is in relation to another place. For example, Kentucky is north of Tennessee and south of Illinois, Indiana, and Ohio.

The other way to describe location is called *exact location.* We use exact location to describe the specific spot where something can be found. When a friend wants to visit your home, you give the friend your address. No other address in your town is exactly like yours. Each address is specific, or exact, for each home. Having an exact location makes it easier for people to find a place.

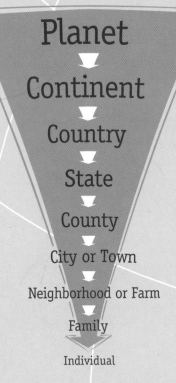

Planet
▼
Continent
▼
Country
▼
State
▼
County
▼
City or Town
▼
Neighborhood or Farm
▼
Family
▼
Individual

Mental Maps

Mental maps are the maps in your mind. They help you remember where things are. You might think maps only show roads and buildings, but that is not true. You know where the rooms in your home are located, right? That means you have a mental map of your home. You also have mental maps of the furniture in your bedroom, the things in your desk, and even the food in your refrigerator.

Draw a mental map of the area surrounding your school. Don't forget to include the parking lot, grassy areas, playground, play equipment, ball fields, and buildings.

The Kentucky Adventure

Where in the World Are We?

1. Our world is the **planet** Earth.

2. Our **continent** is North America.

3. Our **country** is the United States of America.

Illinois
Indiana
Ohio
West Virginia
Missouri
Kentucky
Virginia
Tennessee
Mississippi
Alabama
Georgia

4. Our **state** is Kentucky.

Kentucky's Place in the World

Latitude and Longitude

Latitude and *longitude* lines are another way to describe exact location. These lines are used to describe the location of any place in the whole world. Latitude lines run east and west (side to side). Longitude lines run north and south (up and down). Together, latitude and longitude lines form an invisible **grid** over Earth.

Look at the globe. The latitude line that runs around the middle of Earth is the **equator.** Can you find the longitude line that runs from the North Pole through Greenwich, England and to the South Pole? That line is the *prime meridian.*

Frankfort, our state capital, has a relative location between Lexington and Louisville. Its exact location is 38 degrees latitude and 84 degrees longitude. Can you find Frankfort on a map of our state? Can you find the exact location of your town?

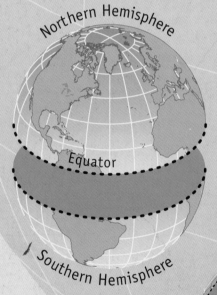

Hemispheres

There is another way to divide Earth so we can find a place. We pretend that Earth is cut in half. We call each half a *hemisphere.*

Look at the picture of the globe to the left. Find the equator. Then find the hemisphere above the equator. It is called the Northern Hemisphere. Find the hemisphere below the equator. It is called the Southern Hemisphere. In which of these hemispheres is Kentucky located?

If Earth was sliced from the North Pole to the South Pole along the prime meridian, it would create a left half and a right half. The left half is called the Western Hemisphere. The right half is called the Eastern Hemisphere. Is Kentucky in the Eastern or Western Hemisphere?

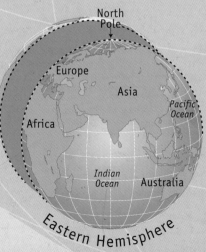

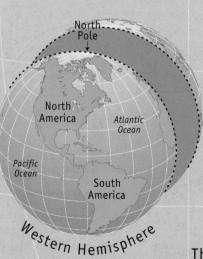

The Kentucky Adventure

Activity

Drawing Lines Around the World

Look at this map of Kentucky. It has lines of latitude and longitude. Here's a way to remember which lines are which:

- **Lat-itude** rhymes with *flat*-itude. Latitude lines lie flat. They run the same direction as the equator and are numbered above and below it.
- **Longitude** lines run up and down, the same direction as the prime meridian. They are numbered to the left and right of it.

Latitude and longitude lines are numbered, and each number has a tiny circle by it. The circle looks like this °. This tiny circle is the symbol for degree. A **degree** is a unit of measure for circles and angles. Study the map below to find the degrees of Kentucky's latitude and longitude lines.

1. The Kentucky-Tennessee border falls between which two degrees north latitude?
2. What is the degree of latitude of the city of Lexington?
3. What is Owensboro's degree of longitude?
4. Which Kentucky town is at about 84° west longitude?
5. Which large city in Kentucky is a little northeast of 38° north latitude and 86° west longitude?

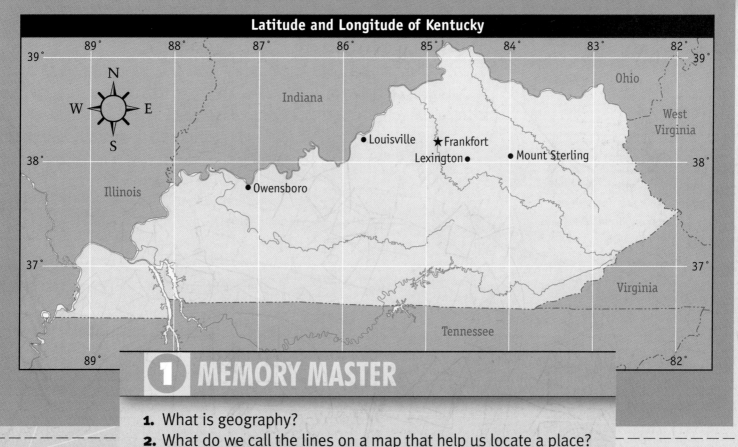

Latitude and Longitude of Kentucky

1 MEMORY MASTER

1. What is geography?
2. What do we call the lines on a map that help us locate a place?
3. What is half of Earth called?
4. What is a degree?

WORDS TO UNDERSTAND

climate
elevation
human feature
natural feature
precipitation

What Do You Think ?

Pretend you have to rename the place where you live with only natural features. What would you name it?

Sometimes places are named for the natural features near them. Do you know of anything named after the Cumberland Gap or the Appalachian Mountains?

Natural and Human Features

Every place is special because it has people and things no other place has. Some of the things that make a place special are natural features, such as climate, landforms, plants, and animals. Other things that make a place special are human features, such as houses, bridges, highways, and shopping malls. Natural features and human features shape every place in the world.

Natural Features

Earth has many kinds of natural features. **Natural features** are things that occur naturally. Mountains and valleys are natural features. Oceans, lakes, ponds, rivers, streams, and even small creeks are, too.

People sometimes use natural features to help describe places. For example, you could tell someone how to find your house by describing natural features. You might say, "To get to my house, you cross the little creek. Then you turn left at the pond. Keep going until you see the big rock with three smaller rocks next to it."

Appalachian**clinic**
WOOTON
care you can trust

Cumberland SeaRay

Climate

Climate is one natural feature of a place. *Climate* is the pattern of weather over a long period of time. Many things affect a place's climate. Some of these things are location, elevation, and precipitation.

Location

One of the things that affects climate is location. If you look at Kentucky on a map or globe, you will see that it is in the middle of North America. It is not very close to the equator, where it is hot all year. It is also far from the North and South Poles, where it is always very cold. Kentucky is in the middle of the continent from east to west. Our central location means we have four seasons: winter, spring, summer, and fall.

Elevation

Elevation also plays a role in climate. *Elevation* is how high the land is above sea level. Places at higher elevations are cooler than places at lower elevations. For example, the winters in Kentucky's mountains are the coldest in the state.

Precipitation

Another thing that affects our climate is the amount of precipitation we get. *Precipitation* is water in the form of rain, sleet, snow, or hail. Kentucky gets enough precipitation that crops and grass grow well here. Our state is often hot, humid, and rainy in the summer and cold and wet in the winter.

This sign has welcomed thousands of visitors to Madisonville. It says the city is the heart of the coal field. Why do you think the people of Madisonville wanted to tell visitors that?

Human Features

People have created many human features on Earth. *Human features* are things people build. They do not appear naturally. Human features are things like roads, homes, schools, railroad tracks, telephone poles, and swimming pools.

Sometimes we use human features to describe places. When we build a university in a city, for example, people will often begin to describe the city as a "college town". What do you think a "railroad town" is? What do you think a "coal town" is?

Planning for Human Features

Builders study a place for a long time before they decide where to build something. They have to know the laws about where buildings can go. They have to think about how the structure will be used. If they were going to build a new school, they might put it near a neighborhood with lots of children. We must consider many factors before we make decisions about where to place things.

2 MEMORY MASTER

1. Name two things that make a place special.
2. What is a natural feature? Name one.
3. Name two things that affect climate.
4. What is a human feature? Name one.

What Are Regions?

The world we live in is very big. One way we can learn about our world is to study smaller parts of it. One smaller part we can study is a region. A **region** is a group of places that have something in common. The things these places have in common may be natural features. For example, there are mountain regions, desert regions, coastal regions, and ocean regions.

A group of places also might be called a region because of similar human features. There are language regions, religious regions, and even housing regions. Some housing regions have homes, and other regions have high-rise apartment buildings.

Regions can be large or small. The entire United States can be a region, or it can be divided into many smaller regions. The map on this page shows our country divided into regions. These regions share common natural features, such as climate and landforms. Which region is Kentucky in?

WORDS TO UNDERSTAND

cash crop
harbor
humid
prairie
region
surveyor
tornado

Regions of the United States

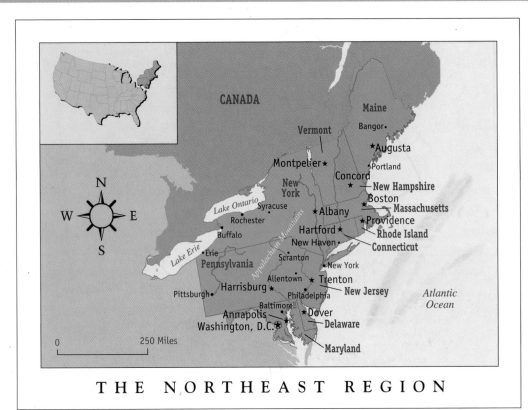

THE NORTHEAST REGION

Natural Features

The Northeast Region is bordered by the Atlantic Ocean, and it has deep, natural harbors. A *harbor* is a protected portion of a body of water. On the coasts of the Northeast, tall grasses grow. Seagulls and other birds soar above the water.

The Northeast has four seasons. In the spring, bright green buds bloom on the ground and in the trees. Then the summers become hot and humid. *Humid* means there is water in the air. High humidity makes the air feel sticky and uncomfortable.

In the fall, trees in the Northeast turn orange, red, yellow, and gold. Then winter comes in cold and wet. Sometimes winter brings ice storms called Nor'easters. These storms coat the streets and sidewalks with a slick layer of ice.

The forests of the Northeast have lots of trees and flowers. In the woods, there are black bears, deer, rabbits, and lots of other animals. The river valleys of the Northeast have rich farmland.

Maine

Connecticut

New Jersey

The Kentucky Adventure

Human Features

Farmers in the Northeast grow corn, apples, peaches, and lots of cranberries. They also raise cows for milk and cheese. Have you ever eaten fish, shrimp, lobster, or crab? If you have, some of it may have been caught in the Atlantic Ocean and shipped to a harbor in the Northeast. Seafood is sent to places all over the nation—even Kentucky!

There is a lot of history in the Northeast, so the region has many historical places to visit. Our nation's capital, Washington D.C., is in this region.

New York City, New York

New Hampshire

The Southeast Region is bordered by the Atlantic Ocean and the Gulf of Mexico. The states in this region are Kentucky, West Virginia, Virginia, Arkansas, Tennessee, North Carolina, South Carolina, Louisiana, Mississippi, Alabama, Georgia, and Florida.

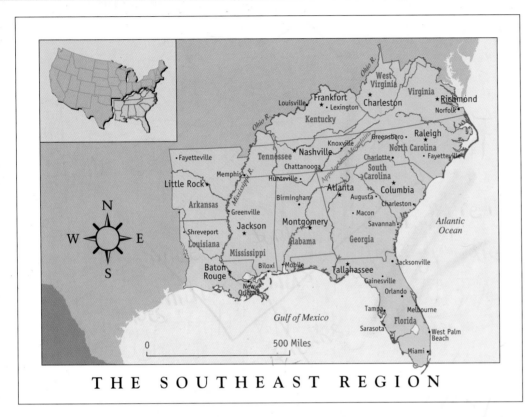

THE SOUTHEAST REGION

In the Southeast, a variety of plants grow. There are pine, birch, walnut, and cypress trees. Kentucky can get lots of snow in the winter, but only a little falls in Florida and Louisiana.

Shrimp, clams, oysters, and fish fill the warm coastal waters. Birds, such as robins, blue jays, and cardinals, come to the Southeast to escape the cold winters in the North. Alligators, snakes, deer, rabbits, and squirrels also live in the Southeast.

What Do You Think?

All states have a certain shape. Kentucky's shape is a little odd because part of it is straight, and part of it is jagged. Why is so much of our border jagged?

Natural Features

The Southeast Region has low mountains and rolling hills. It also has plains, coastlines, and harbors. The great Appalachian Mountains extend from Canada all the way into Alabama. Some of the Appalachian Mountains are in Kentucky. Have you ever visited them?

South Carolina

Tennessee

Miami, Florida

Human Features

People like to travel to the Southeast to visit exciting cities, such as Orlando, New Orleans, Nashville, Atlanta, and Louisville.

Farming is very important in the Southeast. *Cash crops,* such as tobacco, rice, cotton, sugar, fruit, and nuts, thrive in the warm, humid climate.

Another reason people enjoy the Southeast is because of the music. Jazz, Kentucky Bluegrass, blues, country-western, and even rock-n-roll all began in this region. When people think about these styles of music, they often think about the Southeast.

Louisiana

Sanford Duncan's Wedge

Look at the southern border of Kentucky. Can you see the small dip in the border just south of Franklin? That dip exists because a man named Sanford Duncan did not want to live in Tennessee.

In 1830, *surveyors* marked the boundary between Kentucky and Tennessee. Mr. Duncan found that his farm was actually on the Tennessee side of the border. He did not want that, so he paid the surveyors to make a dip in the line to include his farm in Kentucky. That is why that tiny wedge is still there today!

Duncan's Wedge

N W E S

Franklin

Life in the Midwest

The Midwest Region is right in the middle of the United States. The states in this region are North Dakota, South Dakota, Nebraska, Kansas, Minnesota, Iowa, Missouri, Wisconsin, Illinois, Michigan, Indiana, and Ohio. Because it is in the middle of the country, the Midwest is often called "America's Heartland."

THE MIDWEST REGION

Midwest has hot, humid weather that sometimes produces tornadoes. **Tornadoes** are powerful funnel-shaped wind storms that drop out of the clouds and onto the ground.

Much of the Midwest used to be prairie land. A *prairie* is a wide, grassy area with few trees. Prairie animals, such as deer, prairie dogs, and rabbits, scampered across the ground while hawks, owls, and eagles hunted from the sky. Many years ago, thousands of buffalo grazed on the prairies of the Midwest. Now there is very little prairie left.

Natural Features

The Midwest Region is very flat, so it is called the Great Plains. The region has four distinct seasons. The Great Plains can be very cold in the winter. Snowstorms with strong winds, called blizzards, sometimes blow across the plains. In the summer, the

Human Features

Most of the Midwest is ranch and farmland, but there are large cities, too. Some of these cities are Chicago, St. Louis, Omaha,

Iowa

North Dakota

Kansas

and Indianapolis. Have you heard of these places?

Midwestern farms produce corn, wheat, soybeans, and many other crops. The region's ranchers raise cattle, hogs, and chickens. Because the Midwest produces so many kinds of grain and food, it has been called the "Bread Basket of the World."

What Do You Think ?

What would happen to the region, the country, and the world if a bad tornado season hit the Midwest?

Chicago, Illinois

Missouri

Life in the West

The Western Region is bordered by Canada, Mexico, and the Pacific Ocean and includes the Pacific Coast and Rocky Mountain states. The states in this region are Washington, Oregon, Montana, Idaho, Wyoming, California, Nevada, Utah, Colorado, Alaska, and Hawaii.

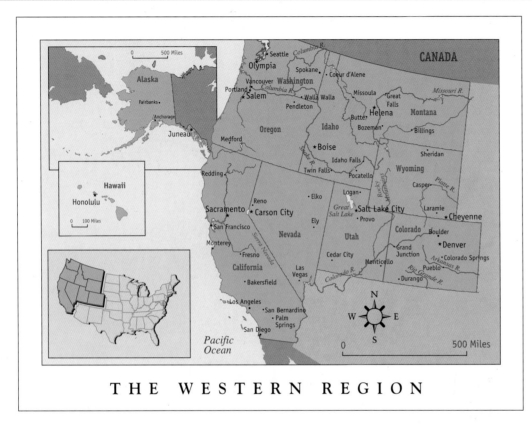

THE WESTERN REGION

The West also contains the Rocky Mountains, which is the longest mountain range in the United States, and the Sierra Nevada Range. Between these two giant mountain ranges is a large area called the Great Basin. In the Great Basin, the sun shines a lot, and there is very little rain. The Great Basin Desert is the largest desert in the United States. It is home to lizards, snakes, and prickly cactus.

The Pacific Ocean is home to whales, dolphins, sea lions, crabs, and many kinds of fish.

Natural Features

The states along the Western Region's northern Pacific Coast receive a lot of rain. The shorelines are rocky and beautiful. This region has large forests filled with redwood, pine, spruce, and oak trees. Some of the largest trees in the world grow in these forests.

Human Features

There are many large cities in the West. Some of them are Seattle, Portland, Los Angeles, San Francisco, Las Vegas, Salt Lake City, and Denver.

Oregon

Utah

San Francisco, California

Outside the cities, western farmers grow fruits and vegetables, such as apples, grapes, strawberries, lettuce, and cucumbers.

Many people in the West love to fish. In the rivers of the Great Basin, they fish for bass, trout, and salmon. People in the West also enjoy outdoor sports, such as skiing, snowboarding, mountain biking, hiking, and rock climbing. They like to camp in Yellowstone National Park.

The Pacific Coast of Southern California is one of the most popular vacation spots in the world. People love to surf, swim, or shop there.

Alaska and Hawaii

Did you know that Alaska and Hawaii are Pacific Coast states? Alaska is the largest state in the United States. In fact, it is almost twice the size of Texas! Alaska is cold most of the year and home to the tallest mountain in North America, Mt. McKinley. People come to Alaska to fish and hike. Did you know Alaska has more elk, bears, and walruses than people?

Hawaii is a group of small islands in the Pacific Ocean. These islands don't have seasons. Instead, the sun shines, and the air is warm all year long. Hawaii's rich soil and warm climate make it a perfect place to grow coffee, sugar, and pineapples. Many people go to Hawaii on vacation. They visit the ocean, walk along the sandy beaches, hike in the mountains, and explore the volcanoes.

Life in the Southwest

The Southwest Region is bordered by the Western Region, the Southeastern Region, the Gulf of Mexico, and Mexico. The states in this region are Arizona, New Mexico, Texas, and Oklahoma.

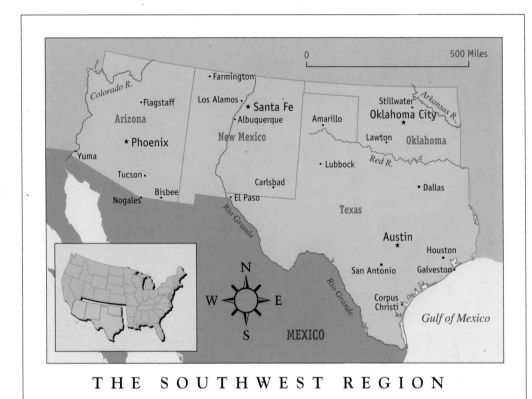

THE SOUTHWEST REGION

The Southwest has a lot of sagebrush and cactus. In the spring, bright flowers bloom. If you look closely, you might find an owl, a lizard, a roadrunner, or a desert tortoise. You should also watch out for rattlesnakes!

Aspen and pine trees cover the mountains, and moose, elk, and deer wander through the woods. In some places, there are mountain lions, bears, and bighorn sheep. The Southwest's streams are full of fish.

Human Features

Many people like to visit the Southwest, especially large cities such as Phoenix, Dallas, and Santa Fe. They also like to visit the beaches, hotels, and restaurants along the Gulf of Mexico.

The Southwest has rich copper and oil resources, so

Natural Features

The Southwest Region has high mountains, flat plains, and low deserts. In the desert, the land and air are very dry. There are only a few lakes and rivers.

The sun shines hot all year round, but the mountains are much cooler than the deserts. The vast Grand Canyon in the Southwest is one of the natural wonders of the world.

New Mexico

Texas

Arizona

Oklahoma

mining is big business. Cattle ranching and farming are also important.

The Southwest has a warm climate that many people enjoy. For this reason, some families are moving to the Southwest. It is one of the fastest-growing regions in the United States.

What Do You Think ?

Temperatures in the summer often soar over 100 degrees. Do you think the Southwest would keep growing quickly if there was no air conditioning?

Dallas, Texas

③ MEMORY MASTER

1. What is a harbor used for?
2. Name two human features in the Southeast.
3. What two mountain ranges lie in the West?
4. Which region is the Grand Canyon in?

Chapter 2 Review

What's the Point?

Geography is the study of the land, water, plants, animals, and people of a place. Places have natural and human features. The United States has five land regions: the Northeast, the Southeast, the Midwest, the West, and the Southwest. All U.S. regions have both natural and human features.

Becoming Better Readers: That's a Surprise!

In your reading journal, write about something from this chapter that surprised you. Explain why it surprised you. It may be something about geography, Kentucky, or any of the regions in the United States.

Our Amazing Geography: Regions All Around Us

Think about your school. Does it have its own regions? It probably has a gym and a playground. It has an area where you can eat. It has rooms where you sit at desks and learn. You do certain things in each region of your school.

What kinds of regions are in your home? You probably have a region for sleeping, a region for bathing, a region for eating, and maybe even a region for reading or watching television. Make a map of your home. On the map, show what kinds of activities take place in each region of your home.

Activity

Giving Direction

In groups, take turns describing where you live. Give directions using relative and exact locations. Have other group members identify which type of directions you are giving, relative or exact. Is one easier to use and understand than the other?

"Sarah" Island

Imagine you were given your very own island. What would you name your island? Would you give it your name? What would you want on your island? Would you want a water slide? How about a roller coaster? What natural features will your island have? Will it have hills, mountains, or rivers?

Draw a map of your island. Write the island's name at the top of the page. Your island needs roads and a place for you to live. You need a place to attend school and a place to shop for the things you need. Your family will need money, so your island must also have at least one place for a family member to work. If you want, you can include railroad tracks, churches, hotels, farms, factories, restaurants, and a police and fire station.

Try to make good decisions about where to place things on your island. Your school should be close to your home. Where should you put the fire station? Remember, if there's a fire, the firefighters need to get to the fire as fast as they can.

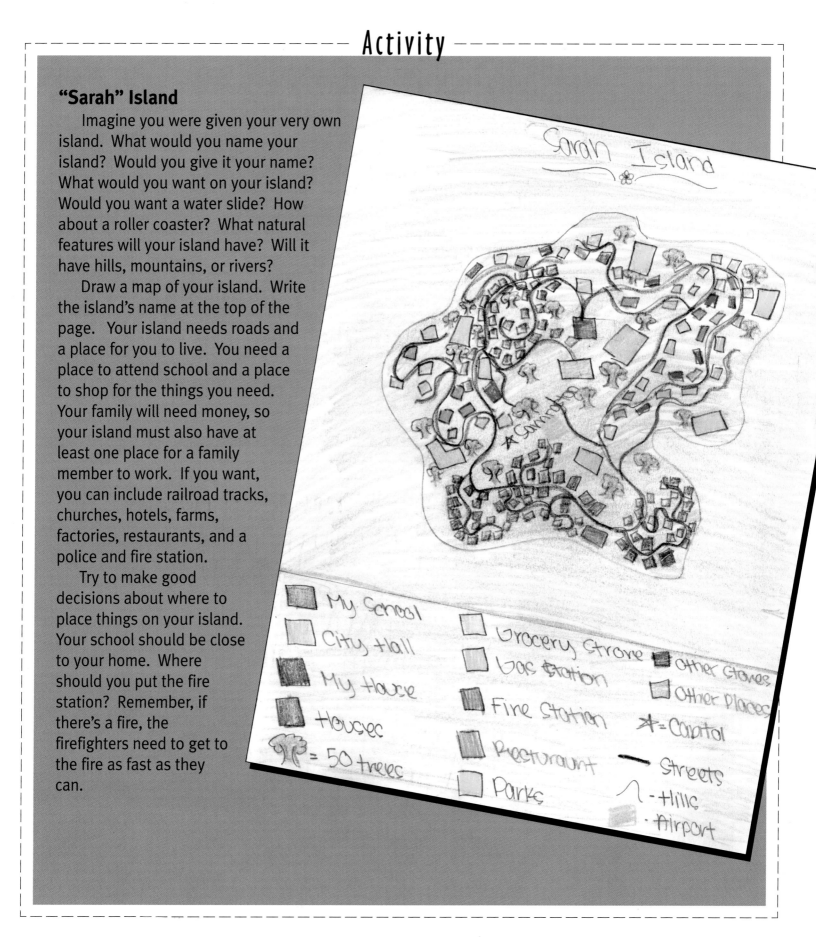

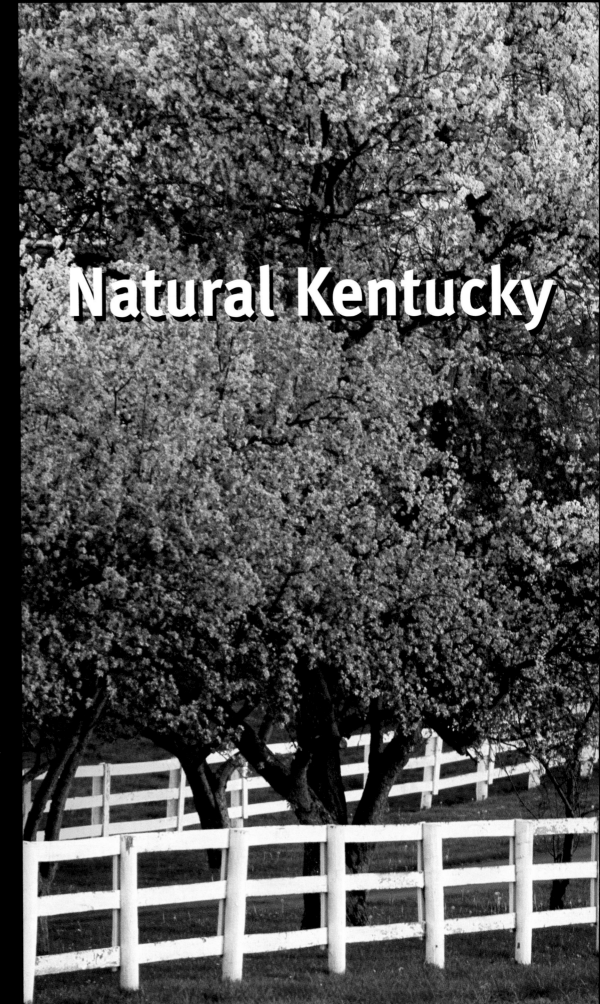

"*It appeared that nature, in . . . her bounty, had spread a feast for all that lives, both for the animal and the . . . world.*"

—*Felix Walker, 1775*

Natural Kentucky

These flowering crab apple trees are on the grounds at Manchester Farms, one of the most famous horse farms in the world.

Chapter 3

It seems like the land around us always stays the same. Actually, our land is always changing. Kentucky did not always look like it does today. It took a very long time for our state to change, and it is still changing right now.

The beautiful Cumberland River
is one of the most popular
places to visit in Kentucky.

The Land Takes Shape

Geologists know that long ago the land in Kentucky was very different from what it is today. *Geologists* are scientists who study the soil and rocks to see how Earth was formed. They study how water, wind, and weather change the land. They predict how the land will change in the future. Though the land is always changing, it is happening so slowly we don't notice.

Under Water

Did you know that Kentucky was once completely covered by water? All natural water contains sediment. *Sediment* is tiny bits of dirt and sand carried in the water. These tiny bits sink to the bottom of the water and form a layer over whatever is lying there. As sediment piles up, plants and the bodies of dead sea creatures become trapped between the layers. Many clues to our past are buried in layers of sediment. Geologists study sediment to learn about Kentucky's past.

Have you ever traveled on Interstate 64? Around Lexington and Frankfort, you can see huge walls of limestone. *Limestone* is a soft, white rock that formed from sediment during the millions of years Kentucky was under water. Limestone is found in much of the state. This rock feeds the soil and makes it rich with minerals.

In some areas, the sediment didn't change into limestone. It changed into coal. In other areas, the sediment was very soft and formed karst. *Karst* is a type of limestone that dissolves easily. Over millions of years, karst washed away under pressure and formed underground holes. We call these holes caves. There are many large caves in Kentucky.

Even though it is millions of years old, the Mammoth Cave is considered "young". This is one of its few rock formations.

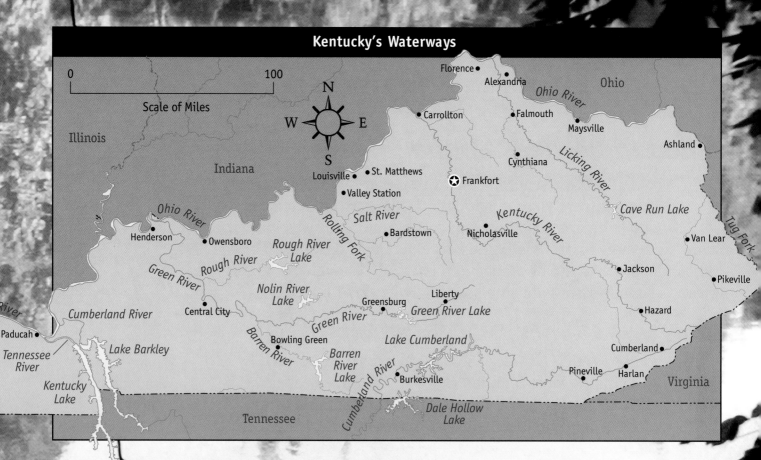

Kentucky's Waterways

The Power of Water

Water is very important to our lives. We drink it, bathe in it, and even swim and splash in it. Living things cannot survive without water. Since we must have water, people built homes and towns near our state's lakes and rivers. The water attracted animals that people hunted, too. Look at all the towns or cities that are near water.

Rivers

You have probably seen at least one river in our state. Kentucky has many rivers. For years, boats have traveled along our rivers to move supplies and crops. We also use our rivers for drinking water, to *irrigate* (supply water to) dry land, to fish, and to make electricity. Kentucky's biggest rivers are the Ohio, Kentucky, Green, Licking, and Mississippi Rivers. Do you live near one of these great rivers?

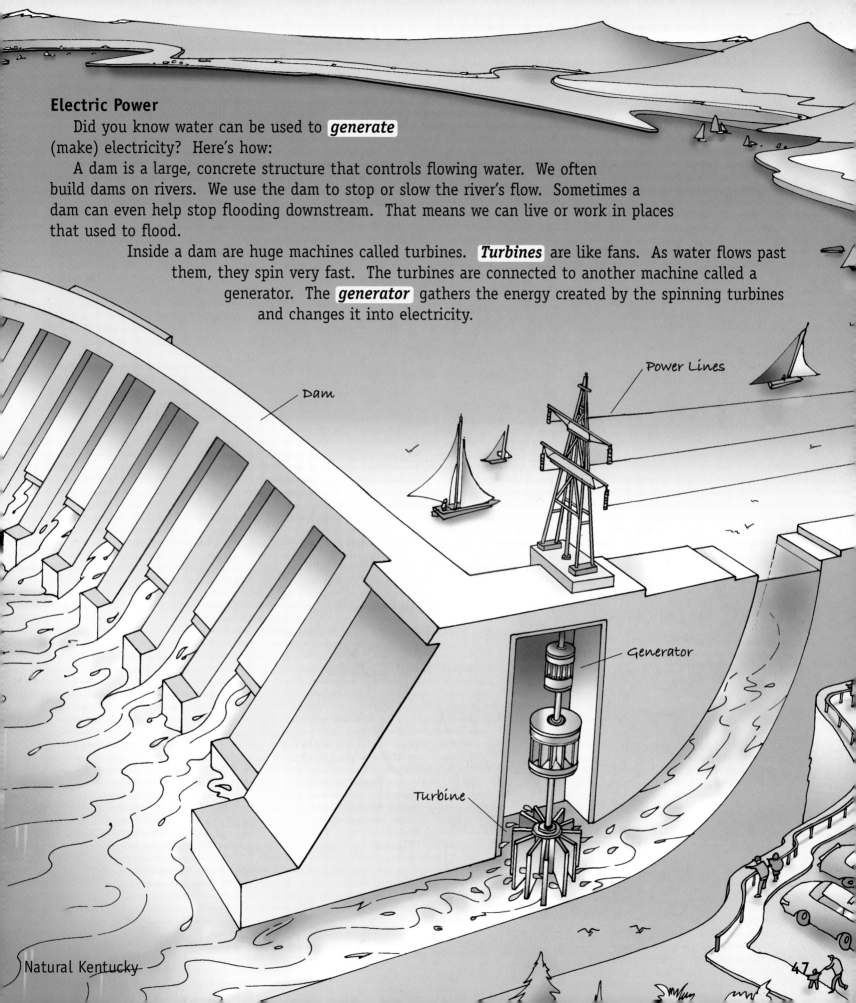

Electric Power

Did you know water can be used to **generate** (make) electricity? Here's how:

A dam is a large, concrete structure that controls flowing water. We often build dams on rivers. We use the dam to stop or slow the river's flow. Sometimes a dam can even help stop flooding downstream. That means we can live or work in places that used to flood.

Inside a dam are huge machines called turbines. **Turbines** are like fans. As water flows past them, they spin very fast. The turbines are connected to another machine called a generator. The **generator** gathers the energy created by the spinning turbines and changes it into electricity.

Dam

Power Lines

Generator

Turbine

Natural Kentucky

This is the Land Between the Lakes. The lakes on both sides of this region are man-made.

Lakes

There are also many lakes in Kentucky. There are big lakes, like Cumberland, Cave Run, and Taylorsville Lakes. And there are small lakes. Have you ever visited a lake in Kentucky?

Some of our lakes are natural lakes. That means they were formed naturally as the land changed over thousands of years. Other lakes are man-made. *Man-made* lakes were created by people. They are used for controlling floods, producing electricity, and just having fun.

What Do You Think ⁇

Can you think of two ways lakes help people? Can you think of two fun uses for lakes?

Floods

At one time or another, most parts of Kentucky have experienced flooding. When rain falls, it fills our rivers and streams. Usually, that is a good thing because we need lots of water. But when rain falls for days and days, the water rises and spills over the sides. This spilling water is called a flood.

Flood waters spread all across the land. They carry diseases and can do a lot of

Do you think it was safe for this horse to drink the flood water?

damage. Sometimes flood waters reach farms and ruin the crops. Other times, the water gets into homes and buildings. If the water is deep and rushing fast, it can wash buildings away. Sometimes people get hurt. Other times, people are safe, but they lose everything they have. Have you ever seen a flood?

Floodwalls and Levees

One way people stop floods is by building floodwalls. *Floodwalls* are concrete walls built around towns and cities to keep flood waters out. The water hits the walls, so the people, roads, and buildings in the cities are safe. Frankfort, Paducah, Newport, Covington, and Pineville all have floodwalls.

Another way to control floods is to build levees. *Levees* are high mounds of earth (or concrete) built in strips along either side of a river or stream. Levees help the water in flooding rivers stay in the river channels.

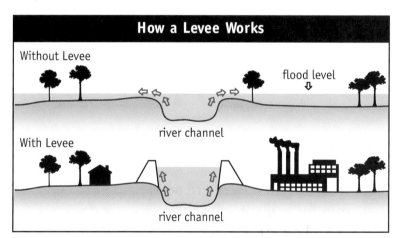

How a Levee Works

Without Levee

flood level

river channel

With Levee

river channel

1 MEMORY MASTER

1. Why do geologists study sediment?
2. Name three ways people use water.
3. What is a turbine?
4. Describe two ways to control floods.

This floodwall is at the end of Broadway in Paducah.

PEOPLE TO KNOW

Stephen Bishop
Andrew Jackson

PLACES TO LOCATE

The Bluegrass
The Eastern Coal Field
The Jackson Purchase
Land Between the Lakes
Mammoth Cave
The Pennyroyal
The Western Coal Field

WORDS TO UNDERSTAND

adapt
county seat
electric-generating plant
moonbow
mountaintop removal
port
reclaim
reclamation fee
strip mining

Kentucky Land Regions

You read in Chapter 2 that the United States has many regions. Kentucky has regions, too. In this chapter, we will explore our state's land regions. A land region is an area that has similar landforms.

Over time, people have adapted to the land regions they live in. To *adapt* means to change something so it works better or fits better. For example, we adapt to changes in the weather. When the weather is warm and dry, we adapt by wearing shorts and t-shirts. When the weather is cold and wet, we adapt by wearing warm coats and using umbrellas.

As we study Kentucky's land regions, we will see how people have adapted. We will learn about the ways people in each region live, work, and play. We will see how life in each region is shaped by nature.

INDIANA

ILLINOIS

Henderson

Owensboro

Sturgis

Western Coalfield

Leitchfield

Beaver Dam

Madisonville

Central City

Princeton

Paducah

Bowling Green

Jackson Purchase

Benton

Hopkinsville

Russellville

MISSOURI

Mayfield

Scottsville

Franklin

Murray

TENNESSEE

Fulton

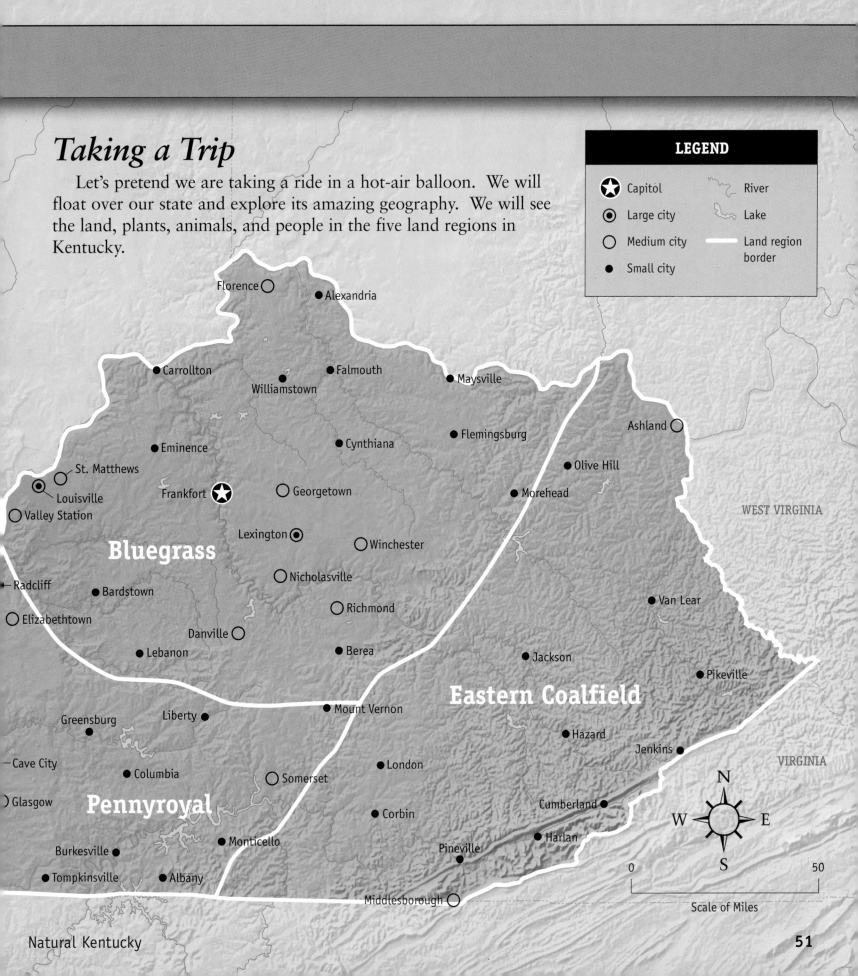

Taking a Trip

Let's pretend we are taking a ride in a hot-air balloon. We will float over our state and explore its amazing geography. We will see the land, plants, animals, and people in the five land regions in Kentucky.

LEGEND

- ⭐ Capitol
- ◉ Large city
- ○ Medium city
- ● Small city
- River
- Lake
- —— Land region border

Florence ○
● Alexandria
● Carrollton
Williamstown ●
● Falmouth
● Maysville
Ashland ◉
● Eminence
● Cynthiana
● Flemingsburg
St. Matthews ○
● Olive Hill
◉ Louisville
Frankfort ⭐
Georgetown ○
● Morehead

WEST VIRGINIA

○ Valley Station

Bluegrass

Lexington ◉
Winchester ○

Radcliff
● Bardstown
Nicholasville ○
● Van Lear

○ Elizabethtown
Richmond ○

Danville ○
● Berea
Jackson ●
● Pikeville

● Lebanon

Eastern Coalfield

Greensburg ●
Liberty ●
● Mount Vernon
● Hazard
Jenkins ●

VIRGINIA

Cave City
● Columbia
Somerset ○
● London
Cumberland ●

) Glasgow

Pennyroyal
● Corbin
● Harlan

Burkesville ●
● Monticello
Pineville ●

● Tompkinsville
● Albany

N
W E
S

0 ————— 50

Middlesborough ○

Scale of Miles

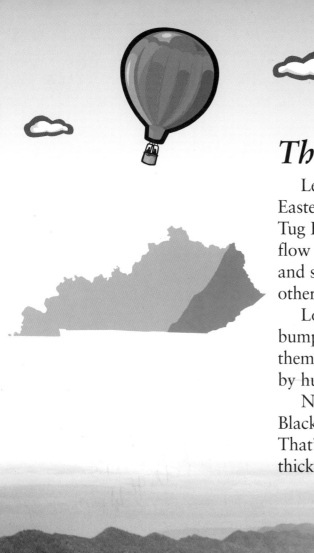

The Eastern Coal Field

Let's begin our balloon ride in the Eastern Coal Field. The Eastern Coal Field is partly bordered by the Ohio, Big Sandy, and Tug Fork Rivers. The Cumberland, Kentucky, and Licking Rivers flow through this region, too. Do you see all the mountains, rivers, and streams? There are more mountains in this region than in any other part of the state.

Look straight ahead! We need to float a little higher so we don't bump into the Appalachian Mountains. What is that deep notch in them? It's the Cumberland Gap, a pass through the mountains used by hunters, explorers, settlers, and animals.

Now we're sailing over the highest point in Kentucky. It's the Big Black Mountain in Harlan County. It stands over 4,000 feet high. That's more than 13 football fields stacked end to end! Look at the thick forests and beautiful trees here, too. The entire region was

The Cumberland Gap

once a great hardwood forest. Today, there are not as many trees as there used to be, but there are still many sawmills. Logging is important in this region.

Think about this region's name. What do you think lies beneath the ground here? If you guessed coal, you were right! Coal is a dark black mineral. From way up here in our balloon, we cannot see the coal under the ground, but we know it's there. Have you ever seen coal? People burn it to produce electricity. Over the years, workers have mined millions of tons of coal from this region.

Cumberland Falls

Cumberland Falls is one of the largest waterfalls in the United States. When the river is at its highest, water drops more than 65 feet into a deep canyon! Cumberland Falls is sometimes called the "Niagara of the South" because its 125-foot wide curtain of water is like Niagara Falls in New York. Over the centuries, the falling water has carved a valley 400 feet deep in the highlands of this region.

One of the most amazing things about Cumberland Falls is the moonbow. A **moonbow** is a special rainbow that appears only at night. It is created when the mist above the falls reflects the moonlight. The moonbow at Cumberland Falls is the only one in the Western Hemisphere. People from all over the world come to see it.

You cannot see the moonbow at Cumberland Falls every night. It only happens when the weather is clear, and the moon is at a certain place in the sky. Have you ever been to Cumberland Falls and seen the moonbow?

The falls in the daylight

The moonbow

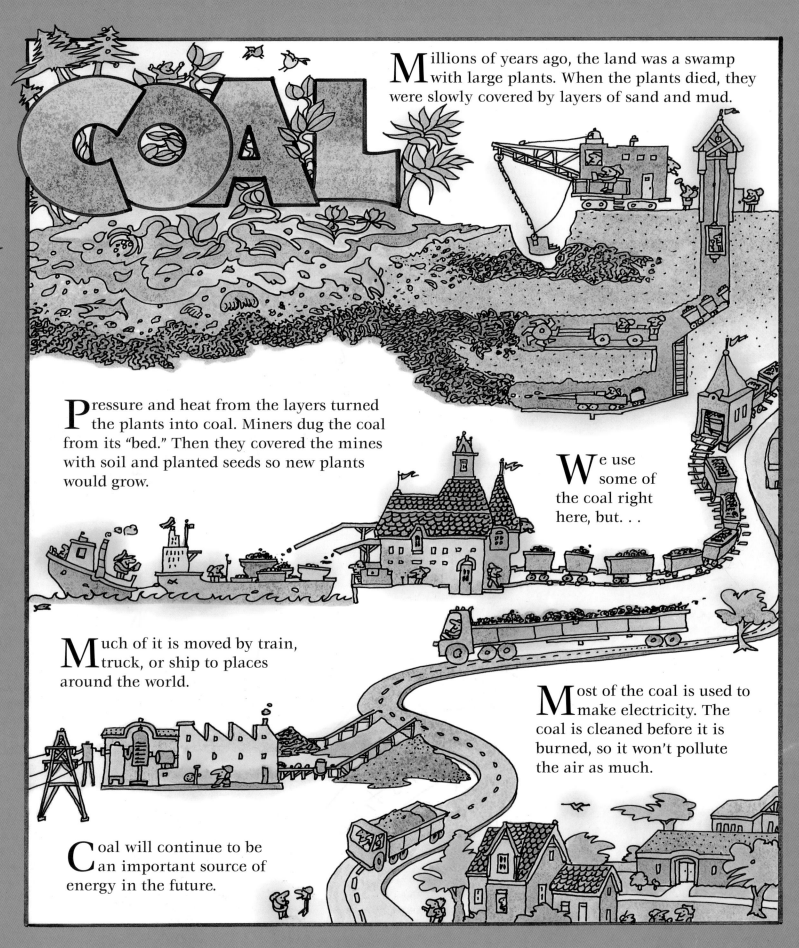

COAL

Millions of years ago, the land was a swamp with large plants. When the plants died, they were slowly covered by layers of sand and mud.

Pressure and heat from the layers turned the plants into coal. Miners dug the coal from its "bed." Then they covered the mines with soil and planted seeds so new plants would grow.

We use some of the coal right here, but. . .

Much of it is moved by train, truck, or ship to places around the world.

Most of the coal is used to make electricity. The coal is cleaned before it is burned, so it won't pollute the air as much.

Coal will continue to be an important source of energy in the future.

Coal

Coal is one of Kentucky's most valuable resources. In fact, only one state produces more coal than our state does. Do you know which state that is? It's Wyoming. Much of the coal produced in Kentucky comes from the Eastern Coal Field.

Natural Kentucky

The Bluegrass

Now we're entering the Bluegrass Region. The two largest cities in Kentucky, Louisville and Lexington, are in this region. As you look out across the land, you can see the grass is not really blue. "Bluegrass" is just a type of a grass that was planted here many years ago. Our state's nickname is "The Bluegrass State".

Look at the gently rolling hills and large, beautiful horse farms. Can you hear the horses whinnying as they graze on the thick, green grass? Horses are very important in the Bluegrass. People from all over the world go to Churchill Downs in Louisville and Keeneland in Lexington to watch horse races.

As we float above the farms, can you smell the fresh-cut hay? This region has some of the finest farmland in the state. Look over there! You can see the cornstalks reaching for the sun and the wheat fields swaying in the warm Kentucky breeze. Just below us now are great fields of tobacco. Tobacco is the major crop in this region.

Have you ever visited a horse farm like this one in the Bluegrass?

Can you see the burley tobacco warehouses? They are built close to the fields so farmers don't have to transport the tobacco very far.

What is that sound? If you listen closely, you can hear rushing water. Can you spot where it's coming from? There it is! It's the Kentucky River flowing through the Kentucky River Gorge, a deep, narrow valley. What is that other sound? It's a train crossing the river on High Bridge! The bridge is very high above the ground. Do you think it would be scary to ride in a train across High Bridge?

Up ahead is Frankfort, our state capital. Just below us is the state capitol building. You can see the building's tall dome. Look up ahead. It's a very large city. Do you know which one it is? If you guessed Louisville, you were right! Many people live in these large cities. In fact, half of all the people in Kentucky live in the Bluegrass.

High Bridge was built in 1877. At the time, it was the highest railroad bridge in the world.

Tall buildings in Louisville light up the night along the Ohio River.

As you look at this picture, imagine you are at Churchill Downs. You can feel the ground shaking as the horses speed around the track. You can hear the pounding of their hooves and the shouts of excited fans. Can you smell the excitement in the air?

The Kentucky Derby in Louisville is the most celebrated horse race in America. Each year on the first Saturday in May, thousands of people pack the stands at Churchill Downs to watch the "Greatest Two Minutes in Sports". These fans include important leaders, famous stars, and many other people— just like you!

The Kentucky Derby is especially important to the people of Louisville. The entire city begins celebrating with decorations and parties two weeks before the race takes place. At Derby time, you can watch a parade, compete in a hot-air balloon or steamboat race, go square dancing, attend a concert, or watch fireworks.

The most exciting part of the celebration is the race itself. Did you know the Kentucky Derby is also called "The Run for the Roses"? That is because race officials decorate the winning horse with roses. Have you ever been to the Derby or watched it on television? It is such a famous event that people all over the United States throw parties and have fun on Kentucky Derby Day!

This is jockey Mike Smith after Giacomo won the Kentucky Derby in 2005.

The Western Coal Field

Now we're heading into the Western Coal Field. Like the Eastern Coal Field, this region is named for the huge amounts of coal that lie under the ground. From our balloon, you can see that the Western Coal Field is much flatter than the Eastern Coal Field.

The flatter land makes this region a good place for farming. Look at all the farms. Can you hear the hogs snorting and the cows mooing? Do you think they can see us up here in our balloon?

The Western Coal Field is bordered on the north by the Ohio River. Below us now is the city of Owensboro. It is one of the largest cities in the region. Can you see the boats gathered around the dock? Owensboro is a port city. A *port* is a place on a shore where boats pick up or drop off goods. As we keep sailing, we can see Henderson. It is a port city, too. Many of the things we buy probably came to Kentucky on a boat.

As we travel south, the rolling hills become steeper. Look up ahead. What is that big factory? Look at the wires and cables coming from it. Can you see all those trucks full of coal driving toward the factory? There are also many empty trucks driving away. What is going on there? Now that we're a little closer, we can see this is the *electric-generating plant* at Paradise. It is a place where coal is turned into power. Almost all of the electric power used in Kentucky comes from electric-generating plants like this one.

Owensboro is the third largest city in Kentucky.

The Kentucky Adventure

This is one of many strip mining sites on Black Mountain, near Harlan.

Strip Mining

People have different ideas about how to use land. In Kentucky, people have argued for years about coal mining. With large earth-moving machines, workers remove whole mountaintops to get to the coal faster. This is called **strip mining,** or **mountaintop removal.**

After an area is stripped, the government often helps the coal companies **reclaim,** or restore, the land. For every ton of coal taken from the ground, the coal companies pay a **reclamation fee.** Sometimes, the government uses money from the fees to build homes or businesses on the stripped land. But in areas that have not been reclaimed, the land looks barren and empty.

Many people are not satisfied with our state's efforts to repair the damage. These people say strip mining hurts Earth forever. They say we are losing our natural resources. Some experts say that when rain hits the stripped land, chemicals mix with the rainwater. They say these chemicals end up in our drinking water and can make us sick.

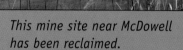

This mine site near McDowell has been reclaimed.

What Do You Think

How do you feel about strip mining? Should coal companies be allowed to continue strip mining the mountains of Kentucky?

"Then the coal companies came
with the world's largest shovel,
And they tortured the timber
and stripped all the land.
Well, they dug for their coal
till the land was forsaken,
Then they wrote it all down
as the progress of man."

—From "Paradise" by John Prine,
courtesy *WB Music Corp.*

The Pennyroyal Region

Now we're sailing into the Pennyroyal Region. Have you ever wondered about this region's name? "Pennyroyal" is the name of a plant in the mint family. The region is named for the plant because pioneer settlers found it growing everywhere. They learned how to use pennyroyal to keep mosquitoes and ticks away.

The Pennyroyal is the largest land region of the state. It touches all of Kentucky's other land regions. The farmers in the Pennyroyal grow apples, tobacco, and soybeans. They also raise dairy and beef cattle.

Look at the rolling hills surrounding Lake Cumberland.

Beautiful Lake Cumberland offers many fun things to do.

Can you see the people fishing and boating on the lake? Can you hear the jet skis? People like to vacation at Lake Cumberland. It is one of the largest lakes in the United States.

As we drift along, we can't see the most famous thing in this region. It is under the ground. Can you guess what it is? No, it isn't coal this time. It is Mammoth Cave, the longest cave in the world. Every year, thousands of people come to Kentucky to visit Mammoth Cave. Have you ever been there? This region has other large cave systems, too.

Look up ahead. Do you see the big lake? The Pennyroyal has more lakes than any region in Kentucky. This lake is Barkley Lake. The land next to it is called the Land Between the Lakes. There, in the distance, is another huge lake. It is Kentucky Lake. Can you see why the land here is called the Land Between the Lakes?

Land Between the Lakes

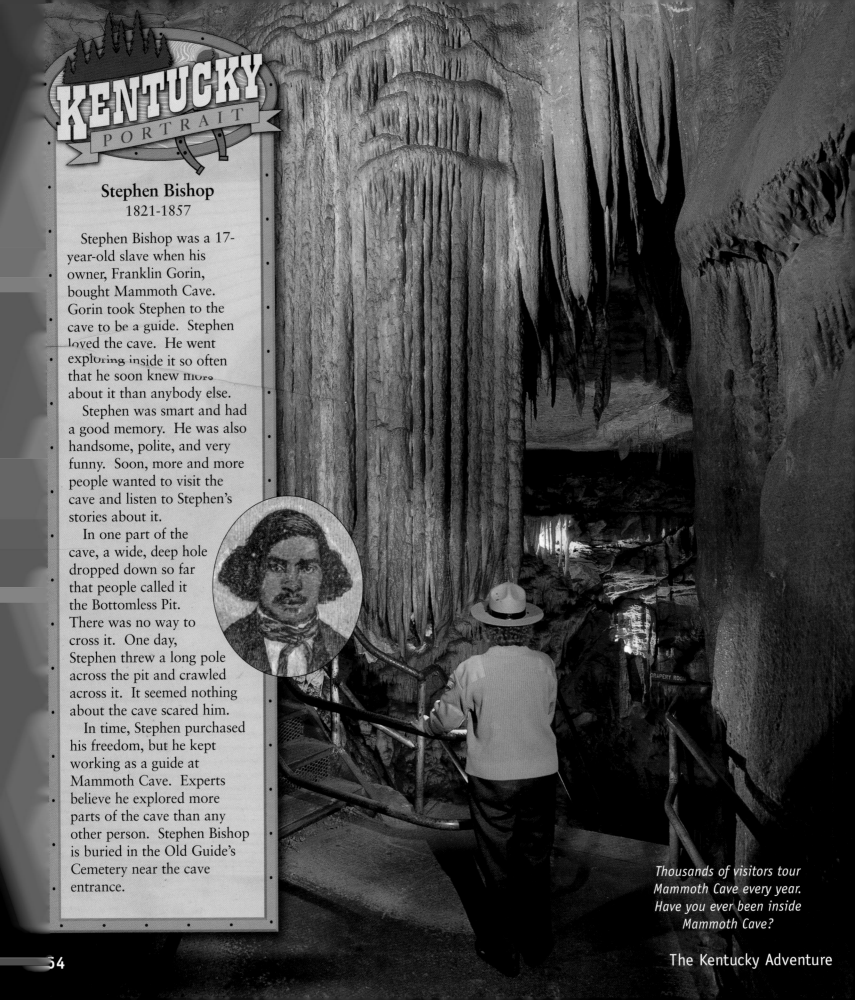

KENTUCKY PORTRAIT

Stephen Bishop
1821-1857

Stephen Bishop was a 17-year-old slave when his owner, Franklin Gorin, bought Mammoth Cave. Gorin took Stephen to the cave to be a guide. Stephen loved the cave. He went exploring inside it so often that he soon knew more about it than anybody else.

Stephen was smart and had a good memory. He was also handsome, polite, and very funny. Soon, more and more people wanted to visit the cave and listen to Stephen's stories about it.

In one part of the cave, a wide, deep hole dropped down so far that people called it the Bottomless Pit. There was no way to cross it. One day, Stephen threw a long pole across the pit and crawled across it. It seemed nothing about the cave scared him.

In time, Stephen purchased his freedom, but he kept working as a guide at Mammoth Cave. Experts believe he explored more parts of the cave than any other person. Stephen Bishop is buried in the Old Guide's Cemetery near the cave entrance.

Thousands of visitors tour Mammoth Cave every year. Have you ever been inside Mammoth Cave?

mammoth cave

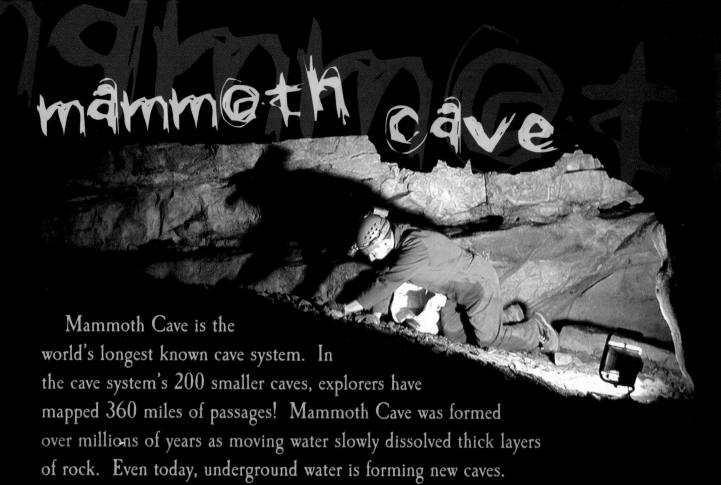

Mammoth Cave is the world's longest known cave system. In the cave system's 200 smaller caves, explorers have mapped 360 miles of passages! Mammoth Cave was formed over millions of years as moving water slowly dissolved thick layers of rock. Even today, underground water is forming new caves.

Mammoth Cave is home to more than 130 types of creatures. One kind of fish has no eyes. That is because deep inside the cave, there is no light. Without light, most living things cannot see. Fish that cannot see do not need eyes. They have adapted to their lightless environment.

The land above the caves is full of holes, too. These are called sinkholes. Rainwater makes its way into these sinkholes, dissolves the limestone, and creates dips in the ground. Sometimes, the dips fill with water. There are many ponds around Mammoth Cave.

Cave fish have no eyes.

Jackson Purchase

Now we're sailing into the Jackson Purchase. This region doesn't get its name from a plant or something under the ground. It is named for Andrew Jackson, who was once president of the United States. Before Jackson became president, he helped our country take control of this piece of land. The Jackson Purchase was added 26 years after Kentucky became a state.

As our balloon floats into the region, you can see the Tennessee River. Do you see the big bridge that connects the Purchase to the rest of Kentucky? Before the bridge was built, it was hard to travel between this region and the rest of Kentucky. For a long time, people in the Jackson Purchase felt separated from other Kentuckians. It is the most southern part of our state.

The Jackson Purchase is also bordered by the Ohio and Mississippi Rivers. All that water has left some of the land in this

region low and swampy. It is some of the flattest land in Kentucky. The lowest point in the state is in Fulton County. It is only 257 feet above sea level.

Look at all the farms in this region, too! Flat, rich, river bottom land is perfect for growing crops. Can you see all the brown plants with fluffy white balls on them? Those are cotton plants. The Jackson Purchase is the only region in Kentucky where cotton grows.

Now we're soaring over Paducah, the largest city in this region. Can you see all the buildings, factories, and railroad yards? Most people in the Jackson Purchase work in farming. But in Paducah, people have all sorts of jobs.

We've come to the end of our balloon ride, and it's time to land. Hold on tight as we glide down toward the ground. Did you enjoy our trip? Did you know that Kentucky was so big and beautiful? Did you know there were so many fun things to see and do in our state? Maybe you will be able to go visit them again one day.

The clothes you are wearing may be made from cotton grown in the Jackson Purchase.

Counties

Another kind of region in our state is a county. A county is a region that has at least one town. Every person in Kentucky lives in one of our state's 120 counties. Each county has its own county seat. The **county seat** is the town or city where the county government has offices. Which county do you live in?

Activity

Where Do People Live?

People live all across our state. In some places, there are lots of people. In other places, there are only a few people. Look at the map to learn more about where people live in our state. Answer these questions:

1. What is the title of the map?
2. What do the lines show?
3. Which county has the most people?
4. Which county do you live in? How many people live in your county?

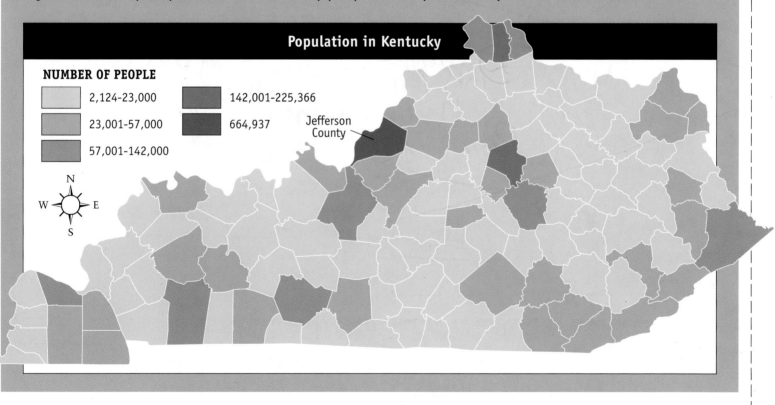

Population in Kentucky

NUMBER OF PEOPLE

- 2,124–23,000
- 23,001–57,000
- 57,001–142,000
- 142,001–225,366
- 664,937

Jefferson County

Having Fun in Kentucky

Can you remember a time when you felt proud of our state or your hometown? Think about some fun things you have done here. Maybe you and your family went to visit Mammoth Cave. Maybe you raked leaves and jumped in the pile. Maybe you have fished in one of our lakes, rivers, or streams.

Divide a poster in half. On one side, attach pictures or drawings that show things you like to do in the land region where you live. On the other side of the poster, attach pictures or drawings that explain things you have done (or would like to do) in another land region in Kentucky. Make your poster colorful and bright. Label each item.

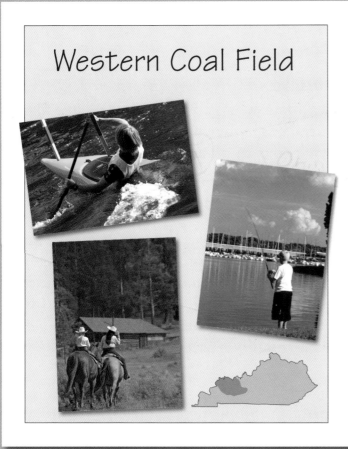

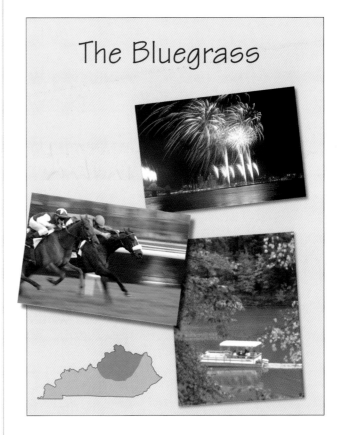

2 MEMORY MASTER

1. The highest point in the state is in which region?
2. What is the largest city in the state?
3. Which region is named after a president?
4. How many counties are in Kentucky?

WORDS TO UNDERSTAND

human system
pollution
technology

Human Systems

After learning about Kentucky's regions, can you see how the land and the people are connected? Some people built towns because they were near rivers, railroad tracks, or roads. Some people started towns because the land in the area was good for farming.

Towns and cities are types of human systems. A *human system* has to do with people working together. A school is a human system. So is a store.

Choosing Where to Live

People have choices about where to live. Most people like to live in places where they can get the things they want and need. Most people also have to work to earn money, so they choose to live close to where they work. If a person has a job in Louisville, he probably wouldn't want to live miles away in Hopkinsville. That would be a long way to drive every day!

Other people choose to live in places because they have family members there. Some people live on property their families have owned for many years. Some people move to certain places because they like the climate there. What is the climate like around your home? Would you prefer to live in a different climate? Where people live tells us much about our natural world.

Using the Land

The land has a lot to do with the way people live. It has to do with the food and crops people grow. It has to do with the kinds of homes we live in. It even affects the clothes we wear.

Over time, people have changed the ways they use the land. Long ago, people ate wild animals, fish, berries, and even grasses. They cut down trees and moved earth and rocks to build shelters. Later, people cleared forests to plant crops and build houses.

Today, we still use the land to grow crops. We cut down trees and use the wood to make paper. We take coal from the ground. We build roads, dams, barns, and shopping malls. We use the land for lots of different things.

Technology and the Land

It is impossible for people to survive in some places. It may be because the place has no fresh water. Or maybe the ground is always frozen. Maybe plants cannot grow, so there is nothing to eat. In the past, people were not able to survive in places like these.

Today, through technology, we have invented things that allow us to live in almost every environment. *Technology* means using man-made things, such as machines, tools, or electricity. You have already read about how people use technology to control the flow of rivers. Dams allow people to now live in areas that used to be flooded.

People have also invented ways to take water to areas where there isn't any. We have invented air conditioning to keep homes and buildings cool. We have built huge pipelines that carry water over hundreds of miles to places that are dry. We even have technology that allows us to survive on the tops of mountains, where the air has little oxygen.

We need things from the land to live, but we also use the land to play.

Las Vegas is a huge city in the middle of a hot, dry desert. How has technology helped people in Las Vegas live more comfortably?

Earth is a living thing. We should all try to protect it from harm.

Taking Care of Kentucky

Our natural world is beautiful, but if we don't take care of it, it won't stay that way. You have read about how people change the land. We build cities and highways. We plant trees, shrubs, flowers, and grass. We build bridges and dams and other man-made features. We dig into the ground to get coal and other minerals. Even though these things change our environment, they are important. We need some of them to survive. If we are not careful, though, we can harm the environment.

People are sometimes careless with the environment. When that happens, plants and animals can get sick and die.

Pollution

When people put harmful things into the environment, it is called *pollution.* There was a time when people did not think it was important to take care of our land. They believed we could never use up all the grass, trees, and other resources. People thought there would always be plenty of fresh air and clean water. Many thought the sky was so big that pollution from cars and factories wouldn't make a difference. We even allowed businesses to dump chemicals and trash into our rivers, streams, and oceans.

Cleaning Up

When people began to understand how important it is to protect our land and air, they worked together to create laws against pollution. Our state set aside land for wildlife and state parks. Today, most people try to keep our state clean. If Kentucky is to remain a healthy place to live, we must take care of it.

You Can Help

How many different types of pollution can you think of? It is up to everyone to help protect natural resources and our environment. Even you can help. You can put trash in the garbage can. You can recycle. You can turn off the lights and TV when you aren't using them. You can be very careful with matches so you don't start a fire. What other things can you do?

③ MEMORY MASTER

1. Name one human system.
2. What are some reasons people choose to live in certain places?
3. How does technology help us live on the land?
4. What is pollution?

Chapter 3 Review

What's the Point?

People and the land are linked together. We use our land in many ways. Kentucky has five land regions. They are the Eastern Coal Field, the Bluegrass, the Pennyroyal, the Western Coal Field, and the Jackson Purchase. We should each do our part to help the land in Kentucky remain healthy and beautiful.

Becoming Better Readers: What's in a Title?

This chapter has a title. Do you remember what it is? It is "Natural Kentucky." Why do you think the author chose that title? What does it tell you about the chapter? There are other titles in this chapter, too. These smaller titles are called main headings and sub headings. Look back through the chapter and make a list of all the smaller titles. Then explain how each title relates to each section. Choose one title from this chapter. Then make up a new one to replace it.

Our Amazing Geography: A Land Region Brochure

Pretend a cousin who lives in another state is coming to visit. You want to tell him or her all about your land region. Make a brochure about it. Create a page to tell about each of the following:

- The land and water
- Plants and animals
- Different kinds of homes
- The jobs people do
- A map that shows the large cities or towns
- Fun things to do

Activity

Why Do I Live Here?

Have you ever wondered why you live where you do? After reading this chapter, you've learned that geography affects where people live. See how it makes a difference in your life.

1. What jobs do the adults in your family have?
2. Is there another place in our state where they could do the same jobs? Why or why not?
3. Which categories best describe their jobs?

Natural Resources Education
Agriculture   Tourism
Manufacturing   Something else (explain what it is)

4. Does the climate affect their jobs? How?

Activity

Act It Out!

Divide into five groups. Each group represents one of Kentucky's land regions: Bluegrass, Eastern Coal Field, Jackson Purchase, Pennyroyal, and Western Coal Field. Shhh! Don't tell anyone else your region. In your group, make up a short skit or play that shows your region. You want the other groups to guess which region is yours. Think about the natural features in your region. What human features stand out? Present your skit to the class. Did they guess your region?

"*When you arise in the morning, give thanks for the food and for the joy of living. If you see no reason for giving thanks, the fault lies only in yourself.*"

—*Chief Tecumseh,*
Shawnee Nation

Timeline of Events

10000 B.C.   8000 B.C.

8000-1000 B.C.
Archaic Indians lived here. They shaped simple tools and weapons. They added fruit to their diet and may have grown squash.

10000-8000 B.C.
Paleo Indians from Asia traveled south into our region. They survived by hunting large animals and gathering wild plants. They may have begun using simple tools.

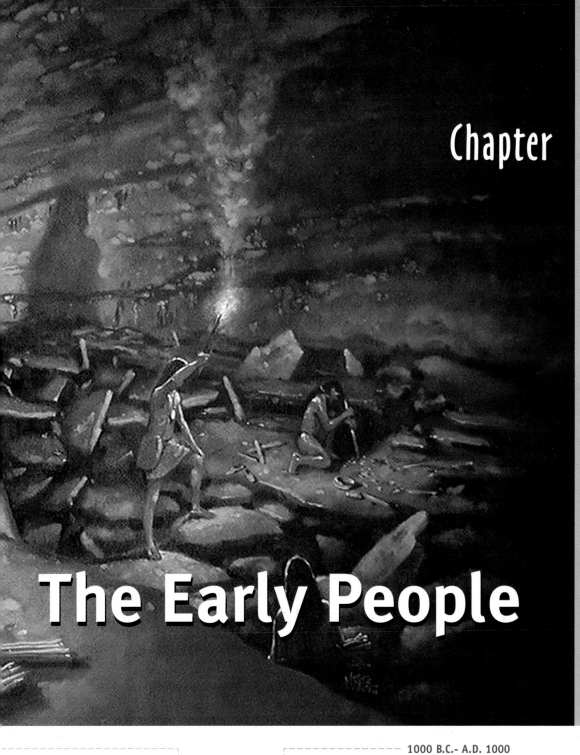

Chapter 4

Long ago, Native Americans lived and hunted on the land we now call Kentucky. They made long trails through the hills and hunted buffalo, elk, and deer. They grew crops, such as corn, beans, and pumpkins. They traveled to far away places to trade.

The Early People

All people need salt to survive. For hundreds of years, Native Americans gathered salt in Mammoth Cave.

1000 B.C.- A.D. 1000
Woodland Indians lived here. They were the first to grow crops and live in villages. They built the first earthen mounds. They learned to make pottery and store food.

2000 B.C.	0	A.D. 2000

A.D.1000-1750
Late Prehistoric Indians (Mississippian Tradition and Fort Ancient Tradition) lived here. They cleared large sections of land and built great villages. They became good farmers. They learned to make better tools, weapons, clothing, jewelry, and pottery. They formed governments and chose leaders. They held feasts and ceremonies, and they played games.

A.D. 1750-present
Historic Indians lived here. The three main groups were the Cherokee, Shawnee, and Chickasaw. They hunted, fished, and grew crops. They traded for their first horses. They became great warriors. They developed written language and told legends.

PEOPLE TO KNOW

Archaic Indians
Paleo Indians

WORDS TO UNDERSTAND

archaeologist
archaic
atlatl
awl
glacier
hide
hunter-gatherer
Ice Age
native
paleo

Native means belonging to or coming from a place. The first people are called Native Americans because they belong to North America. In the next chapter, you will learn why they are also called Indians.

Traveling South

Many scientists believe the first people to live in North America walked here from Asia during the last Ice Age. The **Ice Age** was a time when Earth was very cold. Layers of snow and ice piled up, forming **glaciers,** or frozen rivers of ice. Since most of the ocean was frozen, people could walk to places we no longer can. These first people to cross the bridge are called Paleo Indians. **Paleo** means very old.

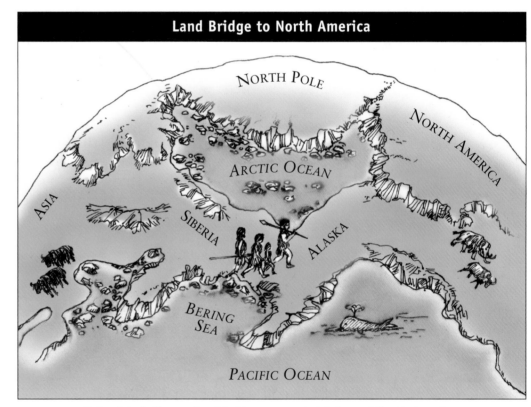

Scientists believe a land bridge connected Asia and North America.

Paleo Indians

The Paleo people hunted huge animals, like mammoths, mastodons, and buffalo, for food. It was hard to survive in such an icy climate. The Paleo people began traveling south, following animals and looking for plants to eat. They traveled great distances. They even traveled in the land that would later become Kentucky.

A large mammoth provided meat for many meals and hides for blankets and clothing.

What Big Teeth They Had!

Mammoths and mastodons had huge teeth! Look at the picture. Between the mammoth and mastodon teeth is a man's shoe. How does the shoe show the size of the teeth?

Look at your teeth in a mirror. How are the teeth in this picture like some of your own? What can we learn about an animal by looking at its teeth?

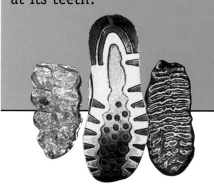

Hunter-Gatherers

The Paleo people were *hunter-gatherers.* That means they had to hunt or gather the food they ate. They did not know how to raise crops. They took from the land everything they needed to survive, so they were always on the move.

Hunter-gatherers used everything they could find. They made tools out of stones. They chipped rocks into sharp points and then tied them to wooden spears. They used pieces of stone, bone, or antler to scrape fur from animal hides. *Hides* are the skins of animals. The women used needles made from bones to sew the hides into clothes and blankets.

Linking the Past to the Present

Have you ever wondered why some of the place names in Kentucky have the word "lick" in them? Much of our soil has salt mixed into it. All living creatures (including people) need salt to live. Animals used to come here and lick the salt from the ground, so people called the places licks. How many places can you think of that have "lick" in their name?

What Do You Think?

You have just read about the food and clothing of the hunter-gatherers. What do you think they used for shelter? Think about what you would use for shelter if you were out in the wilderness. What natural feature in Kentucky could be used for shelter?

Archaic Indians

As time passed, the climate became warmer and drier. The glaciers melted and formed new rivers and lakes. The hunter-gatherers adapted to the warmer climate. They learned new skills and crafted new weapons. These more modern people are known as Archaic Indians. *Archaic* means old—but not as old as Paleo.

Changing Lifestyles

When the weather and land changed, the plants and animals changed, too. Some of the large animals were gone, so people began hunting smaller animals, such as deer and elk. Like the Paleo people, the Archaic Indians traveled in small groups. They didn't have to travel as far as the Paleo people did because more plants grew in the warmer weather. Archaic Indians ate more fruit, vegetables, and nuts than earlier people did. As the people traveled less, they had more children. Their numbers began to grow.

Looking For Clues

How do we know about the early people? They did not leave any written records of their lives. But they did leave other clues. They left things behind when they moved from place to place. They also left things in burial sites and trash pits. Today, these things are called artifacts. Artifacts are tools, baskets, pottery, clothes, toys, and other things made and used by people.

Archaeologists are scientists who study artifacts and other clues to learn how people lived in the past. Most artifacts are found in the earth. Sand and dirt have covered them up over time.

Archaeologists carefully remove one layer of dirt at a time. They keep notes about what they find. Even the smallest item may have a story to tell. It might give clues to what the people ate and what tools they made.

Sometimes, archaeologists find spear points near ancient animals. The points were made by ancient people. They carved pieces of stone until the points were sharp. Then they used the points to hunt. Spear points give us many clues about the first people who lived in Kentucky.

The Archaic people invented many new tools. Archaeologists have found tools used for hunting, butchering, making jewelry, grinding food, and even cracking nuts. One of the most important new tools was an atlatl. An **atlatl** is a long handle that attaches to the end of a spear. When an Archaic Indian used an atlatl to throw his spear, the spear went much farther much faster.

Spear

Atlatl

Using Every Part

Killing a buffalo was very hard work. So, like the Paleo people, Archaic people used every part.

Horns—hooks

Hides—clothing, blankets, moccasins, shelter

Muscle/flesh—food

Long bones—needles, hairpins, awls, tips for carving and chipping

Tendons—thread for sewing

Hooves—jewelry, rattles

① MEMORY MASTER

1. What is a hunter-gatherer?
2. What is a salt lick?
3. What is the difference between the words "paleo" and "archaic"?
4. Name two things Archaic people made out of animal hides.

The Early People

Woodland Indians

More time passed, and Native Americans continued to adapt to the changing environment. They learned more new ways to live and survive, and their numbers grew. The next group to live in Kentucky is known as the Woodland Indians.

Farms and Villages

The Woodland Indians were the first people in Kentucky to farm. They used farming tools made from bones and planted squash and beans in fields near their homes. Growing crops close to home meant the people did not have to travel far to find food. They could stay in one place longer and build small villages. They placed their villages near rivers and streams so they could get water easily.

The Woodland people learned how to make pottery, so they could store food for the cold winter months—a time when crops did not grow. They also learned how to make bows and arrows. The men often left the villages to go hunting. Bows and arrows were even better than atlatls. Bows and arrows kept the hunters safer because they could strike animals from farther away.

Living on the Land

The land had everything to do with the way people lived. People who lived where they could find soft stone were able to carve bowls. Those who lived near rivers or streams ate fish. They also used the water to help their crops grow. If a forest was nearby, the Woodland Indians built their homes of wood. They also made canoes from tree trunks. They burned, chipped, and carved the trunks to hollow out a place for sitting.

These men are making a canoe by hollowing out a tree trunk. Can you see why these boats are called dugout canoes?

The Kentucky Adventure

Indian Mounds

An Indian mound is a pile of dirt. Some Indian mounds are small, but some are very large. The Woodland Indians were the first Native Americans in Kentucky to build mounds—but they were not the last.

Sometimes, Indian mounds were used as burial sites. When village leaders died, they were buried in the largest mounds. Woodland Indians believed the dead needed special things to survive in the next life, so they buried these things with the bodies. Scientists have found food, weapons, jewelry, baskets, and clothing alongside the dead in some mounds. All mounds were sacred places.

Scientists have spent many years studying the artifacts in the mounds. Some of the artifacts are made of materials not found in Kentucky. That means the Woodland Indians must have traded with people who lived far away. When trading, the Woodland people did not use money like we do. Instead, they traded things they had, like furs, pottery, baskets, and jewelry, for things they wanted.

The Wickliffe Mounds lie in Ballard County in western Kentucky. One thousand years ago, the area was the site of a busy Native American village.

What Do You Think

How do you think the Woodland Indians met with other Native Americans to trade? Do you think they went all the way to Illinois or North Carolina? Maybe Native Americans from those places came to Kentucky. Maybe they met halfway. What do you think?

This drawing shows how an Indian burial ground grew over time. How many people are buried in this mound?

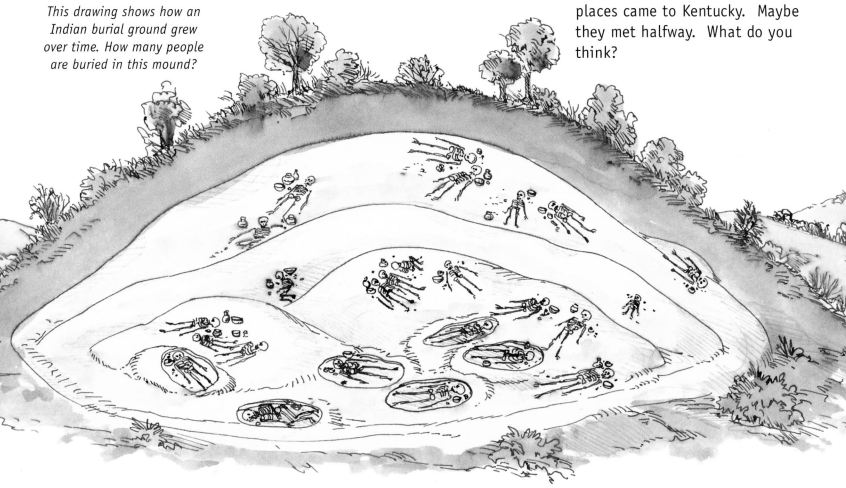

To Dig or Not to Dig

People have learned a lot about our state's history by exploring ancient Indian mounds. However, some people don't think the mounds should be touched. These people believe mounds are sacred. They feel that digging and taking things from them is wrong.

In April of 2005, workers began studying some land near Louisville. They needed to make sure the land was safe before new buildings were built on it. The workers found some pieces of bone from ancient people. A few years earlier, workers had found spear tips, trash pits, seeds, tools, and burned rocks at the same site.

Some people said the building plans should be stopped. They wanted the site to be kept the way it had been for thousands of years. Other people wanted to continue the building project. They wanted to use the new buildings and homes. Still others thought the site should be explored and the artifacts put in a museum. What do you think?

Late Prehistoric

As time passed, life for Kentucky's Native Americans continued to change. The people learned to grow corn, which they called *maize*. They made better tools, like hoes, to *till* the land. They still fished in the rivers and streams and hunted in the woods. Deer was their main source of meat.

The climate in Kentucky was like it is today, and thousands of Native Americans lived here. They had art and culture. They formed governments and nations all across North America. A *nation* is a group of people who live and work together in a community. Sometimes nations are called *tribes*. Several different nations lived in Kentucky.

The Late Prehistoric Indians were divided into two main groups. The Mississippian Indians lived in the southern and western parts of our state. The Fort Ancient Indians lived in the north and east.

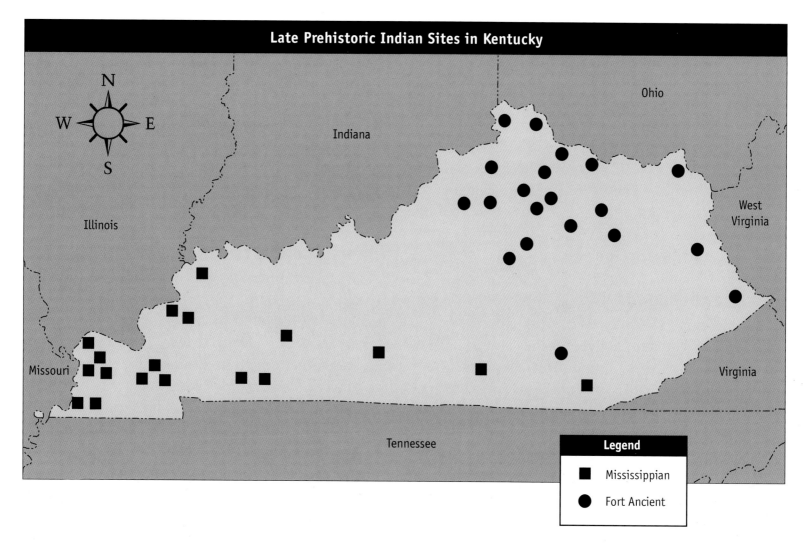

Late Prehistoric Indian Sites in Kentucky

Ohio
Indiana
Illinois
West Virginia
Missouri
Virginia
Tennessee

Legend

■ Mississippian
● Fort Ancient

Living in villages allowed the Mississippians to meet together often.

Painting by Martin Pate, Newnan, GA ▲

The Mississippians

The Mississippian people lived in villages. Sometimes, villages were small and had only a few homes. In other places, villages were large and had lots of homes. The homes in large villages often surrounded an open area. This open area is called a *plaza.* It may have been used for meetings, funerals, or ceremonies.

Homes and Mounds

Mississippians' homes were square or rectangular. The people lived in these homes all year long. First, Mississippians lashed poles together to form walls. Then they covered the walls with mud. This kind of building is called *wattle and daub.* Wattle and daub buildings were strong and sturdy. They were warm in the winter and cool in the summer. The roofs were made of woven grass.

Like the Woodland people, Mississippians were mound builders. Villagers carried hundreds of baskets of dirt from one place to another to build them. The tops of the mounds were flat and may have been used for buildings that all villagers shared. Early on, Mississippians buried their dead in mounds. Later, they buried them in cemeteries much like those we have today.

Farmers and Craftsmen

The Mississippian people worked long and hard to clear the land for farming. Most of Kentucky was covered by thick forests. Crops needed lots of sunlight to grow. That means the trees had to be removed. Sometimes, the men set fires to clear away trees. Other times, they stripped the bark off the trees. This made the trees die. A dead tree is much easier to remove than a living one.

Once they cleared the field, the people had to plant seeds. The most common seed they planted was corn, but they also grew beans, squash,

The Kentucky Adventure

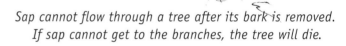

Sap cannot flow through a tree after its bark is removed.
If sap cannot get to the branches, the tree will die.

pumpkins, and sunflowers. The fields did not look like our fields today. The people planted beans, corn, and squash together in mounds. They called these vegetables the "three sisters." The fast-growing corn shaded the squash and provided a stalk for the beans to wind around. The Mississippians also grew tobacco. They dried it and smoked it in pipes during special ceremonies.

The Mississippians learned how to make farming tools, stronger pottery, and better weapons. They learned that seashells could make their pots last longer, so the people mixed shells into the clay as they formed pots. The Mississippians must have been very skilled because making clay pots with shell is not easy. Some of the artifacts found at Mississippian sites are decorated bowls, vases, and pitchers. Archaeologists have also found arrowheads and spear points.

Corn, beans, and squash were the "three sisters".

The Fort Ancient People

Like the Mississippians, the Fort Ancient people lived in homes around the village's plaza. They were great hunters of deer, elk, bear, rabbits, foxes, raccoons, squirrels, and turkeys. They also learned better ways of farming the rich soil. They made hoes from deer and elk antlers and clam shells. Then they used the hoes to clear weeds and break up the soil. The Fort Ancient people even used digging sticks to make holes for seeds.

Society

The Fort Ancient people lived in tribes, and each tribe had leaders. People became leaders by doing special things. For example, if a person was generous or a good hunter, he might become a tribal leader. Leaders helped make decisions for the tribe and led rituals and ceremonies. Sometimes, tribe members did not get along. When that happened, they might have gone to a leader. The leader helped them with their problem.

Traders, Tool Makers, and Potters

The Fort Ancient people spent a lot of time making things. They were great traders and traded with people from far away places. They made hair clips, beads, jewelry, pipes, tools, weapons, baskets, and pottery. They even made robes by sewing animal skins together.

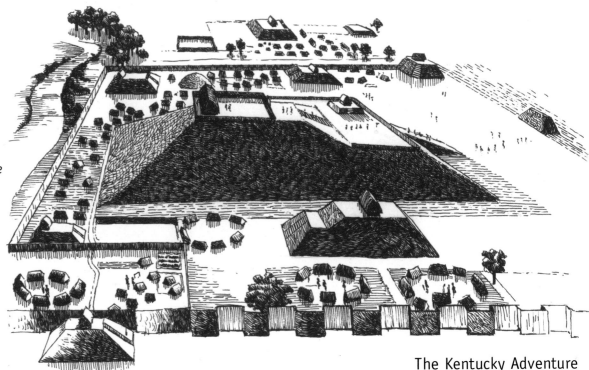

Fort Ancient villages were planned and organized so the people could work together.

The Kentucky Adventure

Making arrowheads, spear points, and knives was slow, hard work. Tool-makers used antlers or bones to chip objects into shape. They had to know exactly where and how hard to hit. If they made a mistake, the piece might break. Then they would have to start all over.

Fort Ancient people used the coil method to make pots. Potters rolled clay into long, narrow pieces that looked like snakes. Then they coiled the pieces into shape. Next, they placed a large, smooth stone inside the pot, bowl, or pitcher being made. They smoothed the outside with a wooden paddle and then added decorations. They carved swirls, lines, notches, or other designs into the soft clay. The last step was baking the pot. Baking made the pot hard and very strong.

Time for Fun

The Fort Ancient people had time to play. One of their favorite games was **Chunkey**. Chunkey was a game of skill. Players rolled a smooth, round, decorated stone on the ground and then threw spears at it as it rolled. The winner was the person who hit the stone or came closest to hitting it. Can you think of any modern games like Chunkey?

The Fort Ancient people made many useful things out of clay.

Activity

Inventing Games

Native American children used everyday objects to make up games, like Chunkey. Look around your classroom or bedroom. Create a game using items around you. How will you decide the winner of your game?

② MEMORY MASTER

1. Why did the Woodland Indians build mounds?
2. What is a nation?
3. Why did the people have to clear away the trees?
4. What is Chunkey?

PEOPLE TO KNOW

The Cherokee
The Chickasaw
The Shawnee

WORDS TO UNDERSTAND

council
cradleboard
historic
prehistoric
sapling
wigwam

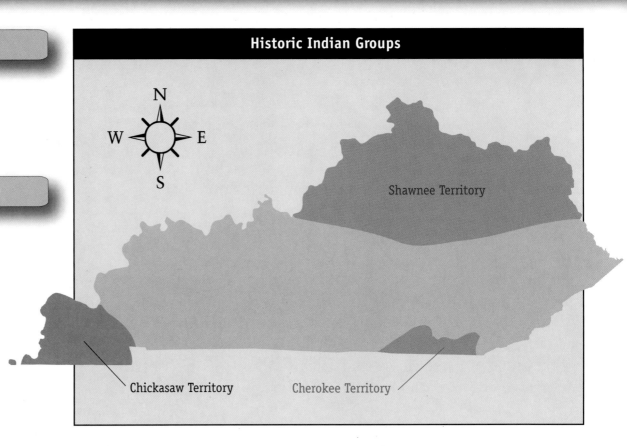

Historic Indian Groups

Shawnee Territory

Chickasaw Territory

Cherokee Territory

Making a Record

When the earliest people lived here, no one kept written records. These people lived before recorded history. That is why the first groups of people are called *prehistoric.* We don't have primary documents that tell us about them. We have only the artifacts they left behind.

Later, when European explorers and settlers came to Kentucky, they wrote about Native Americans in their journals and letters. They described Native American life in Kentucky. That is why we know so much more about the later groups. The later groups are called *historic* because we have written records about them.

Explorers and settlers wrote about three main tribes that made their homes in Kentucky: the Cherokee, Shawnee, and Chickasaw. Each had its own art, dress, and food. Each tribe also had its own stories and music. In some ways, the tribes were all alike. In other ways, they were all different.

The Cherokee

The word Cherokee means "people of a different speech." The Cherokee lived year round in fairly large villages of 30 to 60 houses. In the beginning, they built their homes of wattle and daub. Later, the Cherokee built log cabins with bark roofs.

Cherokee villages had large *council* houses where town leaders met. Council houses were built on top of old Mississippian mounds. The Cherokee did not build new mounds. Inside the council house was a sacred fire. They tended the fire, so it never went out.

The Cherokee had rules and leaders. They created their own government. In later years, a Cherokee man named Sequoyah invented an alphabet, so his people could communicate in writing. The Cherokee even printed a newspaper in their language. It was called *The Cherokee Phoenix*.

A few years after Sequoyah invented the Cherokee alphabet, every Cherokee could read and write.

91

The Shawnee

The Shawnee lived in northern Kentucky and moved often. During the summer, they settled in large villages and raised crops. They liked to live in villages near water, and they often used the same campsites over and over. The men hunted the animals that came to the water to drink.

Shawnee homes, called wigwams, were left standing each winter when the people went off to hunt. When the tribe returned in the spring, the wigwams needed only a few repairs. A *wigwam* is a house made of wooden poles covered with elm or birch bark. The Shawnee built a fire pit in the center of the wigwam. They cut a hole in the roof so the smoke could escape. The family slept on the ground on fur blankets.

Shawnee men and women made jewelry from silver. The men often wore silver medals tied around their necks with strings of brightly colored beads. The women wove silver jewelry into their long black hair.

The Shawnee were tall, strong, and fiercely loyal to one another. The men were great warriors. They were so skilled that other tribes often asked Shawnee warriors to come and protect them from their enemies. Later, the Shawnee fought longer and harder than any other tribe to keep white settlers from taking over their lands.

The word "Shawnee" means "southerner." That may seem strange because the Shawnee lived in the northern part of Kentucky. The reason they had this name is because most Shawnee lived in the southern part of Ohio. Only a few groups lived in northern Kentucky.

Shawnee Babies

Family was very important to the Shawnee. Shawnee men and women wanted their babies to grow up straight and tall. To make sure they did, mothers strapped their babies, even the baby's head, to a *cradleboard.* This kept the baby's body very straight, but it caused a little problem. Every Shawnee had a flat spot on the back of his or her head. The Shawnee also wanted their children to be brave and strong, so they bathed them in cold water every morning—even in the winter!

The Kentucky Adventure

A Step-by-Step Wigwam

1 To build a wigwam, the people cut down young trees called **saplings.** They trimmed off the branches. Then they dug holes in the ground. They put the saplings in the holes. This held the saplings in place.

2 They bent the saplings over, then lashed them together with cord, vines, or animal skins. This made a frame for the wigwam.

3 Finally, they covered the frame with bark or mats made of grasses and reeds. They left a door and a hole in the top so the smoke from the fire could escape.

▼Photos by Suzanne Chapelle, Courtesy of the Irvine Nature Center

The Early People

The Chickasaw

The Chickasaw lived in the region that is now western Kentucky. No one knows exactly what "Chickasaw" means, but many believe it comes from a legend about two brothers, Chisca and Chacta.

The Chickasaw were the fiercest warriors of all the tribes in the Southeast. They shaved off all the hair on their bodies, and they had unusual tattoos. Instead of living in villages, the Chickasaw spread their homes along streams and rivers for many miles. The few villages they did build had high walls, so enemies could not get in. If another tribe attacked, the Chickasaw gathered inside the village.

In the beginning, the Chickasaw traveled in dugout canoes or on foot. They were strong swimmers and fast runners. There were no roads or maps, so the first paths were probably made by herds of buffalo or bison. People followed these well-worn paths to other areas. They also traveled along river banks.

How do you think these Chickasaw warriors felt when they found strangers setting up camp?

Later, the Chickasaw traded with Spanish explorers for their first horses. They worked with the horses and developed a strong, fast breed. This breed was called the Chickasaw Horse. The Chickasaw used these horses when they traveled a long way or if they had a lot to carry.

The Cherokee, Shawnee, and Chickasaw were not the only nations living in Kentucky, but they were the largest. Some of the other groups were the Miami, the Choctaw, and the Delaware.

What Do You Think ?

Some sports teams use Native American tribes or images as their nicknames. Can you think of any? Do you think using these names shows disrespect for Native American cultures? Why or why not?

Activity

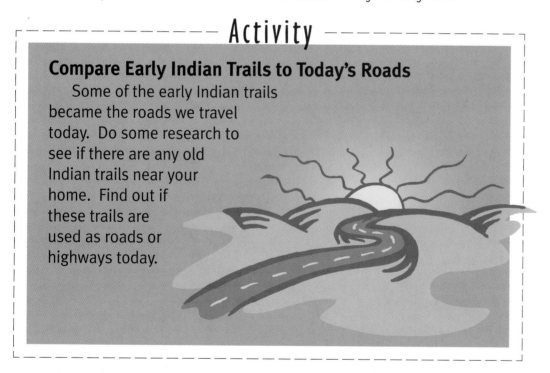

Compare Early Indian Trails to Today's Roads

Some of the early Indian trails became the roads we travel today. Do some research to see if there are any old Indian trails near your home. Find out if these trails are used as roads or highways today.

③ MEMORY MASTER

1. Why are the early groups of Native Americans called prehistoric?
2. Were the Cherokee mound builders?
3. Which nation had the fiercest warriors?
4. Name the three main Indian nations explorers and settlers found in Kentucky.

Ways of Life

Even though they were in different tribes, Kentucky's Native Americans were a lot alike. For example, most tribes had the same beliefs about the land. Tribe members also hunted the same animals and grew the same kinds of crops. The men usually hunted, and the women usually cared for the crops and raised the children.

The tribes also had differences. Each had its own language. In some ways, their religions, customs, and traditions were alike. In other ways, they were very different.

Respect for Nature

The tribes that once lived in the land we call Kentucky had great respect for Earth. The sky above them, the water they drank, the soil that provided food—all these things had great spiritual meaning.

The first Kentuckians also believed the animals they hunted had spirits and should be respected. The people saw themselves as part of nature. The land was for all to use, care for, and protect. They believed the spirits of Earth gave them everything they needed, and the people gave thanks for all they received.

What Do You Think❓

How do you feel about the land? Should people be able to own it? Should landowners be able to tell other people to stay away? Should we be able to change the land? Should we try to live more like early Native Americans did? Why or why not?

When historic Indian tribes lived here, the Kentucky wilderness looked just like it does today.

Spirituality

All Native Americans believed in a Great Spirit. The Great Spirit made the world and watched over it with loving care. Other spirits watched over the animals, the plants, the wind, the stars, and the rain.

Every morning, Indian men, women, and children prayed to the Great Spirit. They asked it to guide their day. They also prayed before they began important work like planting, hunting, or going to war.

The Bread Dance and the Green Corn Dance

Native Americans also prayed to the Great Spirit by dancing. The most important ceremony was the Bread Dance. It was held in the spring, and each tribe had its own special way of doing it.

For the Bread Dance, all the people danced in a circle. They beat their drums and sang joyfully. They asked the Great Spirit to give them plentiful crops. Then they feasted on corn bread, fruit, vegetables, and deer meat. The women ate first because their job of farming was so important in the summer. On the next day, they planted their crops with the blessing of the Great Spirit.

The Green Corn Ceremony was held when crops ripened. They danced the Green Corn Dance in early summer when the first corn was ready for picking. It was a way to rejoice about the new crop. It also marked the beginning of the new year in the nation.

The Feast of Small Grain

In the fall, all the people gathered again at the Feast of Small Grain. They danced and sang. They asked the Great Spirit for a good harvest and for good hunting in the winter. Then they feasted. This time, the men ate first because their job of hunting was so important in the winter. During the next few weeks, they harvested all their crops. When the men left on the hunt, they believed they left with the blessing of the Great Spirit.

There were many other Indian dances. The people danced before battle. They danced in memory of the dead. They also danced just for fun.

Most Native Americans were very spiritual. They danced and held ceremonies to ask for blessings and to give thanks.

The Kentucky Adventure

Green Corn Ceremony

It is a feast,
A ceremony of thanks,
For the corn that grows
Along the river banks.

This is the staple,
That keeps us in health,
Of sun-baked yellow gold,
A mountain of wealth.

We sing praises to Mother Earth
For blessings only you can give,
For without your guidance,
We could never live.

Stories, Legends, and Folktales

Many times during the year, people gathered together by a warm fire and told stories. Storytelling was a time for sharing and for being close. It was a time for telling about the good things people had done. It was a time of laughing and listening.

Some stories repeated the history of the people so it would not be forgotten. Some stories explained things like why the stars were in the sky and why wolves howl at the moon.

Children learned about their world by listening to legends. **Legends** are stories that tell about the past. Through legends, children learned important lessons. They learned to treat all living things with respect.

What Do You Think ?

What do you think your day as a Chickasaw child would be like? Have you ever heard a legend told by anyone in your family?

No Lost Children—A Chickasaw Legend

So well taught and so much a part of the land and wilderness were the children of the Chickasaw that parents never worried about them going out into the woods and hills alone. Little Indian boys roamed at will from village to village or in the woods with their bows and arrows or blow-guns. They would be gone all day, and the mothers were not uneasy about them.

A Chickasaw boy went quietly through the wilderness taking note of every bush, tree, and rock, so he would always know his way back. His sense of direction was so good that he never became lost.

No "Lost" Children—A Chickasaw Legend
from Ann Sheffield papers,
Chickasaw Council House Museum.

Leadership

Every Indian village had two leaders. One leader was the village chief, who helped make important decisions. The chief was usually a man, but there were a few women chiefs. Each village also had a war chief. The war chief was always a man. He was the bravest warrior in the village. The war chief led the men of the village into battle.

Sometimes all the villages of one tribe would gather in a council. They would talk about their plans and then vote on what to do. Meetings were not over until everyone agreed, so they sometimes lasted for weeks.

Families

Family was very important to Native Americans. Everyone worked together to survive. Children had great respect for their parents and other older people.

If you were a Native American child, your mother's brother would teach and train you as you grew. Your real father would be more like a special friend. He would come to visit and play with you, but you wouldn't see him very often. He would be busy raising his sister's children. In this way, families followed the mother's line. They stayed very close.

Native American leaders did not make decisions alone. They helped everyone decide together.

Learning to Survive

If you were a historic Native American in Kentucky, you and your friends learned skills that would help your family survive.

If you were an Indian boy, you learned about the woods, rivers, and mountains. You learned how to tell rabbit tracks from turkey tracks. You learned to be quiet in the forest. You learned how to listen and watch for animals. You sharpened arrow points and practiced your aim. You dreamed about becoming a leader or a warrior when you grew up.

If you were an Indian girl, you learned about working in the fields and garden. You learned which wild plants you could eat. You learned how to cook over a fire. You learned to take care of younger children. You helped your mother weave baskets and form pottery. When you grew older, you learned how to sew clothes.

There was time to play, so you and your friends splashed in the rivers and streams. You roamed the fields. You danced and sang and played games. You challenged your friends in races and contests. You ran and laughed and shouted when the village held celebrations.

The Great Encounter

By 1700, thousands of Native Americans lived in what is now Kentucky. At the time, they did not know their world was about to change. English settlers from the East began crossing the Appalachian Mountains into present-day Kentucky. These settlers thought they had discovered a new land. But native people had lived here for centuries.

The Conflict Begins

The ways Native Americans and settlers met is an important part of Kentucky's history. Both groups had different beliefs about religion, government, and how to use the land. They did not always agree, and they grew frustrated and angry with one another. As troubles developed, the settlers and Indians often fought. In the next chapter, you will read about the ways settlers changed the lives of Indians in Kentucky forever.

4 MEMORY MASTER

1. Where did Native Americans get everything they needed?
2. Name two reasons Native Americans danced.
3. Name two jobs for Native American boys and two jobs for Native American girls.
4. Why did Native Americans and settlers disagree?

Chapter 4 Review

What's the Point?

Many different Native American groups lived in Kentucky. Native Americans took everything they needed from the land. They adapted to the changing climate. They organized societies and cultures.

Becoming Better Readers: Different for a Day

Pretend you are a Native American boy or girl for a day. Review the section "Learning to Survive". Draw a picture of something you made. Then write in your reading journal about what you will do with the thing you made.

Our Amazing Geography: Blazing a Trail

Pick a nation you'd like to belong to: Cherokee, Shawnee, or Chickasaw. Now imagine you are the leader of your tribe. You must lead your people from one side of Kentucky to the other. Plan your trail. Where will it start and end? What landforms will you cross? How will you do it? What will you eat? Where will you sleep? Use a map of Kentucky to draw your trail (even though Kentucky state lines didn't exist then).

Activity

What Changed and What Stayed the Same?

Look at the chart below. Charts help us organize and compare information. On a piece of paper or on the chalkboard, copy the chart. Fill in the blank spaces to compare the different groups of people. Look back in the chapter if you need help. The first one is done for you.

	Paleo	Archaic	Woodland
Homes	Caves and shelters made of rock or brush	Caves and shelters made of rock or brush	Wigwams or longhouses
Food			
Tools			
Clothes			

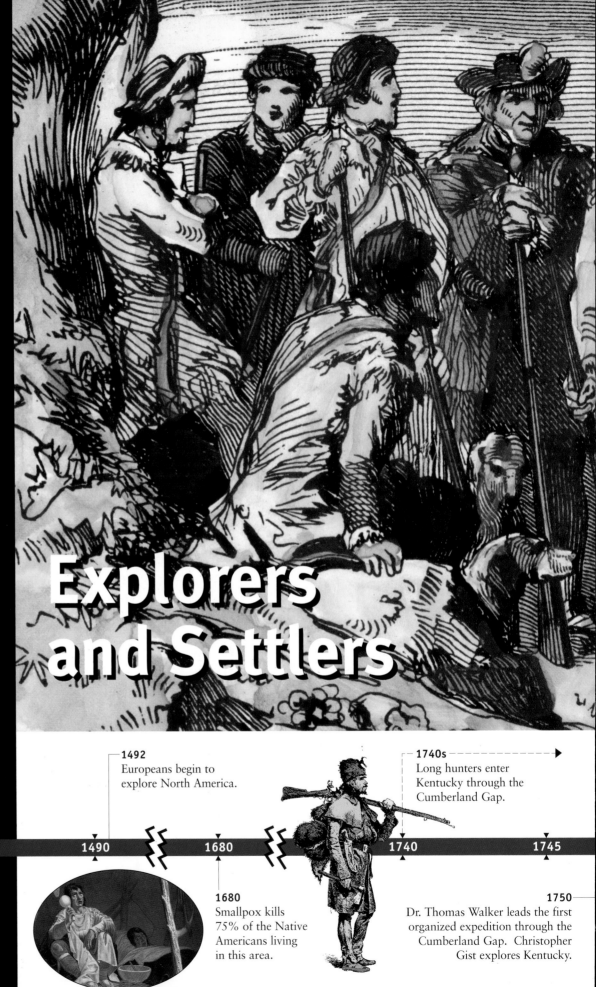

"The whole white race is a monster who is always hungry and what he eats is land."

—Chiksika,
older brother of Tecumseh

"Stand at Cumberland Gap and watch . . . the buffalo following the trail to the salt springs, the Indian, the fur trader and hunter, the cattle raiser, the pioneer farmer— and the frontier has passed by."

—Frederick Jackson Turner

Long hunters, like Daniel Boone, blazed the trail for the thousands of settlers who came after them.

Explorers and Settlers

Timeline of Events

1492
Europeans begin to explore North America.

1740s
Long hunters enter Kentucky through the Cumberland Gap.

1490   1680   1740   1745

1680
Smallpox kills 75% of the Native Americans living in this area.

1750
Dr. Thomas Walker leads the first organized expedition through the Cumberland Gap. Christopher Gist explores Kentucky.

The next period in Kentucky's history is full of exciting adventures—and long, bloody wars. More people from the East pushed through the Cumberland Gap and settled on the land that would later become our state.

But thousands of native people already lived here. They grew angry when white settlers moved onto their lands. Read the quotes on the opposite page again. What points of view do they show? Can you understand why the two groups fought?

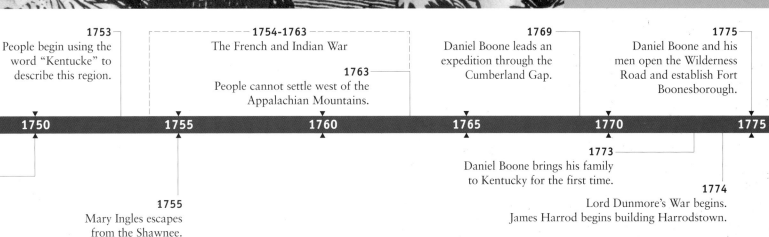

1753
People begin using the word "Kentucke" to describe this region.

1754-1763
The French and Indian War

1763
People cannot settle west of the Appalachian Mountains.

1769
Daniel Boone leads an expedition through the Cumberland Gap.

1775
Daniel Boone and his men open the Wilderness Road and establish Fort Boonesborough.

1750   **1755**   **1760**   **1765**   **1770**   **1775**

1773
Daniel Boone brings his family to Kentucky for the first time.

1774
Lord Dunmore's War begins.
James Harrod begins building Harrodstown.

1755
Mary Ingles escapes from the Shawnee.

PEOPLE TO KNOW

John Cabot
Christopher Columbus
Queen Elizabeth
Sir Walter Raleigh
Amerigo Vespucci

PLACES TO LOCATE

Asia
Atlantic Ocean
Europe
The Indies
North America
South America
Virginia

WORDS TO UNDERSTAND

colony
European
smallpox

In this chapter, you will read a lot about "Kentucky." When this land was first explored, it was not a state. The region you are reading about is the land that later became the Commonwealth of Kentucky.

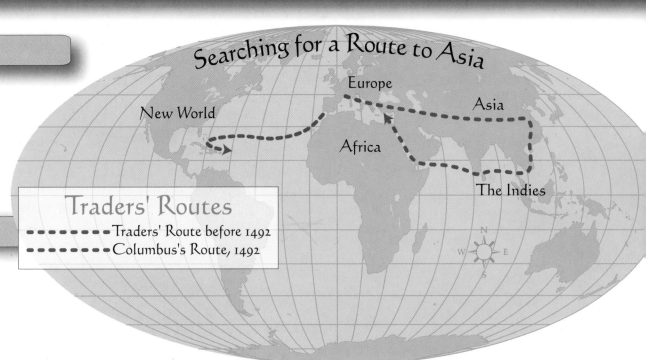

Searching for a Route to Asia

Traders' Routes
— — — Traders' Route before 1492
— — — Columbus's Route, 1492

Explorers Come from Far Away

The first European settlers who came to Kentucky followed explorers. The explorers came because they were looking for a faster way to get to Asia. *Europeans* had long been trading with people in Africa, Asia, and the Indies. They traded for goods such as spices, silk, gems, and furs. They also traded slaves.

The journey between Europe and Asia was long and very dangerous. There were often robbers along the way. If a quicker route could be found, many people would become very rich.

Christopher Columbus

Christopher Columbus began to wonder if he could reach the Indies faster if he traveled west across the Atlantic Ocean. He had no idea North and South America were even there. He thought there were only miles and miles of ocean.

Columbus and his crew sailed for over a month. Finally, they arrived at some islands. They thought they had reached a part of Asia. Actually, he and his men were not far from Florida. But since they thought they were in the Indies, Columbus and his men called

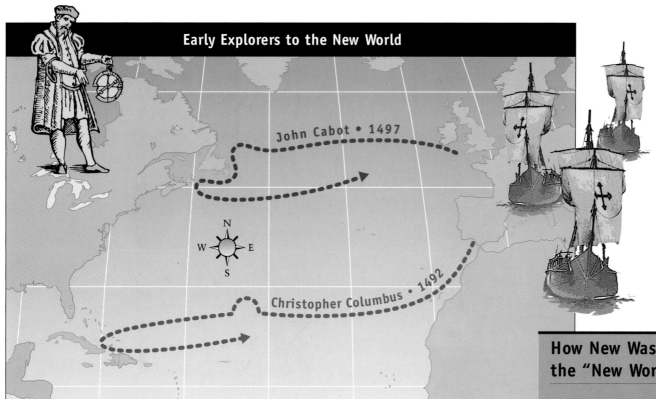

Early Explorers to the New World

John Cabot • 1497

Christopher Columbus • 1492

the people they found "Indians". From then on, Europeans used the word "Indian" to describe the people who lived here.

Other Explorers

When Columbus returned to Spain, he told people about the place he had found. His stories made others want to explore the area. Explorers from Italy, Spain, Holland, and Portugal came to North America. They thought they would find gold and treasure.

One explorer's name was Amerigo Vespucci. Look closely at his first name. The continents of North and South America were named after him.

How New Was the "New World"?

Europeans called the land here the "New World". But it was not really new. People had been living here for thousands of years. The "New World" was only new to Europeans.

Activity

Out of This World!

Traveling to other countries in the days of the early explorers was exciting and scary. We might compare it to modern times by thinking about traveling to space. Imagine you are going to travel to outer space. Write a letter to the president asking for money for your trip. What do you hope to find in space? Explain why you need to go and why your trip will help our country.

John Cabot landed in what is now eastern Canada.

The English

In time, Europeans learned North America was a whole continent they hadn't known about. Many Europeans wanted to come here because they thought the land would make them rich. The Dutch, French, Spanish, and Portuguese all established colonies. A *colony* is a settlement owned and governed by a distant country. Some colonies did not survive. England built more successful colonies in North America than any other country.

John Cabot

England sent John Cabot to North America only five years after Columbus's first trip. He, too, was looking for a route to Asia, but he did not find it. He instead found a different treasure—fish! Many people could be fed by those fish, so England claimed land in the New World. The British, or English, started settling all along the East Coast of North America.

Raleigh and Roanoke

One Englishman, Sir Walter Raleigh, established a colony in modern-day North Carolina. He sent about 100 people to his new settlement, which he called Roanoke. When a supply ship docked at Roanoke a few years later, no settlers could be found. What happened to these first English settlers is still a mystery. But Raleigh succeeded in getting people in England interested in the land he named Virginia.

Sir Walter Raleigh convinced the queen to let him name the land after her. Her name was Elizabeth. Since she was not married, she was known as the Virgin, or pure, Queen. Raleigh named the land Virginia in her honor.

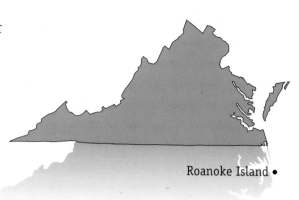

Roanoke Island •

Virginia? But This Is Kentucky!

You may be wondering why you are reading about Virginia. The reason is simple. During this time, modern-day Kentucky was part of Virginia. Virginia remained an English colony for more than 150 years.

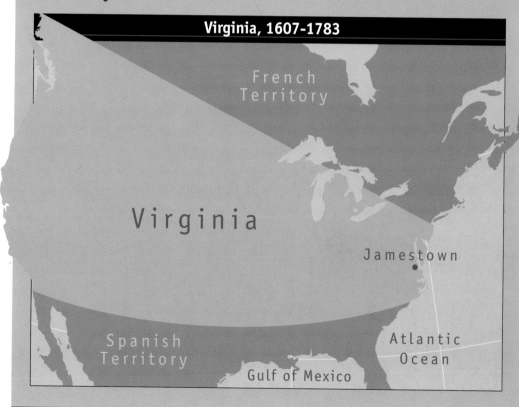

Virginia, 1607–1783

French Territory

Virginia

Jamestown •

Spanish Territory

Gulf of Mexico

Atlantic Ocean

What Do You Think?

What do you think happened to the colonists at Roanoke?

Queen Elizabeth was often called "Good Queen Bess".

People became upset when the government told them how they should worship.

Why They Left England

When Englishmen came to North America, it was a time of many new ideas. The printing press had been invented, so people began reading more. Much of what they read was about the New World.

People wanted to get away from the things they did not like about England. The New World seemed like a place where they would be able to do that. Making the deadly, 3,000-mile journey from England to North America was dangerous, but people believed it would be worth the risk.

Too Many People

One of the main reasons the English came to North America was because 4 million people lived in England. Many people longed to live in a place with more space and fewer people. Most of these people did not know about the thousands of Native Americans already living here.

Poverty

Another thing people hoped for in the New World was farmland. Many English farmers had lost their land and had no place to live. They longed to build homes and raise families on the rich land in the New World. Treasure-seekers also hoped to find gold here.

Religion

Still another reason people left England was religion. England had a state religion. A state religion means that everyone in the state (or country) belongs to the same church. But not everyone believed what the Church of England taught. Some people longed to live in a place where they could worship the way they chose.

The Kentucky Adventure

Deadly Diseases

The explorers and settlers who came to Kentucky brought diseases with them. The native people had never been around diseases like **smallpox** or measles. Their bodies could not fight off the illnesses. Smallpox spread quickly, and many people died. Sometimes, almost everyone in a village died. Within 200 years of Columbus's first landing, 75% of the Native Americans in Kentucky had died from disease.

A Shaman, or medicine man, tried to heal the sick.

1 MEMORY MASTER

1. Why did the first explorers come to North America?
2. Where did Columbus actually land?
3. Who named Virginia after Queen Elizabeth?
4. What happened to 75% of the Native Americans after Columbus came?

PEOPLE TO KNOW

Daniel Boone
Christopher Gist
Thomas Walker
George Washington

PLACES TO LOCATE

Appalachian Mountains
Barbourville
Cumberland Gap
Walker's Line

WORDS TO UNDERSTAND

adventurous
long hunter
predict
scalp
survey
trespass

Cumberland Gap

Exploring "The West"

The region known today as Kentucky was once considered "The West". That's because it was across the Appalachian Mountains, on the western side of Virginia. Lots of settlers made their homes in Virginia, but very few traveled into these "western areas". Most people did not even know the land continued westward for thousands of miles.

Kentucky Long Hunters

The first white people to explore Kentucky were *long hunters.* These men came across the mountains in small groups. Most did not actually climb the mountains. Instead, they passed through an opening in the mountains called the Cumberland Gap, or Gap for short. They hunted and explored for months—or even years—at a time.

What Is a Long Hunter?

Long hunters came here because they could sell animal furs and hides for a lot of money. They were also very *adventurous.* They did not want to stay in one place. They did not want to farm and ranch. They wanted to hunt and explore. Strong and brave, they were able to survive in even the worst conditions.

Most long hunters packed up and headed through the Gap in March. Some died in the wilderness, so they never returned. Those who did return usually came home in late October. That was a very long time to go hunting. That is why they were called long hunters.

What Do You Think?

What is the farthest distance you have ever traveled? How did you make the trip? Did you ride in a car or airplane? Do you think you would want to walk that far?

Many long hunters named places and landforms they discovered. For example, the Clinch River was named by a long hunter whose last name was Clinch.

Knowing the Land

Long hunters had to learn about the land. If they didn't, they could not survive. Some long hunters knew the land so well they could look at the sky and tell how the weather would be the next day. They could smell the wind and tell if it was going to rain. Long hunters could tell time at night by the location of the stars. By looking at plants, they could tell which direction was north.

Long hunters knew how to use, repair, and sometimes even make rifles. They knew how to make horseshoes for their horses. They could hunt and skin animals with nothing but a knife.

Long hunters spent so much time in nature that they learned the habits of animals and birds. They could *predict* what animals would do. Long hunters could even tell a true animal sound from a false one made by a human.

A long hunter's life depended on his knowing the land.

Food, Clothes, and Shelter

Do you like beef jerky? Long hunters ate dried meat for almost every meal. But most of the time their dried meat wasn't beef. It was deer, buffalo, rabbit, or even fish. Have you ever eaten dried fish?

In warm weather, long hunters wore moccasins, leggings, a loincloth, and a shirt. They did not wear pants.

Long hunters used poles and bark to build three-sided huts. They left the fourth side of the hut open to the fire pit. These huts did not offer much protection from wind, rain, and cold, but they were better than nothing.

Many long hunters got sick from being cold and wet. They also suffered from gun shots, animal bites, and broken bones. The most common problem they faced was lack of food. But there was something even more dangerous than hunger.

Conflict with Indians

Most Indians did not like long hunters. They felt the long hunters were *trespassing* on their lands. Indians used every part of an animal, but long hunters wanted only the furs and hides. Sometimes, long hunters killed hundreds or even thousands of buffalo in a single day. Then they took only the hides. They left the rest of the buffalo rotting on the ground.

When the Indians came upon such a scene, it made them very sad and angry. They needed the buffalos for food. The Indians wanted to stop the long hunters from wasting animals. Sometimes, Indians captured long hunters or *scalped* them.

Long hunters made and repaired all of their clothing.

When one minister tried to tell his people what heaven was like, he repeated the words of a long hunter. He said heaven was a "Kentucky of a Place".

The Kentucky Adventure

"The Best Poor Man's Land"

The first long hunters went home and told people about Kentucky. They described the wild game, endless waterways, forests of large trees, and lush land with rolling hills. More and more settlers crossed the mountains. After learning about Kentucky's beauty, they wanted to come here.

Many people had heard that Kentucky was "the best poor man's land". This early promise excited settlers, and more people began traveling through the Gap. They hoped they could get some of the good land. The Indians who already lived or hunted here were not happy that strange, new people were taking over their lands.

Barbourville ●

Land Companies

Most of the early long hunters and explorers who came to Kentucky worked for land companies. Wealthy Englishmen owned the land companies. The king had given these men land in Kentucky, but they had never seen it. They hired long hunters, like Daniel Boone, to tell them what their land was like. As payment, the long hunters were supposed to receive some of the land.

The Loyal Company

One of the first land companies in Kentucky was the Loyal Company. It hired Dr. Thomas Walker to find the best farming sites in southeastern Kentucky.

Though many had come before, Dr. Walker led the first organized group of men through the Cumberland Gap. They built a cabin near Barbourville. After exploring the mountains for a few weeks, the group returned to Virginia.

Linking the Past to the Present

Thomas Walker visited Kentucky many times. Our state's southern boundary with Tennessee is named Walker's Line because Walker helped **survey** it.

Do you remember what you read in Chapter 2 about the southern boundary of our state? Do you suppose Walker was the surveyor Sanford Duncan paid to keep his farm in Kentucky?

This is a model of the cabin Walker and his men built near Barbourville.

More Explorers

The next organized group through the Gap was Christopher Gist and his 17-year-old black servant. The English hired Gist to make friends with the Indians. He was also supposed to find out if the French were building a colony here.

On his third trip into Kentucky, Gist brought a guest—George Washington! Do you know who he is? He later became the first president of the United States. You've probably seen his picture on the one-dollar bill. Gist and Washington became very good friends. In fact, Gist once saved Washington's life.

Activity

Why Did They Come?

Many people explored and settled Kentucky during this time. Look back through Lesson 2 and find five reasons people came here. If you were living then, why would you want to move to Kentucky?

What's in a Name?

Have you ever wondered what the word "Kentucky" means? One legend says it means "a dark and bloody ground". The name is probably an Iroquois word that means "place of meadows" or "land of tomorrow".

Some of the early settlers called the land here "Kentucke". After a while, the "e" was replaced with a "y". Settlers liked this name better than the Shawnee name, which was "Skipaki-Thiki". That means "town of the Blue Lick". Maybe settlers liked the Iroquois name better because it was easier to pronounce. Can you imagine eating at Skipaki-Thiki Fried Chicken?

What Do You Think?

Does Kentucky seem like a "place of meadows" to you? If you had to rename Kentucky, what would you call it? Why?

2 MEMORY MASTER

1. Why was Kentucky once known as "the West"?
2. How did Indians and long hunters disagree about the buffalo?
3. What are land companies? Who owned them?
4. Who did Christopher Gist bring on his third trip to Kentucky?

The British and the colonists fought against the French and Indians in the French and Indian War.

PEOPLE TO KNOW

Daniel Boone
Chief Cornstalk
Chief Dragging Canoe
Lord Dunmore
James Harrod
Richard Henderson
Mary Draper Ingles
Colonel Andrew Lewis

PLACES TO LOCATE

Big Bone Lick
Fort Boonesborough
Harrodstown
Ohio River
Point Pleasant
Wilderness Road

WORDS TO UNDERSTAND

militia
permanent
pound
Proclamation of 1763
rival
treaty

The French and Indian War

England had 13 colonies in North America. France claimed the land around the colonies. England and France were *rivals*. Each hoped to become the greatest power in the New World. The two countries began fighting. The winner would have the largest empire in the world.

The Indians also wanted the land. It was their home. They wanted everyone except the French to leave. The Indians still wanted to trade furs with the French. Many warriors helped the French fight the British.

People who lived in the 13 colonies were still citizens of England. They agreed to help England fight the French in North America. One of these men was George Washington. At the time, he was a young officer in the Virginia *militia*. The colonists called the war the French and Indian War because they were fighting the French *and* the Indians.

Mary Draper Ingles

1731-1815

Life in a New Land

Mary Draper's parents came to the New World from Scotland. Mary was born soon after they arrived in Philadelphia. The Drapers wanted to start a new life on the frontier. They took their family to western Virginia. They built a home at a place they called Draper's Meadows. The Ingles family lived nearby. When Mary was 19, she married William Ingles. Soon, they had two sons and a home of their own.

An Attack

After the French and Indian War began, a group of Shawnee attacked Draper's Meadows. They killed many settlers and took some as prisoners. Mary and her two sons were taken. William Ingles was out in the fields and saw the attack. He ran for home, but he did not get there in time to save his wife and children.

The Shawnee took Mary and the boys far from their home. As the group traveled, Mary gave birth to another child. But the Shawnee took the baby and the two boys. Mary did not know if she would ever see her children again.

Escape!

After several weeks, the Shawnee took Mary and some other prisoners to gather salt at Big Bone Lick in Kentucky. While they were there, Mary and an older woman decided to escape. Mary knew she could not take her baby with her. She had to leave the baby behind.

The two women went toward the Ohio River. Mary did not know how to swim, so crossing streams and rivers was scary. They had to climb steep hills and mountain ridges. It was early winter, so the nights were bitterly cold. The only food they had were the berries, nuts, and roots they could find. Their shoes wore out.

The Last Part of the Journey

Later, Mary and the other woman went separate ways. Mary found an old canoe by the New River. It was hard work to clean the mud out of it, and Mary was tired and very weak. After finding a stick to use as a paddle, Mary went across the river in the canoe.

It had been over a month since she escaped. She knew home was not far, but a tall rock cliff stood in her way. There was no way around it. She gathered her strength and began to climb. It was not easy. She was hungry and very tired. Her hands were torn and bleeding. But Mary knew she would live if she made it to the top of the cliff. At last, she reached the top. She saw a cornfield and a hunting cabin. It was not long until she was home with her husband again.

A Woman of Courage

Mary became famous for her courage. Newspapers in the colonies printed stories about her adventure. One paper wrote, ". . . the woman that was taken Prisoner from New-River, has come back, . . . she had lived all the Time on Grapes and Nuts."

Mary and William Ingles did not leave their frontier home. They had more children and built a new home that they called Fort Hope. Mary lived to be 83 years old. Her life was filled with adventure, struggle, and sorrow.

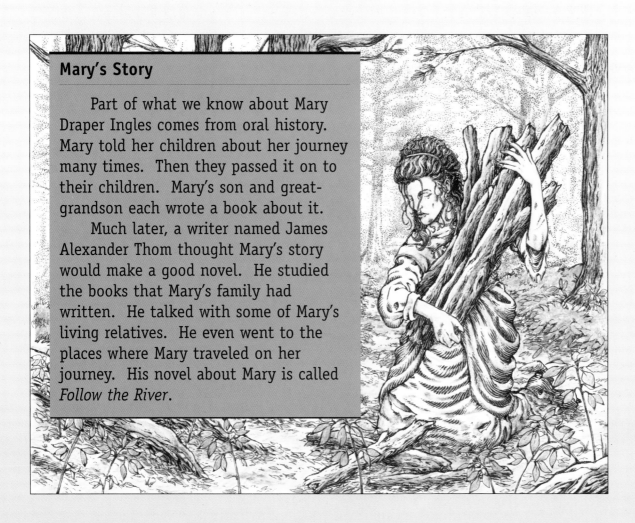

Mary's Story

Part of what we know about Mary Draper Ingles comes from oral history. Mary told her children about her journey many times. Then they passed it on to their children. Mary's son and great-grandson each wrote a book about it.

Much later, a writer named James Alexander Thom thought Mary's story would make a good novel. He studied the books that Mary's family had written. He talked with some of Mary's living relatives. He even went to the places where Mary traveled on her journey. His novel about Mary is called *Follow the River*.

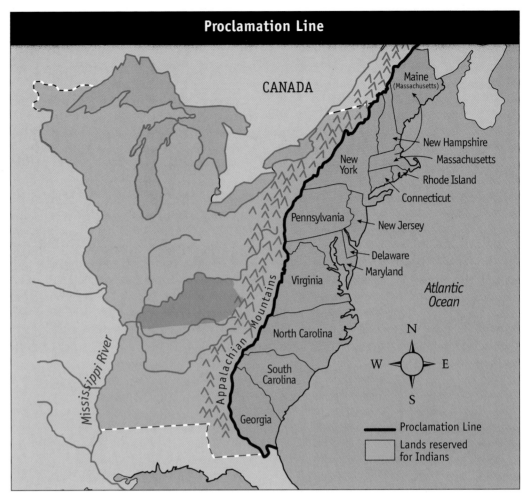

Proclamation Line

The new law created the Proclamation Line. Colonists were not allowed to live west of that line. Find the land that is now Kentucky. Can you see why colonists did not like the Proclamation of 1763?

What Do You Think

The British government made the Proclamation of 1763 because England did not want to fight any more Indian wars. How would you feel if a distant country told your family to move? Do you think the settlers had a right to be angry? Do you think there was another way to solve the problem?

The Proclamation of 1763

After nine years, England and the colonies won the French and Indian War. England gained control of all the land east of the Mississippi River. Finally, France was no longer a threat. The colonists thought they would be able to move farther west. But the British did not want to fight more Indian wars. They passed a law called the ***Proclamation of 1763.*** This law said colonists could not settle west of the Appalachian Mountains. The law also said settlers living west of the mountains had to move to the East.

The new law made settlers angry. They did not think it was fair for the British government to make decisions about the land without talking to them first. They did not want to leave their homes and farms. Most people just ignored the new law. They stayed on their farms. Those who left made slashes on trees to mark the boundaries of their land. They planned to one day return.

The Kentucky Adventure

Fort Boonesborough

The most well-known land company was the Transylvania Company. Its owner was Richard Henderson. He hired long hunter Daniel Boone to cross the Cumberland Gap and explore the wilderness on the other side. Henderson also wanted Boone to establish a settlement there.

Boone and about 30 other men cut down trees and brush to make a road. They called it the Wilderness Road. It wasn't a road like the roads we have today. It was more like a trail. The new trail made the journey to Kentucky much easier. After opening the road, the group built Fort Boonesborough along the Kentucky River.

Fort Boonesborough

Wilderness Road

Activity

Studying a Painting

This painting shows Daniel Boone entering the Cumberland Gap. Is it a primary or secondary source? Look at the clothing, the scenery, and the people. Which one is Daniel Boone? How can you tell? Why do you think the artist chose to paint this view?

JAMES HARROD

1746? **1792?**

Old Fort Harrod

James Harrod was born in Pennsylvania. When conflict with Indians grew, his family moved to Ohio. Over the years, Indians killed his brother and his stepson. But even those events never caused Harrod to hate Indians. In fact, he became friendly with them.

Harrod was a tall, slender man. He was smart and spoke French and several Indian languages. Harrod was also a fine hunter. He served in the military as a guard and then became a ranger. Harrod also became a great explorer and traveled west to Kentucky, where he met Daniel Boone.

Hoping for land in the rich Kentucky Bluegrass, Harrod established the first **permanent** settlement in Kentucky. He called the settlement Harrodstown. Now it is called Harrodsburg. Leaders in Virginia soon made Harrodstown the county seat of Kentucky County.

Harrod became a successful farmer. He owned more than 20,000 acres of the best land in our state. Harrod also owned six slaves. These people cared for his land, cattle, sheep, hogs, and horses. When he was in his 30s, he married a widow who had a son.

After Indians kidnapped and murdered his stepson, Harrod began taking long hunting trips. It was on one of these trips that he disappeared. No one knows what happened to him, but he was never seen again.

DANIEL BOONE

1734 **1820**

Daniel Boone's cabin in High Bridge

Daniel Boone

No long hunter in Kentucky is more famous than Daniel Boone. Many exciting stories are told about him, but some of them are not true.

Boone was not born or raised in Kentucky. He was born in Pennsylvania, and he spent most of his youth in North Carolina. He became skilled with a gun and fought in the French and Indian War. He married Rebecca Bryan, and they had ten children.

Boone was not the first settler to come to Kentucky, and he probably never wore a coonskin cap. He heard about "Kanta-ke" from other long hunters. Boone and his men passed through the Cumberland Gap. They collected hundreds of furs and pelts. Shawnees stole the furs and warned Boone and his men never to return.

The Shawnee warning did not stop Daniel Boone. Boone and his men blazed through the Cumberland Gap once again. They opened the Wilderness Road and built Fort Boonesborough. It was the second permanent settlement in our state. A few years later, Boone brought his family to Kentucky.

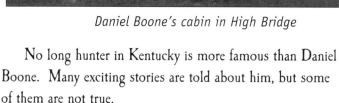

At Point Pleasant, Native Americans fought long and hard to try to keep white settlers off their land.

More Fighting on the Frontier

After the French and Indian War, there was still a lot of fighting on the frontier. More and more settlers moved onto western lands—even though it was against the law. They built forts and turned Indian hunting grounds into farms. Indians and settlers fought many times.

Lord Dunmore's War

The governor of Virginia, Lord Dunmore, grew tired of the fighting and concerned about his land. He went to Pennsylvania and led nearly 2,000 soldiers down the Ohio River. Dunmore then sent Colonel Andrew Lewis to gather a second army to fight the Indians. Lewis and his men marched over the mountains and across the rough countryside. At Point Pleasant, they met Chief Cornstalk and his Shawnee warriors. The two sides fought a deadly battle.

Linking the Past to the Present

Sometimes, when two groups meet, they have a hard time understanding each other. There is conflict. Conflict is a struggle or disagreement. Do conflicts happen today? How can they be solved?

The Battle of Point Pleasant was the biggest battle of Lord Dunmore's War. Many people on both sides were killed, but the settlers won. They forced the Indians to give up their land. All the Shawnee had to move north of the Ohio River.

The Treaty of Sycamore Shoals

The Shawnee were not the only native people who were struggling to keep their land. The settlers fought the Cherokee, too. After Lord Dunmore's War, Daniel Boone urged the Cherokee to sign the Treaty of Sycamore Shoals. A *treaty* is an agreement written on paper.

The treaty gave 17 to 20 million acres of wilderness to the Transylvania Company. In return, the Cherokee received 10,000 *pounds* (British dollars). But they could no longer live in Kentucky.

Before Cherokee Chief Dragging Canoe led his people away, he warned Richard Henderson about the land. He said it had a dark cloud over it. That is probably how the legend about the name Kentucky meaning "a dark and bloody land" first began.

After Lord Dunmore's War and the Treaty of Sycamore Shoals, most Native Americans in Kentucky had to move to other places. More white settlers came. After these events, very few Native Americans lived on the land that later became our state.

What Do You Think ?

The Proclamation of 1763 forced people west of the Appalachians to move. Settlers thought the law was very unfair. After Lord Dunmore's War, the Shawnee had to move off their Kentucky lands. Then, after the Treaty of Sycamore Shoals, the Cherokee had to move off their lands in Kentucky, too. Do you think the Shawnee and Cherokee felt the same way the settlers had? Do you think forcing Indians off their lands was fair?

❸ MEMORY MASTER

1. How many colonies did England have in America?
2. Who won the French and Indian War? What did they get?
3. Who won the Battle of Point Pleasant? What did they get?
4. What was decided in the Treaty of Sycamore Shoals?

WORDS TO UNDERSTAND

card
flax
homespun
loom
lye
shear
stockade

Life in the Settlements

The first settlers came to Kentucky on the Wilderness Road. They traveled to settlements such as Harrodstown and Boonesborough. What do you suppose daily life was like for those early frontier families?

Frontier life was hard and often dangerous. Pioneers had to be strong and brave. They had to grow their own food. They also had to make their own clothes, tools, and furniture. Most pioneers couldn't afford to buy finished goods from the cities in Virginia.

The Fort

The first thing settlers needed was protection from weather, wild animals, and Indian attacks. That is why most of the early settlements were forts. These forts were almost always built near rivers or streams. Settlers could not survive without fresh water.

A fort is a large area surrounded by a wooden stockade. The *stockade* had tall, log walls that went all the way around the settlement. To make the stockade walls, men first cut huge trees. Then they stood the logs next to each other in holes in the ground. Every fort had a front gate. It also had small openings in the walls so the settlers could keep watch.

Linking the Past to the Present

Crossing the country during frontier times was not easy. Compare it to moving today. Have you ever moved? Would you rather move today or during frontier times? Why?

Strong forts helped protect the settlers from harm.

The Kentucky Adventure

On the frontier, every member of the family had to help.

Building a Home

Building a simple cabin was very hard work. First, a family had to clear the land of trees. The men cut down the trees and dug the stumps from the ground. Then they had to cut the logs into sections and split them.

The men stacked rows of split logs on top of each other. Then they put clay or mud between them. That sealed the cracks and helped keep out the wind and rain. Most cabins had only one room. Sometimes, there was a loft. Children often climbed up a ladder to sleep in the loft.

Perhaps the most important item in the house was the fireplace. Pioneer women had to cook over the open fire. The whole family depended on the fire to keep them warm when the weather was cold. But the fireplace was dangerous, too. Sometimes chimneys caught fire.

Cabin furniture was simple and handmade. Most families had only a table, benches, and one or two beds. There might be a few chairs and a cradle for the baby. There was no plumbing for sinks or toilets, and there was no electricity. Those things hadn't been invented yet.

Wheat and corn were the most important crops on the frontier.

Corn!

The settlers prepared corn in many different ways. Sometimes, they cooked it over the fire. Other times, they made it into whiskey. Most often, they dried it and ground it into cornmeal. Then they used the meal to make cornbread and mush. Sometimes, they poured the mush into a pan. After sitting for a while, it became firm, like gelatin. Then the settlers sliced it and fried it in animal fat. Eating a piece of fried corn mush with a bit of honey was a real treat!

Farming

Most of the families who settled in Kentucky were farmers. They had to raise enough food to feed their animals and everyone in the family. The farmer used a team of oxen or a horse and plow to break up the soil. Then he planted.

Growing Food

Besides wheat and corn, other important food crops were squash, pumpkins, beans, and potatoes. Children helped pick berries and nuts. To make their food sweeter, families made syrup from the sap of maple trees. They also gathered honey from wild bees.

Many settlers raised animals, especially hogs and chickens. What do you think they were used for? Frontier families hunted deer, elk, wild turkeys, rabbits, and bears for food.

The Kentucky Adventure

Pioneer women cooked every meal from scratch. There was no fast food.

Frontier Women

Pioneer women were in charge of taking care of the home and family. Most families were large, so making one meal sometimes took many hours. A pioneer woman's day was long and filled with hard work.

The Frontier Home

Women helped grow food in small "kitchen gardens" near the cabins. Here, a pioneer woman planted vegetables and herbs for cooking and making medicines. If there was a cow, the woman milked it and used the cream to make butter and cheese.

When her husband came home from a hunt, a pioneer woman salted or smoked the animal meat to make it last. Like the Indians, pioneers used every part of an animal. They even learned how to make candles from animal fat.

Lye Soap

Pioneer women made soap from animal fat. All year long, they saved ashes from the fireplace in barrels. At soap-making time, pioneer women poured water into the barrels. The liquid that oozed out was called **lye.** The women put the lye in a big kettle, added animal fat, and cooked the mixture over the fire. After it cooled, they molded the gooey liquid into bars of soap.

Making Clothes

"I learned to card and spin both cotton and wool. I learned to make shirting, sheeting, and cotton for dresses, counterpanes, table-cloths, jeans, linsey, and every other fabric; and as for knitting, I could do that in the dark."

—Susannah Johnson, Kentucky Pioneer

Pioneer mothers and daughters made all the clothes for the family. They often used deerskin to make pants, shirts, and coats for the men and boys. But they needed cloth to make blankets, sheets, and their own dresses.

Do you know how frontier women got cloth? They had to make it themselves from a plant called *flax.* Flax had fibers pioneers used to make linen. They used a spinning wheel to turn the flax into thread.

Pioneers also raised sheep so they could have wool. They had to **shear,** or cut, the wool off the sheep. Then they washed and **carded** the wool with special tools to make it smooth. Next, they used a spinning wheel to spin the wool into yarn.

Pioneer women sometimes colored the yarn or cloth by dyeing it. To make dye, they boiled leaves, stems, bark, or berries in water. Then they dipped the yarn or cloth into the dye. The longer they left it in, the darker the yarn became.

Finally, pioneer women used a **loom** to weave the thread or wool into cloth. Weaving was almost always done by the daughters. Once the cloth was finished, pioneer mothers still had to measure, cut, and sew it into clothes for each family member. Because it took so much work to make, **homespun** cloth was very precious. Can you imagine how careful mothers were to cut only as much cloth as they needed? What do you think they did with the scraps?

Linking the Past to the Present

How do we get clothes today? Has your mother or grandmother ever made something for you? Where do women who sew get cloth?

This woman is spinning wool into thread. The square paddles in the basket on the floor were used to card wool.

Pioneer boys and girls often watched over the animals and made sure none of them got lost.

Frontier Children

On the frontier, people married young and had large families. More children meant more help on the farm. But many babies and young children died from disease. It was rare for every child in a family to live to become an adult.

Daily Chores

Parents were strict with their children. Children always had to be polite and obedient. They had to complete their many chores without complaining. The sons learned to farm. They gave the animals food and water, chopped wood, and helped plant and tend crops. They learned to hunt and fish.

Young girls learned how to cook; care for children; preserve food; make soap and candles; and spin, weave, sew, and repair clothing. Most frontier villages did not have schools. Children learned reading, writing, and math from their mothers.

Working Together

It took a lot of hard work to survive on the frontier. Everyone understood that they would be safer if they helped one another. They also knew they would be able to get more done. The frontier was often a lonely place. It was good to have friends and family nearby.

Cabins and Quilts

Pioneers worked together to clear land and to build forts and cabins. In a single day, four men could move enough heavy logs to build a cabin. The next day, they notched and stacked the logs while other men built the floor. By the end of the third day, the roof was on.

Women worked together, too. They had quilting parties. Young children played under the quilts while their mothers sewed. Whole families got together to gather sap, shuck corn, harvest fields, or make syrup or molasses.

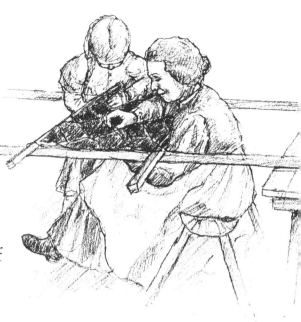

A quilting "bee" (meeting) was a time to visit and laugh.

This quilt piece was made following a log cabin pattern. The pattern is based on a small square, called the "chimney", surrounded by rectangular "logs".

Having Fun!

What did settlers do for fun? Most men and boys liked to hunt and fish. Girls played with dolls made from cloth or cornhusks. All children had fun with the carved wooden toys their fathers made. They also liked to tell jokes and riddles. Boys and girls played outdoor games like tag, hop-scotch, hide-and-seek, and leapfrog.

The settlers often gathered together. They sang songs, played homemade instruments, and danced. They also liked to tell ghost stories, Bible stories, and folktales. The folktales were often about other settlers. Their brave deeds made the pioneers feel safe and less lonely.

Activity

PARTY TIME!

You are planning a party for your class. You are in charge of food, activities, and decorations. The rule is that you must use only things found or made during pioneer times. Review the sections of this chapter that describe pioneer life. Here are some ideas to help you get started:

Food-corn, butter
Activities-storytelling, outdoor games
Decorations-candles, leaves

As part of your planning, do some research to find games and recipes from pioneer days. Then have the party. What was it like to attend a pioneer celebration?

4 MEMORY MASTER

1. What is a stockade?
2. Name three kinds of food pioneers ate.
3. Name two chores pioneer children had to do.
4. Where did pioneers get clothes?

Chapter 5 Review

What's the Point?

Explorers came to North America and called it the "New World." Settlers came looking for new opportunities and a better life. Long hunters and pioneers had to work hard for food and shelter. There were many fights about the land. The Indians were forced off the land in Kentucky. Some nations received money.

Becoming Better Readers: Reading Detectives

If your friends ask you about your weekend, do you tell them every little detail? No! If you described everything, it would take a whole weekend to tell it! Authors do the same thing when they write. They do not write every detail. They give the most important information.

You, the reader, must be a detective to fill in details from what the author says. Go back and review the portrait of James Harrod. The author does not tell you why Harrod was friendly toward Indians or how he felt during his life. Choose three events from Harrod's portrait. How do you think Harrod felt during these three times in his life?

Activity

Famous Kentuckians

Sometimes songs or poems are written to honor famous people. Do you know any songs or poems about the people in this chapter? If you don't, here's your chance to make up one yourself!

Choose one character from this chapter, and write a chant, rhyme, poem, or song about him or her. Below are some examples of first lines. You can use one of them, or you can make up your own. Your verse doesn't have to rhyme.

"Sir Walter Raleigh came for the queen . . ."
"Christopher Gist brought Washington . . ."
"James Harrod was a man who tried to make peace . . ."
"Daniel Boone was a true long hunter . . ."
"Chief Cornstalk fought with his Shawnee warriors . . ."
"Mary Ingles escaped by running away . . ."

"*Every nation has a right to govern itself . . . under what forms it pleases, and to change these forms at its own will.*"

— *Thomas Jefferson*

Timeline of Events

1775-1783
The American Revolution

1775
The First Continental
Congress is held in
Philadelphia.

1778
Settlement of
Louisville begins.

1779
Settlement of
Lexington begins.

1774   1776   1778   1780

Dec. 31, 1775
Kentucky County is established.

1776
The Second Continental Congress is held. The American
colonies declare independence from England.
Jane Coomes organizes the first school in Kentucky.

1778
Shawnees capture Daniel Boone.
Indians and settlers fight at Fort Boonesborough.

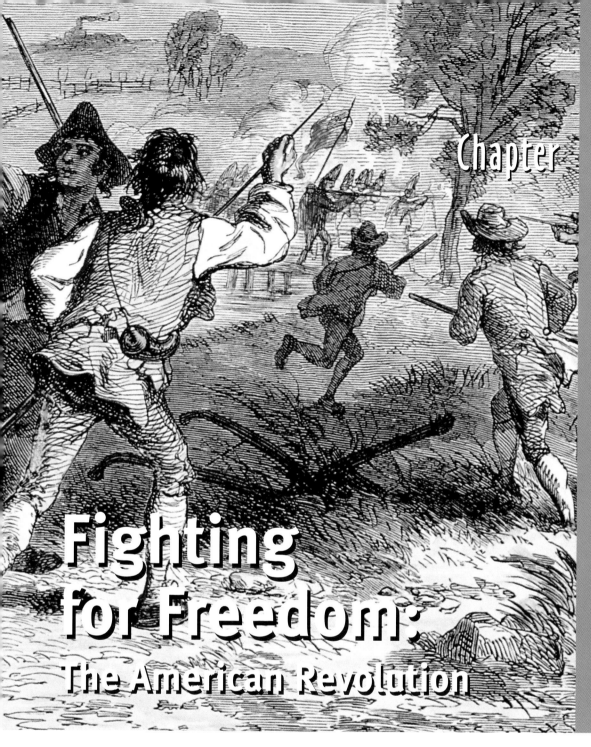

6

Men on the Kentucky frontier left their wives and families to fight for liberty. Most of them were not trained as soldiers. Instead, they were hunters, farmers, and ranchers who wanted to be free of unfair leadership. When the time came, they grabbed their guns and joined the fight.

Fighting for Freedom: The American Revolution

When the men left to fight, their wives and children sometimes cried. They knew they might never see each other again.

1782
Monk Estill becomes the first freed slave in Kentucky.

1783
The Virginia General Assembly creates the District of Kentucky.

1786
The city of Frankfort is established.

1789
The Chenoweth Massacre takes place.

1782	1784	1786	1788	1790

1780
Dr. Thomas Walker creates Walker's Line. Indians attack Martin's and Ruddell's Stations.

1784
The Spanish close the Mississippi River to American trade.

1787
The Spanish Conspiracy takes place.
The Kentucke Gazette is published.

PEOPLE TO KNOW

Abigail Adams
John Adams
George Rogers Clark
Thomas Jefferson
John Gabriel Jones
George Washington

PLACES TO LOCATE

Boston, Massachusetts
England
Kentucky County
Philadelphia, Pennsylvania

WORDS TO UNDERSTAND

ammunition
boycott
declare
delegate
independence
Loyalist
Patriot
revolution
tax
treason
unalienable

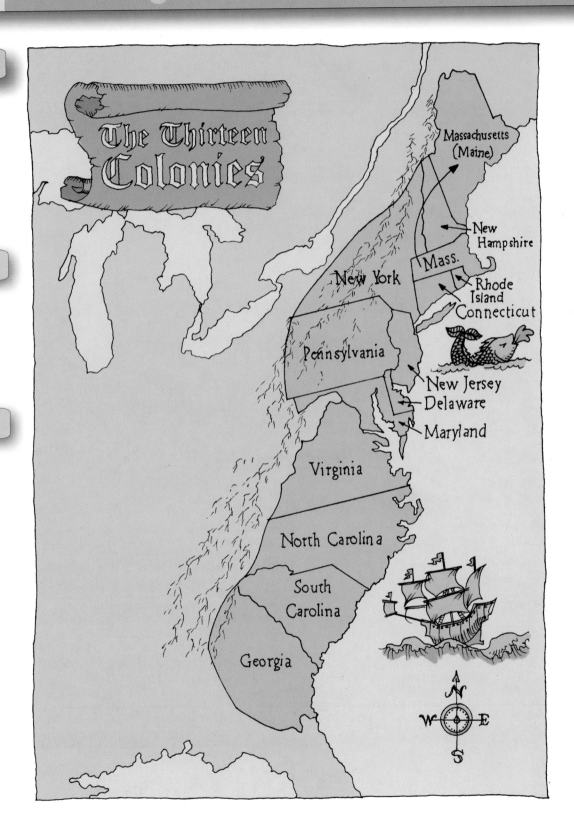

The Thirteen Colonies

Massachusetts (Maine)
New Hampshire
Mass.
Rhode Island
Connecticut
New York
Pennsylvania
New Jersey
Delaware
Maryland
Virginia
North Carolina
South Carolina
Georgia

The Most Important Colony

By the mid-1700s, the most important colony was Virginia. It was the largest and had the most people. Many of the colonies' most important leaders came from Virginia. Two of them were George Washington and Thomas Jefferson. Have you ever heard of these men? Do you know what they did for our country?

Kentucky County

The land that is now the Commonwealth of Kentucky was in the western part of the Virginia Colony. The people in Kentucky wanted to govern themselves. They wanted to make decisions about their homes. They didn't think it was fair for people in eastern Virginia to decide how they should live. Life on the western frontier was much different than life in Virginia's cities.

England is sometimes called Great Britain. English people are sometimes called British.

George Rogers Clark and John Gabriel Jones traveled to eastern Virginia. They asked the leaders there to separate Kentucky from the rest of Virginia. The leaders agreed, and Kentucky became its own county on December 31, 1775.

Kentucky County, Virginia

This is the shape of Kentucky County. How is it different from the shape of our state today?

Trouble with England

Being part of an English colony was not easy. Several things made people in all the colonies unhappy:

- They did not want to leave their homes in western Virginia—even though the Proclamation of 1763 said they had to.
- They wanted a chance to help make the laws that would affect them.
- They did not want to pay high taxes.
- They did not want to pay high prices for British goods.
- They did not want to provide housing for British soldiers.

Colonists were angry over the taxes. In this picture, they are arguing with the tax collectors.

New Taxes

A ***tax*** is money given to the government to pay for things. Taxes pay for the army, police, and other government workers. The British thought the colonists should help pay for the French and Indian War. But many colonists felt they had paid enough. They had also fought in the war and given food to soldiers.

To raise money, England taxed the colonists. Here are some of the taxes the colonists had to pay:

- **The Sugar Act** taxed sugar and molasses. The colonists used these items every day. They put sugar in their tea. They used molasses for baking.

- **The Stamp Act** required colonists to buy special stamps and place them on many papers. Letters, newspapers, and even playing cards had to have stamps.

- **The Tea Act** taxed tea. Tea was a very popular drink.

The Colonists Have No Say

The colonists were not angry only about the taxes. They were also angry that they could not help make new laws and rules. The colonists grew frustrated because they could not talk to their leaders about the things they needed.

These are examples of colonial playing cards. Cards were very popular, so they were taxed by the Stamp Act. The British hoped to make money from the taxes on playing cards.

The Kentucky Adventure

The colonists who dumped the tea didn't want anyone to know who they were. They dressed up like Indians and boarded the ship at night.

The Colonists Protest

The colonists wanted to show how unhappy they were. They held meetings and talked about what they could do. Many colonists ignored the Stamp Act and refused to buy the special stamps. They also **boycotted** British goods. That means they stopped buying things made in England. It was hard to get everyone to go without these things, but the boycott worked. The British ended some of the taxes, but they did not end the tax on tea.

One night in Boston, a group of colonists boarded a British ship loaded with tea. They dumped all the tea into the harbor. When the newspapers wrote about what happened, they called it the Boston Tea Party. Now the British were angry, too. They closed the port of Boston until the colonists paid for the tea they had destroyed. The colonists became even more upset.

Boycotts could not solve all the problems with Great Britain. In fact, the colonists felt their problems were getting worse. People throughout the colonies began calling for **independence**. This means they wanted to become a separate country. They wanted to form their own government. They did not want to be citizens of England anymore.

What Do You Think?

Why do you think it was called the Boston Tea Party? Do you think the colonists were right to dump the tea? Can you think of another way they could have tried to solve their problems with England?

Linking the Past to the Present

What kinds of taxes does our government use to raise money? Have you ever paid a tax? What kinds of taxes have you paid? Do you think taxes are fair? Why or why not?

In this painting, there are many more British soldiers than American soldiers. Does it look like the Americans will win the war?

The Colonies Come Together

The colonists knew they needed to work together. They sent *delegates,* or men to speak for each colony, to a meeting in Philadelphia, Pennsylvania. This meeting was called the First Continental Congress. In the meeting, the delegates talked about what the colonists should do about England.

England had the strongest army in the world. A war against British soldiers would be bloody and dangerous. But the delegates felt independence was worth the cost. The delegates decided the colonists should begin collecting guns and *ammunition.* They wanted to be prepared to fight. At the same time, England was sending more soldiers and ships to America. England was getting ready to fight, too.

A *revolution* is a time when citizens decide they want changes in government. They may also want a new way of life. In a revolution, people are usually willing to fight for the things they want.

The Kentucky Adventure

The Fighting Begins

The colonists formed an army. They chose Virginia's George Washington as their general. Washington had earned great respect as a leader in the French and Indian War.

In one city named Lexington and another city named Concord, both in Massachusetts, shots were fired between British soldiers and the colonists. Men on both sides were killed. The American Revolution had begun.

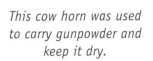

This cow horn was used to carry gunpowder and keep it dry.

Loyalists and Patriots

Some colonists did not think they should go to war with England. They wanted to be loyal to England. These people were called *Loyalists.*

The colonists who wanted freedom from England were called *Patriots.* The king of England said that anyone who was a Patriot was committing treason. *Treason* means turning against your country. English law stated that anyone who committed treason could be put to death.

What Do You Think ❓

Do you think it took courage to be a Patriot? Do you think Patriots were committing treason?

This painting shows George Washington crossing the Delaware River. The artist shows Washington leading his men out of a dark storm. They are heading for the light of freedom. Do you think freedom is like a light?

The Declaration of Independence

Once the war started, more colonists wanted independence. They sent delegates to meet in Philadelphia again. This meeting was called the Second Continental Congress. The delegates wanted to *declare* independence from England. But how would they do it?

The delegates wanted everyone to know—especially the king of England—why the colonies wanted to be a separate country. A statement had to be written by someone who was a very good writer. He also had to understand all the problems. Which one of the 55 delegates would that be?

Thomas Jefferson and the Declaration of Independence

Congress finally chose a young Virginian named Thomas Jefferson. Jefferson worked hard to find the best words. He wrote in a clear way that made sense. He explained that because the colonies had been treated unfairly, they were cutting all ties with Great Britain. The statement he wrote became known as the Declaration of Independence. It is one of the most important documents in history. Jefferson wrote:

" . . . that all men are created equal, that they are endowed by their Creator with certain *unalienable* Rights, that among these are Life, Liberty, and the pursuit of Happiness."

This was a bold statement. In England, the king was above everyone else. No one was allowed to question his power. Jefferson wrote that the colonists were equal to the king. He also explained that governments should get their power from the people.

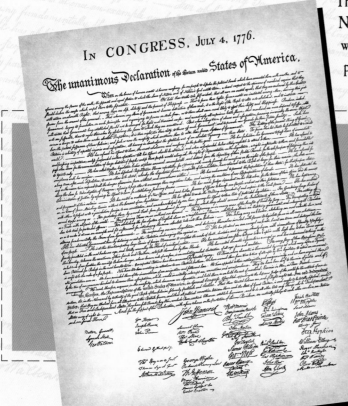

Activity

Declaration in Your Own Words

Thomas Jefferson understood that the Declaration of Independence was very important. He was careful to choose words that said exactly the right thing. Re-read the quote above that begins, "that all men". Some of the words Jefferson used may be new to you. Look up those words in the dictionary. Then rewrite the quote in your own words. Which do you like better: your words or Jefferson's words? Why?

The Kentucky Adventure

July 4, 1776

On July 4, 1776, the declaration was approved by all the delegates. The Continental Congress printed copies and sent them to all the colonists. The colonies were on their way to becoming independent states, but it was not going to be easy. They still had to fight a war.

What Do You Think ?

"All men are created equal . . ." What do these words mean to you? Do you think women and slaves should have had equal rights, too? Abigail Adams was the wife of John Adams. John was an important delegate to the Congress. Abigail asked John to "remember the ladies" when the delegates helped write the Declaration of Independence.

At that time, women were not allowed to vote. They were not allowed to serve in government. They could not own land. Abigail Adams wanted these things to change. She wanted women to have more rights.

After the declaration was written, nothing changed for women or slaves. Do you think the delegates remembered the ladies? Many delegates owned African slaves. What do you think "all men are created equal" meant to enslaved people?

Linking the Past to the Present

When something important happens in the world today, how do we hear about it? We watch the news on television, read newspapers, or check the Internet. We hear about things as soon as they happen. Long ago, it took a while for news to travel. Riders on horseback had to carry messages from place to place.

1 MEMORY MASTER

1. Where was the First Continental Congress held?
2. What is a delegate?
3. What was the Boston Tea Party?
4. Who wrote the Declaration of Independence?

PEOPLE TO KNOW

Chief Black Fish
Daniel Boone
Jane Coomes
Monk Estill
Richard Henderson

PLACES TO LOCATE

Estill's Station
Fort Boonesborough
Harrodstown

WORDS TO UNDERSTAND

accuse
compromise
enslaved
replica
slave
slave owner
station
trial

Kentucky Escapes the Early Battles

When the American Revolution began, there were less than 200 settlers living in Kentucky. Most of the early battles were in eastern Virginia and other colonies. Even though there was no fighting here at this time, other important things happened.

KENTUCKY PORTRAIT

Jane Coomes
1740(?)-1816

Jane Coomes was Kentucky's first schoolteacher. She grew up in a Catholic family in Maryland. After Jane got married, she moved to Harrodstown with her husband. Settlers were so happy to have a trained schoolteacher that they built a small but sturdy log schoolhouse. Jane began teaching her first group of students there in 1776.

The school in Harrodstown was very poor. Parents had to pay for their children to attend. Jane didn't earn very much money, and the school had almost no equipment. Students didn't have any textbooks. Jane had to think of a way to teach her students without books. She began making ink from the juice of ball-shaped fruits that grow on oak trees. She used the ink to write lessons on smooth wooden boards.

Long after Jane died, she was honored by a special Catholic group. In Harrodsburg, the group created a monument to her. The monument was a *replica* of the little log schoolhouse.

Students used hornbooks to learn the alphabet and numbers. Hornbooks were made of wood and shaped like paddles. A sheet of paper with words printed on it was attached to the paddle. Then the paper was covered by a very thin layer of animal horn. Once students could read, they studied song books and the Bible.

Daniel Boone and Fort Boonesborough

Do you remember reading about Daniel Boone in the last chapter? By this point in Kentucky's history, he had spent a lot of time here. He wanted his family to join him in the beautiful wilderness. He went back to North Carolina, gathered his family, and led them through the Cumberland Gap.

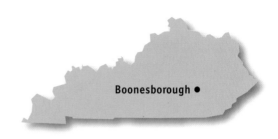

Boonesborough ●

Fort Boonesborough

While the Boone family traveled, one of Boone's sons was killed in an Indian attack. Boone decided to take his family back to North Carolina. He then returned to Kentucky and built Fort Boonesborough. Boone believed the fort would keep his family safe. He brought them back to Kentucky to stay.

The Capture of Jemima Boone

Fort Boonesborough was attacked several times by Native Americans. One warm Sunday afternoon, Daniel Boone was taking a nap. Boone's daughter, Jemima, and her friends, Betsey and Fanny Callaway, decided to take a ride in a canoe. They pushed the canoe onto the river. Suddenly, an Indian burst out of the water and grabbed the boat. The girls screamed and fought, but the Indian dragged the boat to shore. Other Indians were waiting there, and they kidnapped the girls.

The men in Fort Boonesborough heard the girls' screams. They left the fort and ran after the girls. As the girls traveled through the forest, Betsey Callaway dropped tiny bits of cloth. This helped the men follow their trail. Within three days, the men caught up to the group. They attacked the Indians, and the girls were soon home with their families.

Three of the settlers who had followed the kidnappers were Flanders Callaway, Samuel Henderson, and John Holder. These three young men were the girls' boyfriends. A few years after the event, the girls married the three brave young men who helped rescue them!

The Shawnee took Daniel Boone without a fight.

The Capture of Daniel Boone

One day, Daniel Boone and some other men from Fort Boonesborough left the fort to gather salt. While they were at the salt lick, a Shawnee war party surrounded them. The Indians were led by Chief Black Fish. Boone knew the Indians would kill his men if they tried to escape.

Boone told the chief that the frontiersmen would not fight. They would go as prisoners of the Indians. Chief Black Fish had to promise the men would not be harmed. The chief agreed, so Boone explained the agreement to his men. Boone had to talk for a long time. The men finally understood. They did not try to fight as they left the salt lick as prisoners of the Shawnee.

Two Escape

When the Shawnee first attacked the group at the salt lick, two settlers escaped! They ran back to Fort Boonesborough and told the settlers what had happened. A group of men soon left the fort to try to rescue Boone and the others.

The rescuers discovered Boone's group was already across the Ohio River. They were certain their friends must be dead. They returned to the fort with the sad news.

Chief Black Fish Adopts Daniel Boone

But Daniel Boone was not dead. Chief Black Fish had noticed how the men listened to Boone when he talked. The men had done what Boone said. The chief knew Daniel Boone was special. He invited Boone to stay in his home. He even adopted him as his own son. The tribe gave Boone a new name, Sheltowee. It means Big Turtle.

For the next six months, Boone lived the life of an Indian. This worried the other men who had been captured. They wondered why he didn't try to escape. One night, Boone heard British officers talking with Chief Black Fish. The war with England was still raging. British soldiers were moving closer to Kentucky. In fact, they were making plans to attack Fort Boonesborough! Boone knew he had to escape.

Daniel Boone Escapes!

The next day, Boone made his move. In four days, he traveled 160 miles. Part of the time, he rode an Indian pony. The pony soon became too tired to go farther. Boone walked or ran the rest of the way. When he finally reached the fort, the settlers thought he was an Indian because he was wearing Indian clothing. They almost shot him!

What Do You Think

Why do you think Daniel Boone didn't try to escape sooner? Why could staying with the Indians for a while be a good thing?

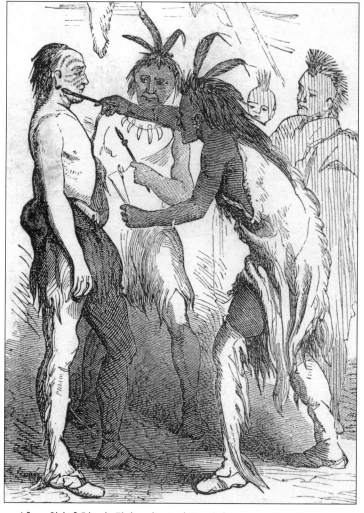

After Chief Black Fish adopted Daniel Boone, the Shawnee gave him a makeover. They wanted Boone to look like they did.

The Battle of Fort Boonesborough

After a few weeks, the Indians and British soldiers arrived at the fort. They called out to Daniel Boone, "Sheltowee, Sheltowee, your father wants you." Boone left the fort to talk with Chief Black Fish. The two men talked and finally reached a *compromise.*

No one is certain what happened next. The Indians walked toward the settlers. Maybe they just wanted to shake the settlers' hands. Maybe they were angry because they did not think the compromise was fair. The Indians and the settlers began to fight. The settlers ran back to the fort, and the two groups fought for ten days. Finally, the Indians gave up. Over the next 20 years, Indians attacked the settlers many times, but they never bothered Fort Boonesborough again.

What Do You Think ?

Why do you think the battle at Fort Boonesborough began? Why do you think Indians never attacked the fort again?

After the Battle of Fort Boonesborough, the fort was a very safe place to live.

Daniel Boone
Is Charged with Treason

After the battle at Fort Boonesborough, some of the settlers began to question Daniel Boone's loyalty. They wondered why he stayed with Chief Black Fish for so long. They wondered if he cared more about the Indians than he did about the settlers. Two men from the fort *accused* him of treason. Do you remember what treason is? It is turning against your own people or country.

The Trial

Daniel Boone had to stand *trial.* That means he had to prove he did not turn against the settlers at Fort Boonesborough. He had to prove that he cared more about the settlers than Chief Black Fish.

At the trial, officers from the Kentucky army listened to people talk about Daniel Boone. Then the officers listened to Boone tell his side of the story. After that, the officers went into another room to discuss all the things they had heard. When they came back, they said Daniel Boone had done nothing wrong. They thanked him for being so helpful in the battle at Fort Boonesborough. They even made him an officer in the Kentucky army.

No Land for Daniel Boone

Richard Henderson, the owner of the Transylvania Company, organized a meeting of people from Fort Boonesborough and other settlements. They met under an elm tree to discuss what kind of government they wanted for Kentucky County. Settlers were pleased with the meeting. They thought they would have fair leadership. Daniel Boone hoped he would get a large piece of land since he had done so much for Kentucky.

That never happened. Land company leaders were not fair to the settlers. They raised the price of land, so most settlers could not afford to buy any. Daniel Boone found himself without any land. Angry and discouraged, he left Kentucky for Missouri. Boone stayed there until he died. He was buried in Missouri. Later, his family had his body moved to Frankfort, our state capital.

What Do You Think ?

Do you think Daniel Boone was guilty of treason? Why or why not?

What Do You Think ?

Do you think Daniel Boone deserved to have some land in Kentucky? Do you think he should have been buried in Frankfort, or some other place? If another place, where? Why?

Monk Estill
1750?-1835

Monk Estill was an enslaved African man. His owner was Captain James Estill. He and Monk became good friends. Monk and Captain Estill arrived at Fort Boonesborough in the early days of the settlement.

Monk was a charming person. He was not very tall, but he weighed 200 pounds, and he was very strong. He had three wives and 30 children! One of those children was the first African American child born in Kentucky.

After Captain Estill founded Estill's Station, Monk moved there. One day while Captain Estill was hunting, a group of Indians attacked the settlement. They captured Monk and asked him questions about the fort.

Monk did not answer the questions truthfully. He told the Indians that the settlement had many men, guns, and weapons. Actually, it had only a few. The Indians decided not to attack until they had more weapons. Two days later, Captain Estill, Monk, and other settlers attacked the Indians.

Captain Estill was killed in the battle, but Monk escaped. He carried a wounded man nearly 25 miles back to Estill's Station. Captain Estill's son was so impressed with Monk's courage that he gave Monk his freedom. Estill's son gave Monk money so he lived comfortably for the rest of his life.

After he was freed, Monk learned to make gunpowder. This was a very important skill. Soon, Monk was making all the gunpowder for Fort Boonesborough and Estill's Station.

In his later years, Monk lived in Shelbyville and became a Baptist preacher. He is remembered for being the first freed slave in Kentucky.

Frontier Slavery

The first African slaves came to Kentucky with explorers. A *slave* is a person who is owned by another person. The people who owned slaves were called *slave owners*.

By the time the American Revolution began, many *enslaved* people lived in Kentucky. They helped with farming, salt processing, housework, and other duties. However, more slaves lived in states that were farther south than ever lived here.

Most enslaved people were not treated like human beings. They were bought and sold like property.

Monk Estill

Enslaved children and parents were sometimes sold to different owners. They might never see one another again. Slave owners often abused their slaves, too. It was impossible for parents to protect their children.

• Estill's Station

A *station* was a settlement of cabins surrounded by a stockade.

2 MEMORY MASTER

1. Who was Kentucky's first schoolteacher?
2. Who captured Daniel Boone?
3. Why did Daniel Boone move to Missouri?
4. Who was Monk Estill?

The War Comes to Kentucky

As the American Revolution continued, the battles moved closer to Kentucky County. Settlers became worried. They did not want British soldiers to *invade* their homes. They wondered how the war would affect life in Kentucky.

As the war moved into Kentucky, many frontiersmen joined the colonial army. They were trained by other soldiers.

PEOPLE TO KNOW

Henry Byrd
George Rogers Clark
King Louis
John Martin
Robert Patterson

PLACES TO LOCATE

Blue Licks
Corn Island
Falls of the Ohio
Lexington
Louisville
Martin's Station
Ruddell's Station
Yorktown, Virginia

WORDS TO UNDERSTAND

erosion
invade
surrender

George Rogers Clark

George Rogers Clark had become famous during Lord Dunmore's War. He was bold and daring. Clark asked the governor of Virginia if he could gather an army. He wanted to invade the British forts north of the Ohio River. The governor approved. Clark took 175 men and headed north.

Clark and his men built a stockade and several cabins at Corn Island, near the Falls of the Ohio. In late June, they left Corn Island

A Vanishing Island

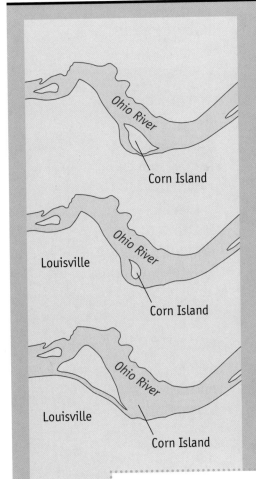

Did you know that Corn Island no longer exists? Four events caused the island to disappear. The first event was early builders taking limestone from around Corn Island. The builders used the rock to make buildings and roads. They took so much limestone from the island's shores that the whole island began to shrink.

The second event was **erosion.** Removing the rock from the beaches killed the plants and grasses that grew there. These plants protected the shores from erosion. Once the plants were gone, the moving water of the Ohio River began washing away the shores. The island shrank more.

The third event has to do with cement. Workers discovered that the limestone around Corn Island was perfect for making cement. They began removing tons of rock every year. Workers even dug out the rock that was under water. The island shrank even more.

The last event was the building of a dam. By the early 1900s, very little of Corn Island was left. Then the government built a dam to generate electricity. The dam caused the Ohio River to rise and flood the last traces of Corn Island. By 1924, the site of Louisville's first settlement was deep under water.

Linking the Past to the Present

After Clark's army left Corn Island, the settlers moved to the Kentucky shore. They built a stockade and cabins. Now they had to choose a name for their new settlement. They thought about the king of France. The king was sending thousands of French soldiers to help the colonists fight the British. To thank him, the settlers named their city after the king. Do you know which large Kentucky city this is? The king was Louis, and the city is Louisville!

and marched northward. Ten days later, they began capturing British posts. The English army knew Clark's soldiers would win if there was a fight. They often **surrendered** without firing a single shot.

Clark Attacks the Shawnee

After capturing the British posts, Clark's army attacked a Shawnee village near what is now St. Louis, Missouri. Clark led the attack for two reasons. First, the Shawnee were helping the British. Second, warriors often traveled into Kentucky even though they had agreed not to.

Before the attack, the Shawnee learned Clark's army was coming. Everyone in the village escaped before the soldiers arrived, so no one was killed. The troops did, however, destroy the village and the tribe's winter supply of corn.

The Battle of Blue Licks

Kentuckians attacked the Shawnee many more times. One major attack was called the Battle of Blue Licks. Some called it the "last battle of the American Revolution." One of the soldiers who fought in this battle was Daniel Boone.

The Shawnee had many more men than the Kentuckians, so the Kentuckians lost the battle. Some people said it was Clark's fault. But even though this battle was lost, George Rogers Clark helped Kentucky fight the British more than any other person.

George Rogers Clark was a soldier and a pioneer. He also was excellent at math and worked as a surveyor.

The Battle of Blue Licks was one of the worst military disasters on the Kentucky frontier.

Fighting for Freedom: The American Revolution

Martin's and Ruddell's Stations

John Martin was an early Kentucky pioneer. He started a station on Stoner Creek. Less than a year later, British captain Henry Byrd and his soldiers captured Martin's Station. The settlers did not try to defend themselves. Instead, they allowed the British to take them prisoner.

The following year, Captain Byrd gathered a larger army that included nearly 1,000 Indian warriors. Byrd's group attacked a settlement called Ruddell's Station. This time, the settlers tried to defend their home. About 20 of them died, and the rest were taken prisoner.

Settling Lexington

Shortly after the war began, a group of pioneers and explorers from Pennsylvania camped in the Bluegrass near McConnell Springs. They named their camp site Lexington after the battle in Massachusetts. Several years later, Colonel Robert Patterson built a block house on the site. It was the first home in the city of Lexington. After the war was over, Patterson helped plan the new town.

After the war was over, people cheered and waved as George Washington and his men returned.

The End of the War

While settlers in Kentucky still fought, the war was coming to an end in Virginia. George Washington's army surrounded the British near Yorktown, Virginia. The British general had no where to go, so he surrendered. The American colonies won the war!

During the war, many people believed the British would win. The British had more men, better weapons, and better training. The colonial army was made up of farmers, merchants, and frontiersmen. They were not trained to fight. But the colonists were very committed to freedom. They fought to protect their homes and families from unfair laws. During the surrender, a British band played music called "The World Turn'd Upside Down".

What Do You Think?

Why do you think the band played "The World Turn'd Upside Down"? What do you think seemed upside down to the British? Do you think the country with the stronger army should have won? Why or why not?

A Treaty and a New Nation

The United States and England signed the Treaty of Paris. England allowed the United States to become an independent country. British soldiers had to leave all the colonies—including Kentucky County, Virginia.

The British also agreed that the United States' western border would be the eastern shore of the Mississippi River. Even though Spain controlled the river, Kentuckians would not have to leave their homes. The Proclamation Line was gone.

What Next?

The new nation now had a different set of problems. How would the country be governed? How should the states work together? Could regions like Kentucky County become states? How would they do it? These were things our country's citizens and leaders still had to decide.

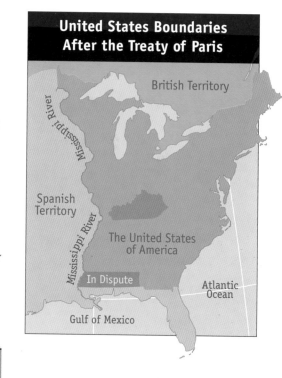

United States Boundaries After the Treaty of Paris

Mississippi River

British Territory

Spanish Territory

Mississippi River

The United States of America

In Dispute

Atlantic Ocean

Gulf of Mexico

---

3 MEMORY MASTER

1. Who built a stockade at Corn Island?
2. Who is Louisville named after?
3. Who won the Battle of Blue Licks? Why?
4. After the Treaty of Paris was signed, where was the United States' western border?

Land Claims

The war brought thousands of new settlers to Kentucky. Through the Cumberland Gap, they came by wagon, horse, or even on foot. Those who came from the North floated down the Ohio River on flatboats or in canoes. Everyone hoped for a piece of the "best poor man's land."

As more and more settlers claimed land, they began to argue over *boundaries*. Settlers could claim land in one of three ways: military claims, land company claims, and squatter's claims.

Military Claims

Soldiers who had fought in battles were supposed to get paid. But the government didn't have any money to pay them. Instead of money, the government gave them land. This payment of land was called a *military claim*. Military claims rewarded soldiers for risking their lives.

Land Company Claims

The land companies paid workers with land instead of money. This was called a *land company claim*. But when British governors had been in charge, they had often refused to allow the settlers to keep the land. These people were left with no land at all. This is what happened to Daniel Boone.

Squatters

Some settlers felt they should be able to own land if they had lived on it for a while. They felt they had earned the right to keep it by clearing it and building homes on it. These people were called *squatters*.

Who Deserves the Land?

Each family felt it deserved land more than anyone else. Men who had served as soldiers had protected the land. Some had terrible scars or were missing limbs. They had been promised land

for their time and effort. Squatters had worked the land for years.
They had survived hunger, Indian attacks, and terrible storms. They
had worked hard to build their homes.

These settlers became angry when the government passed a law
called the Land Act. This law said settlers had to pay for land—
even though they had been promised free land. Some settlers had
established successful farms in the rugged wilderness, but they had
very little money. They could not afford to pay for the land.

Deeds and Maps

Have you ever seen a *deed?* It is a piece of paper used to prove
someone owns a piece of land. A deed shows the land's boundaries
and the name of the person who owns the land. Deeds are stored at
the county courthouse. On the frontier, there were no deeds and no
courthouses. Families weren't sure where their land ended and their
neighbor's began.

The maps of Kentucky made things difficult, too. Many of the
early map-makers used natural features, such as trees or rocks, to
describe the land. Over time, the natural features changed or
disappeared. Soon, the maps did not show the land like it really
was. Boundaries often overlapped, so people claimed the same
pieces of land. Sometimes, they even fought about it.

Linking the Past to the Present

How do we mark boundaries
today? How do you know
where your property lines
are? What property belongs
to everyone?

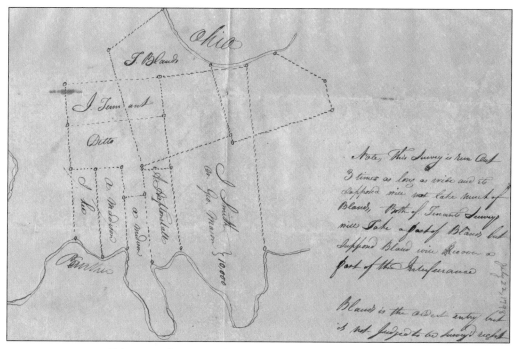

*This map shows overlapping land claims. Such claims
caused many problems on the frontier.*

Creating the District of Kentucky

The arguments about land claims got worse. Settlers had to travel all the way to eastern Virginia to get help. Kentucky County needed judges and courts of it own.

The Virginia Assembly finally changed Kentucky County to the District of Kentucky. This change solved many problems. The new district had courts that could make decisions about land claims, treason, and other problems. Finally, Kentucky settlers didn't have to travel so far to get help with their land claims.

The First Steps Toward Statehood

Creating the District of Kentucky helped with some problems, but Kentuckians still argued. Do you know what they were arguing about? It was statehood. Some people wanted the District to become a separate state from Virginia. Others didn't want to become a state at all. They didn't want to be part of the United States.

At this time, people in Kentucky were divided mostly into three groups. The three groups were landless farmers, landowners, and *politicians,* who were often landowners, too.

Landless Farmers

Landless farmers were people like Daniel Boone. They wanted the government to take some of the land away from people who had a lot. Virginia's leaders refused to do that, so these men wanted to separate from Virginia. They wanted the District to become a new state. They hoped new state leaders would help them get land.

This is the old courthouse in Williamsburg, Virginia. Kentuckians wanted a courthouse closer to home.

The Kentucky Adventure

Landowners

Landowners usually owned thousands of acres and many slaves. These men were very rich. They did not want anyone to take their land away from them. They thought a strong state government would protect their claims. They wanted the District to separate from Virginia, too.

Politicians

The politicians were mostly lawyers and judges. Most of them did not own land, but they wanted some. A man named James Wilkinson told them they would become rich and powerful if the District of Kentucky joined with Spain. Some politicians began to wonder if Kentucky should remain part of the United States.

Conflict Between the Groups

The three groups wanted different things. Leaders of the District of Kentucky decided to hold meetings to talk about problems in the district. The meetings gave the groups a chance to discuss their problems together.

John Bradford

The Kentucke Gazette

The District of Kentucky had a printing press and hired John Bradford to run it. He set up a shop in Lexington and printed the first newspaper in Kentucky, *The Kentucke Gazette*.

The Kentucke Gazette kept people informed. They read about statehood. They read about events taking place all across the world. The *Gazette* didn't print stories about events in Lexington. That was because Lexington was so small nearly everyone already knew what was going on!

The Kentucke Gazette's *first office was this little log cabin.*

After Kentucky became a state, even more people read the *Gazette*. That was because it was the only newspaper for 500 miles—but not for long. Soon, another printer began printing *The Kentucky Herald*. Now people had a choice.

John Bradford went on to publish other things. He published *The Kentucky Almanac* and a book of poems by a Kentucky poet. After 60 years and many changes in ownership, *The Kentucke Gazette* published its final issue in 1848.

The Spanish Conspiracy

The Mississippi River was very important to the District of Kentucky. It was the fastest and safest way to move goods in and out of the region. If people couldn't sell their goods, they couldn't make any money. The river was so important that countries sometimes fought for control of it.

Spain Controls the Mississippi River

Spain controlled the huge piece of land to the west of the United States. This piece of land was called the Louisiana Territory. It was named after the place in the South where the Mississippi River emptied into the Gulf of Mexico.

During the colonists' fight for independence, the Spanish did not control the Mississippi River—but they wanted to. The Spanish knew they could destroy the economy of the United States if they had control of the river. With no money, the United States would become very weak. Then Spain could take over.

After the American Revolution, the United States was forced to give **right of control** of the river to the Spanish. Spain quickly passed a law that said Americans could not use the river. It became very hard for Kentuckians to buy or sell goods.

Kentuckians had a hard time selling their goods when Spain refused to let them use the Mississippi River.

James Wilkinson

James Wilkinson was a Kentucky politician. He urged Kentuckians to separate from Virginia and become part of Spain. If Kentucky did this, the region would be able to use the river again.

Wilkinson traveled to New Orleans and met with Spanish governor Esteban Miró. Wilkinson told Miró that Kentuckians would soon separate from Virginia and become part of Spain. The Spanish governor was so pleased that he let Kentuckians begin using the Mississippi River again!

There was a problem, though. Wilkinson had lied to the Spanish governor. Most people in Kentucky did not want to become part of Spain. They did not want to leave the United States. They only wanted to separate from Virginia.

When Kentuckians found out what Wilkinson had done, they became very angry. They wanted to use the river, but they did not want to become part of Spain. Wilkinson's plan, known today as the *Spanish Conspiracy,* failed.

James Wilkinson

Frankfort, Our State Capital

James Wilkinson did do one important thing for our state. He started Frankfort, the city that became our state capital. Before Kentucky became a state, Wilkinson bought a large piece of land on the north side of the Kentucky River. That same year, the Virginia legislature turned 100 acres of it into the town of Frankfort.

A few years later, Wilkinson sold the entire piece of land to Andrew Holmes. Kentucky then became a state and needed to choose a capital. State leaders couldn't decide which city would be best. They finally told Kentuckians that the city that offered the most land, money, and other benefits would become the capital.

Andrew Holmes wanted Frankfort to become the capital city. He called a meeting of all the people in the town. The townspeople wanted the capital, too. They offered several plots of land, $3,000 cash, building supplies, and a few other things. The offer from the people of Frankfort was more than any other city's offer. Three days later, state leaders named Frankfort as the capital of the Commonwealth of Kentucky!

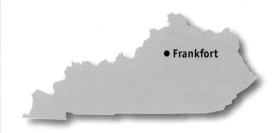

Kentucky Bourbon Whiskey

The first settlers in Kentucky noticed that the corn they planted grew strong and healthy. They also found hundreds of freshwater springs bubbling out of the limestone. Top-quality corn and spring water became the two main ingredients in whiskey. Kentuckians soon set up **stills** and made some of the finest bourbon whiskey in the United States.

All bourbon whiskey is made from corn. But not all whiskey is the same. The quality and taste of the water makes a big difference. So does **aging.** Elijah Craig was the first person to age corn whiskey in a **charred** white oak barrel. The longer the whiskey stayed in the barrel, the more the wood flavored it. People loved the "smooth" taste, and the business of making whiskey became very popular here. In fact, Kentucky still has more **distilleries** than any other state in the nation!

166

The Kentucky Adventure

The Chenoweth Massacre

One fateful summer night, Indians made their last major attack on Kentuckians. The family of Richard Chenoweth was gathering for supper when the Shawnee invaded. The Shawnee killed three of the Chenoweth children, a guard, and all the farm animals.

Margaret (Peggy) Chenoweth, the wife and mother, was shot by an arrow, wounded by a tomahawk, scalped, and left for dead. Somehow, she made it to the family's well house, where soldiers found her the next day. She survived and lived to be over 80 years old! For the rest of her life, she wore a small white cap to cover her baldness.

This is the well house where Peggy Chenoweth was found.

A Faded Dream

By the time Kentucky was approaching statehood, 73,000 people lived here. Yet most of them owned no land. The dream of the "best poor man's land" quickly faded. Many, like Daniel Boone, left the state disappointed that their dream had not come true.

Many Kentuckians were also disappointed that the District of Kentucky was still part of Virginia. They were tired of having to travel to eastern Virginia if they wanted to talk to their leaders. Settlers also felt most Virginians did not understand the needs of people on the frontier.

The colonists had once wanted independence from England. They fought for eight long years to gain it. Now the settlers in the District of Kentucky wanted independence from Virginia. What would it take for that to happen?

Linking the Past to the Present

You can still visit the stone well house where Peggy Chenoweth escaped. It is in Middletown.

• Middletown

4 MEMORY MASTER

1. What is a deed?
2. Settlers who fought in the army were paid something instead of money. What was it?
3. What new name did the Virginia Assembly give Kentucky County?
4. Who printed the first newspaper in Kentucky? What was the paper called?

Chapter 6 Review

What's the Point?

Kentucky becomes a separate county of Virginia. The 13 colonies want freedom from England. Colonial delegates meet in Philadelphia to decide what to do. Thomas Jefferson writes the Declaration of Independence. The American Revolution is fought.

In Kentucky, problems with land and Indians continue. Later, Kentucky enters the war. The colonists win the war against England. Kentucky becomes the District of Kentucky.

Our Amazing Geography: Bounding Along

In Lesson 4, you learned about boundary lines. In geography, a boundary is a line that divides one area from another. Can you think of how boundaries are used in your community today? Make a list of six ways boundaries are used today. Then look at your list carefully. Divide your list into two groups:

1. Boundaries that help bring order
2. Boundaries that create problems

Now look back through this chapter and see how boundaries helped Kentucky. How did they cause problems with the land? Using a blank map of Kentucky, draw a map of how you would divide land rights among Native Americans, squatters, land companies, explorers, and settlers.

Activity

From County to State?

At the end of this chapter, we learn that Kentuckians wanted freedom from Virginia. Can you think of reasons why Kentucky should be a separate state? Can you think of reasons *not* to separate? Make a list called "Pros" (reasons to be a new state) and "Cons" (reasons *not* to be a new state). Then think about Thomas Jefferson writing the Declaration of Independence. Write a letter to Virginia leaders declaring why you want Kentucky to be a state. Choose your words carefully, and write clearly!

Becoming Better Readers: A Letter from George Rogers Clark

The following is from a letter written by George Rogers Clark. It was written on November 19, 1779 while Clark and his men were at the Falls of the Ohio. Read the letter, and then answer the questions below it.

On the evening of the 4th of July, we got within three miles of the town (of) Kaskaskia, having a river of the same name to cross to the town. After making ourselves ready for anything that might happen, we marched after night to a farm that was on the same side of the river, about a mile above the town, took the [British] family prisoners and found plenty of boats to cross in, and in two hours transported ourselves to the other shore with the greatest silence.

I learned that they had some suspicion of being attacked and had made some preparations —keeping out spies—but they, making no discoveries, had got off their guard. . . . Nothing could excel the confusion these people seemed to be in, being taught to expect nothing but savage treatment from the Americans. Giving all for lost . . . they were willing to be slaves to save their families.

It was certain that they were a conquered people, and, by the fate of war, was at my mercy, and that our principle was to make those we reduced free, instead of enslaving them as they imagined; that if I could have surety of their zeal and attachment to the American cause, they should immediately enjoy all the privileges of our government.

No sooner had they heard this than joy sparkled in their eyes. . . . [T]hey told me that they had always been kept in the dark as to the dispute between America and Britain. . . .

1. What British post did Clark take over?
2. How did Clark and his army take over the post?
3. Were the British ready to fight Clark?
4. Was Clark going to enslave the conquered people or set them free?
5. Why does Clark write "joy sparkled in their eyes"?
6. Do you think Clark shows he is a good leader in this letter? Why?
7. What events were important for Clark to tell about?
8. What does he NOT talk about in the letter?

"The idea of perfection in government is a mere [fantasy]. The most to be hoped for is the great, not the perfect, good."

—George Nicholas

1790   1792   1794   1796   1798   1800

1792
Kentucky becomes the 15th state.
Isaac Shelby becomes the state's
first governor.

1796
The Pinckney Treaty allows free
use of the Mississippi River.

1799
Transylvania Seminary (later University) is established.
The state's second constitution is adopted.

Statehood —At Last

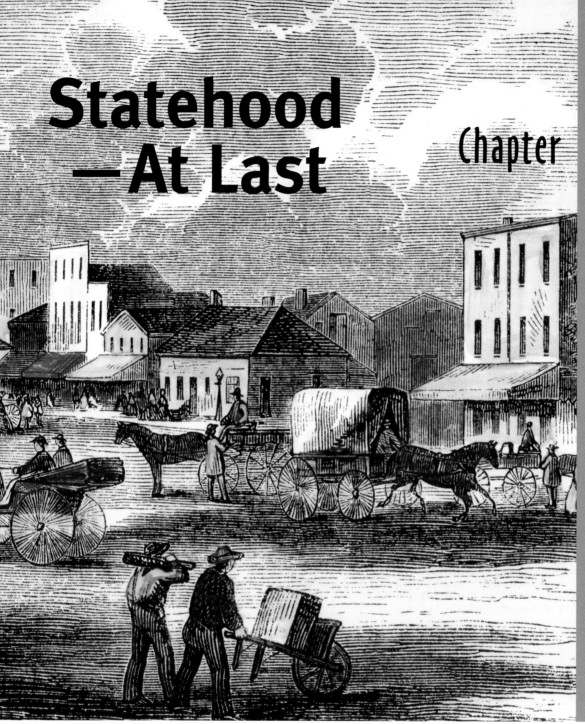

The years just after statehood were good ones for Kentucky. People from many parts of the world moved here. They brought with them new religions, new traditions, and new lifestyles. New towns sprang up, and existing towns grew much larger. After the United States bought land in the West, Kentucky was no longer considered "the frontier".

This is the marketplace in Covington. The town square was always the busiest place in the city.

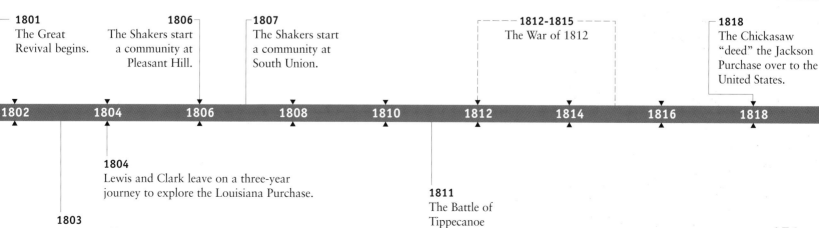

1801
The Great Revival begins.

1806
The Shakers start a community at Pleasant Hill.

1807
The Shakers start a community at South Union.

1812-1815
The War of 1812

1818
The Chickasaw "deed" the Jackson Purchase over to the United States.

1802   1804   1806   1808   1810   1812   1814   1816   1818

1804
Lewis and Clark leave on a three-year journey to explore the Louisiana Purchase.

1811
The Battle of Tippecanoe

1803
Thomas Jefferson signs the Louisiana Purchase Treaty.

172

Working Toward Statehood

For many years, Kentuckians had wanted to separate from Virginia. The Virginia Assembly had made Kentucky a district, but the district was still part of the state of Virginia. The people of Kentucky were not satisfied. They wanted Kentucky to have all the rights of a state. They wanted their own state government. They wanted more control over their region. They decided it was time to make a change. Kentuckians sent delegates from across the state to Danville for a special meeting called a *statehood convention.*

Petitioning the U.S. Congress

At the convention, the delegates talked about the reasons Kentucky wanted to become a state. Then they wrote a letter to the U.S. Congress. The letter asked Congress to recognize Kentucky as a state. But national leaders did not think Kentucky was ready. They said no.

Kentuckians did not give up easily. Again and again, the delegates gathered in Danville for meetings. After each convention, the District of Kentucky *petitioned* Congress for statehood again. Each time, Congress refused.

One Condition

Shortly after the U.S. Constitution was *ratified,* delegates petitioned for statehood again. President George Washington urged Congress to approve the petition. Congress agreed to make Kentucky a state, but the delegates had to do one more thing. They had to write a state *constitution.*

◄ *This is a model of the building at Constitution Square in Danville, where the delegates met.*

PEOPLE TO KNOW

Alexander S. Bullitt
James Garrard
George Nicholas
Reverend David Rice
Isaac Shelby

PLACES TO LOCATE

Danville
Frankfort

WORDS TO UNDERSTAND

committee
constitution
elector
legal
legislature
petition
ratify
restrict
statehood convention

Danville ●

Reverend David Rice
1733-1816

David Rice was born in Virginia. He had 11 brothers and sisters. When he was a young man, he went to school to become a minister. He then married Mary Blair, and they had 12 children.

After David finished school, he received a letter from 300 people in Kentucky. They wanted a minister to teach them. David talked with his family about the letter. They decided to move to Kentucky.

Many Kentuckians grew to love David Rice. He was honest and kind. He was also well-educated, and he was a good organizer. David started three Presbyterian churches in Kentucky, including one in Danville. He also helped start Transylvania Seminary.

David Rice felt strongly about slavery. He thought it was a terrible thing. He often wrote about it and preached about it in his sermons. He worked hard to end slavery in Kentucky, but he did not succeed.

David died at the age of 83. He and Mary are both buried in Danville at the old cemetery next to the Presbyterian church.

The First State Constitution

Kentucky delegates gathered in Danville for the tenth time. They began writing the state's first constitution. The constitution made rules for the state. It also described how state and local governments would operate. The constitution said the new state's name would be the Commonwealth of Kentucky.

David Rice and the Slave Debate

Some of the delegates who helped write the constitution were George Nicholas, James Garrard, Alexander Bullitt, and Reverend David Rice. Have you ever heard these names before? If you have been to Garrard or Bullitt County, you probably have.

There is no Rice County in Kentucky. That may be because David Rice did something that upset other state leaders. He spoke out against slavery. Reverend Rice thought slavery was wrong. He wanted the state constitution to make it illegal in Kentucky. He hoped the other delegates would agree with him, but they didn't.

George Nicholas was one of the delegates who did not agree. He did not think slavery was wrong. Nicholas and many of the delegates owned slaves. They did not want to pay workers. They wanted to continue using slave labor because it cost less.

The delegates talked for a long time. Then they voted. Sadly, the result was 26 votes for slavery and 16 votes against it. Reverend Rice and six other delegates were so upset that they left the convention. They did not want to be part of a group that supported such a hurtful practice.

The state constitution made slavery **legal,** or allowed, in Kentucky. More and more people used slaves on their farms and ranches. By 1800, one out of every four families in Kentucky owned at least one slave.

Slavery and the First Constitution

26 votes for slavery
16 votes against slavery

RESULT: Slavery is legal

Statehood!

When the constitution was finished, the delegates sent it to Congress. They soon received word that it had been approved! On June 1, 1792, Kentucky became the 15th state in the United States of America.

There were no parades or parties that day. Most Kentuckians spent the day just like any other. They probably did not know that joining the United States was one of the most important events in Kentucky history!

What Next?

Kentucky was now a state. But the new state *legislature* still had a lot of work to do. It had to manage a brand-new state government.

What Do You Think?

Why do you think becoming a state was so important? What would change now that Kentucky was a state?

Activity

Historical Events Have Many Causes

It is important to realize that events do not occur for only one reason. Most of the time, there are many reasons, or causes, for a single event. For example, when you go to the store with someone in your family, do you buy only one thing? Not usually. Maybe you need milk. Maybe you need dog food. One trip to the store usually has many causes.

History is like that, too. The state of Kentucky was settled for many reasons. In your reading journal, draw and complete a diagram like this:

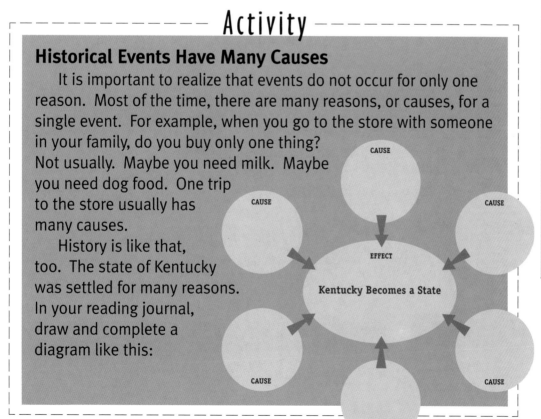

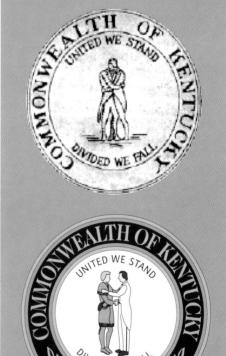

The State Seal

Over the years, our state seal has changed several times. The seal on top is an old one. The seal below it is the one we use today. Some people say the old seal represents Kentucky better than the new one. What is different about the two seals? Which one do you like better? Why?

Isaac Shelby
1750-1826

Isaac Shelby was born in Maryland. He became a war hero when he served as a soldier in Lord Dunmore's War and the American Revolution. After the Revolution, Isaac married Susannah Hart and moved to Knob Lick in Lincoln County.

Kentuckians sent Isaac to Danville to work on the petitions for statehood. Once Kentucky became a state, the electors voted to make Isaac the first governor. He worked hard to make the new state strong.

Isaac served one term as governor and then spent 16 years building a successful farm. When the War of 1812 began, Kentuckians asked Isaac to become governor once again. As governor, Isaac gathered 3,500 troops and led them to join the fight. He was 62 years old, but he was still very brave.

Three years after the War of 1812 ended, Isaac Shelby helped our state again. This time, he worked with Andrew Jackson to buy the Jackson Purchase from the Chickasaw.

He then retired to his farm, where he lived until his death at the age of 75.

Kentucky's First Government

The first governor of Kentucky was Isaac Shelby. Shelby did not win an election to become governor. Instead, he was chosen by a small group of men called *electors.*

Voting Rights

When people vote for leaders or laws, they have to consider what is best for everyone in the state. The delegates who wrote the state constitution did not trust Kentuckians to make good choices. In the constitution, the delegates *restricted* voting rights. That means only some Kentuckians were allowed to vote. The people who were allowed to vote were mostly white men who owned land.

What Do You Think?

Do you think it is wrong to limit voting rights? Should people be allowed to elect their leaders and judges? Who should be allowed to vote? Who is not allowed to vote today?

The State Capital

Every state has a capital city. This is the place where state leaders meet. Kentucky's new state government had to choose a capital city. Some people thought it should be Lexington. Others thought it should be Boonesborough, Louisville, or Frankfort. The first constitutional convention had taken place in Danville, so many thought that was the right city.

State leaders asked a group of Kentuckians to serve on a *committee* that would choose the capital city. The committee held a contest and finally chose Frankfort. Frankfort is located in the center of the state, along the Kentucky River. The river allowed people to travel there easily.

1794

1813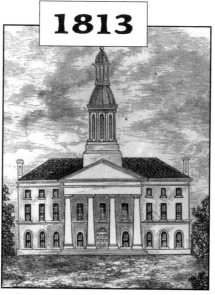

1824

Have you ever seen the capitol building in Frankfort? It is pictured below. It was built in the early 1900s. Kentucky had three other capitol buildings before the one we have today.

The people of Frankfort wanted their city to become the capital. They offered many things to the committee. They even offered 1,500 pounds of nails to help build the capitol building! Do you remember what else they offered? (If you don't, turn back to page 165.)

Today

① MEMORY MASTER

1. What was the one condition for Kentucky to become a state?
2. What was the state's new name?
3. Who was Kentucky's first governor?
4. Which city became the state capital?

PEOPLE TO KNOW

Asa Blanchard
Matthew Jouett
Jim Porter

PLACES TO LOCATE

Danville
Lexington
Louisville

WORDS TO UNDERSTAND

ambassador
apprentice
barge
hemp
jockey
landmark
population
portrait
sewer
silversmith
tavern
toll

What Do You Think?

Look at the drawing on this page. Do you think it was made by a Native American person or a white person? How can you tell? How might the drawing be different if someone else made it?

By this time in history, problems between Native Americans and settlers were mostly in western Kentucky.

Changing Life in Kentucky

Even though there was a new state government, daily life for most Kentuckians remained the same. The cities were growing and changing. But most of the state was still frontier.

On the Frontier

On the frontier, daily life continued to be a struggle. There was still conflict with Native Americans. Common illnesses, like colds and fevers, took many lives each year. Most men farmed or worked on the rivers. Women raised the children and made almost everything the family needed. There was no indoor plumbing or electricity.

For the Rich

Life for wealthy people—in the city or in the country—was much different from life on the frontier. Wealthy men in cities paid others to do work. They took time to hunt, read books and newspapers, visit their friends, and travel. They lived in large mansions filled with expensive furniture. They owned slaves who worked in the fields.

Wealthy men's wives did not cook meals or care for children. They wore stylish gowns, ate delicious foods, and visited with friends. They had very comfortable lives. Enslaved people did all of the cooking, sewing, cleaning, and caring for children.

For Children

Most children in Kentucky did not go to school. There were no public schools, and the private ones were very expensive. When some counties finally built schools, they were very small and had only one room. Most schools did not have books. If they did, the books were very old.

Many parents did not think education was important. They wanted their children to stay home and work on the farm. Less than one-fifth of all the children in Kentucky went to school during this period in history.

In our state, there was no law against enslaved children attending school. However, schools did not accept black children. This did not stop them from trying to learn, though. They knew education would give them power.

Kentucky's blacks tried hard to educate themselves, but it was not easy.

No Rights for Women

At this time, women did not have the same rights as men. Women could not vote, and they could not go to college. The very few who became educated were allowed to work only as teachers or nurses.

Most women married at a young age. The moment a girl said, "I do," everything she owned became her husband's property. She even lost her name. If a girl named Jennifer Brady married a man named James Petersen, she became known as Mrs. James Petersen. Only her closest family members still called her Jennifer.

Some women in Kentucky felt they were being treated unfairly. They wanted the same rights as men. To survive on the rugged frontier, a woman had to be strong and brave. Kentucky women later used their strength and bravery to fight for their rights.

Louisville

The city of Louisville was growing fast. It became a stopping place for people who traveled on boats and barges. **Barges** were large, flat platforms that floated down the river. They carried tons of goods. Most of the men who worked on them lived rough lives. Sometimes they came to Louisville. They would often drink too much and get into fights.

A Growing Economy

Over time, river travel became much easier. More people and businesses came to Louisville, so it grew even more. In ten years, Louisville's *population* jumped from 329 to 4,200! Then, over the next ten years, the city's population doubled again. Louisville became one of the most important river cities in the nation.

Whiskey makers and tobacco farmers built huge factories in Louisville. These people became very rich. Some of them earned so much money that they built homes as large as palaces!

The Falls of the Ohio was a dangerous place for boatmen and travelers. They often stopped in Louisville to rest.

Floods and Disease

Because Louisville was on the river, it sometimes flooded. Most of Louisville's poorest people lived near the river. When the water rose, their homes flooded. Some people lost everything they owned.

The floods also left pools of water in the city. Then mosquitoes laid eggs in the water. When the eggs hatched, the air filled with thousands of mosquitoes. Many people became very sick. Some even died.

Disease was a problem all over Kentucky—not just Louisville. Even the best doctors did not know very much about germs. They did not know that mosquitoes or dirty water could make people sick. Sometimes, *sewers* emptied into the water that was used for drinking and bathing. Germs spread so quickly that hundreds of people died at a time.

Lexington

Lexington was different from Louisville because it was not near a river. People could not travel there by water. Yet Lexington grew quickly, too. That was partly because two major roads through the frontier crossed one another there. Hundreds and hundreds of people passed through Lexington.

Hemp Production

Lexington also grew because it was near the best hemp and tobacco farms in Kentucky. Factories were built to make the hemp into rope and to cure the tobacco.

Hemp is a plant that grew well in the fertile soil of the Bluegrass. It was used mostly to make rope and cloth. People paid a lot of money for rope and cloth because they were hard to make. The hemp industry made some people in Lexington very rich.

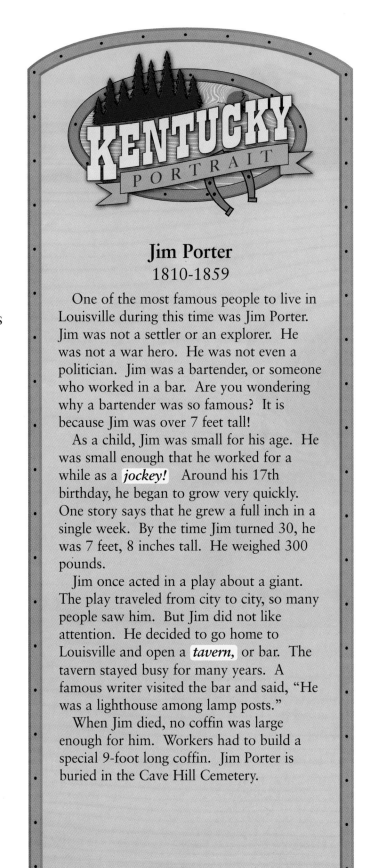

KENTUCKY PORTRAIT

Jim Porter
1810-1859

One of the most famous people to live in Louisville during this time was Jim Porter. Jim was not a settler or an explorer. He was not a war hero. He was not even a politician. Jim was a bartender, or someone who worked in a bar. Are you wondering why a bartender was so famous? It is because Jim was over 7 feet tall!

As a child, Jim was small for his age. He was small enough that he worked for a while as a *jockey!* Around his 17th birthday, he began to grow very quickly. One story says that he grew a full inch in a single week. By the time Jim turned 30, he was 7 feet, 8 inches tall. He weighed 300 pounds.

Jim once acted in a play about a giant. The play traveled from city to city, so many people saw him. But Jim did not like attention. He decided to go home to Louisville and open a *tavern,* or bar. The tavern stayed busy for many years. A famous writer visited the bar and said, "He was a lighthouse among lamp posts."

When Jim died, no coffin was large enough for him. Workers had to build a special 9-foot long coffin. Jim Porter is buried in the Cave Hill Cemetery.

TU had the first medical school in "the West". Students came from all across the nation to learn how to take care of sick people.

The name *Transylvania* is Latin. It means "across the woods."

Linking the Past to the Present

The medical school at TU is now closed, but other colleges stayed open. Students still attend Transylvania University today. It is one of the most famous **landmarks** in Lexington.

Transylvania University

Before Kentucky became a state, the Virginia Assembly set aside land in Lexington for a school. But the school was not built until many years later. In fact, the first classes at Transylvania Seminary were held in a cabin near Danville. School officials then decided to move the school close to the growing city of Lexington.

Later, the school changed its name to Transylvania University (TU). Teachers at TU taught classes on language, law, business, and even medicine.

Many important government leaders went to school at Transylvania University. Two U.S. Supreme Court justices, two vice presidents, 50 U.S. senators, 101 U.S. representatives, 36 governors, and 34 **ambassadors** to foreign countries graduated from TU!

The Arts

Many of the citizens of Lexington were wealthy and well-educated. They spent money on beautiful music, fine art, and entertainment. Lexington became home to many musicians, artists, craftsmen, and actors.

KENTUCKY PORTRAIT

Matthew Jouett
1788–1827

Matthew Jouett was born and raised in Kentucky. He graduated from Transylvania University with a degree in law. But he did not want to be a lawyer. He wanted to be an artist. Matthew was very talented, and he soon began painting portraits.

A *portrait* is a picture of someone. Cameras had not been invented yet, so people could not take photographs. Good artists could paint portraits that looked just like the people they were painting.

Matthew set up a studio in Lexington and became famous for his fine portraits.

Matthew Jouett traveled down the Mississippi River to New Orleans, painting portraits all along the way. He married at the age of 25 and had nine children. By the time Matthew died, he had painted 334 portraits.

Asa Blanchard
1770(?)–1838

Asa Blanchard was a talented silversmith. A *silversmith* is a person who makes spoons, tea sets, bowls, pitchers, and other things out of silver. Asa opened his first silversmith shop in Lexington in 1809.

Asa's silver was the finest in Kentucky. His pieces were beautiful and very well made. One of the most famous pieces of Blanchard silver is a set of candlesticks he made especially for Governor Isaac Shelby.

Over the years, Asa taught several young men how to work with silver. These boys were called *apprentices.* Apprentices lived and worked with their teachers. Several of them grew up and became famous silversmiths, too.

Asa died in Lexington when he was about 70 years old. Before he died, an artist painted his portrait. Can you guess which famous artist it was? If you guessed Matthew Jouett, you were right!

Linking the Past to the Present

Would you like to see Governor Shelby's silver candlesticks? You can! They are on display at the Speed Art Museum in Louisville. A Blanchard silver bowl is also on display as part of the Harned Collection in Frankfort.

Matthew Jouett's paintings are all around the United States. You can see some at the University of Kentucky Art Museum in Lexington.

Travel and Tolls

To make travel easier, Kentucky needed more roads. But who would pay for them? During these years, the government did not pay for roads. Private citizens had to. The owners of the roads charged a *toll,* or fee, for people to use them. Many people in Kentucky did not think tolls were fair.

What Do You Think?

Many roads in the United States still charge tolls. Do you think tolls are fair? Why or why not?

The Lexington and Winchester Turnpike Company

Tolls to Use This Road Are as Follows:

20 head of sheep, hogs, or small stock	6.25 cents
10 head of cattle	6.25 cents
Every horse, mule, donkey, or other 4-footed large animal except cattle	4 cents
2-wheeled pleasure carriage (not including driver and passenger)	8 cents
4-wheeled pleasure carriage (not including driver and passenger)	16 cents
Cart, wagon, or carriage	25 cents
Every person	2 cents

Moving On

Less than 30 years after Kentucky became a state, half a million people lived here. Some of them had come because they hoped for a piece of "the best poor man's land". But the land was too expensive. Many families traveled on to Indiana, Ohio, or Illinois, hoping for land they could afford.

2 MEMORY MASTER

1. What was life like on the frontier?
2. What is hemp?
3. What was the name of the first medical school in "the West"?
4. Why were painted portraits important?

The Pinckney Treaty

Kentucky was growing quickly. Most of the wilderness was claimed, and the cities were filling with people. Kentuckians were growing more crops and making more goods than they could use. They wanted to sell these goods, called *surplus* goods, to people in other states. But they couldn't use the Mississippi River to ship them. Spain still controlled the river. State leaders and business owners grew more and more frustrated.

The Right to Use the River

A group of men in Lexington wrote a letter to President George Washington. They told Washington that he must help them get the rights to the Mississippi. The men said they would attack Spain or leave the United States if the government didn't help.

Washington grew very concerned. He did not want a war with Spain. He also did not want to lose Kentucky. Washington sent Thomas Pinckney to meet with Spanish officials. The Spanish finally agreed to the Pinckney Treaty. This treaty gave Kentuckians free use of the Mississippi River.

PEOPLE TO KNOW

John Adams
Thomas Jefferson
Ann Lee
Thomas Pinckney

PLACES TO LOCATE

Cane Ridge
Mississippi River
Pleasant Hill
South Union

WORDS TO UNDERSTAND

abolish
criticize
Kentucky Resolutions
missionary
Sedition Act
spiritual
states' rights
surplus
synagogue
tannery

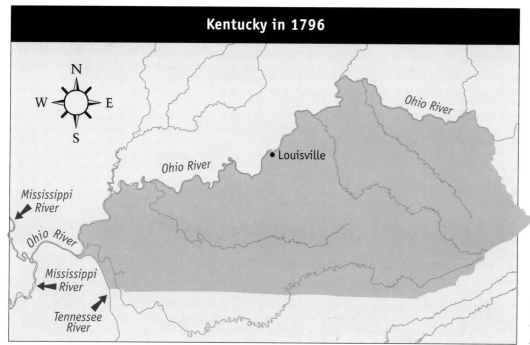

Kentucky in 1796

The Mississippi River connected Kentucky to customers in the North and in the South.

The Idea of States' Rights

The United States finally had control of the Mississippi River, but another crisis was looming. American leaders were arguing with French leaders. Some citizens became angry that our leaders had not declared war on France.

The Sedition Act

John Adams became the new U.S. president. Many people in Kentucky did not like him. They *criticized* the things he did. They also wrote stories in the newspapers about him. Congress passed a law called the *Sedition Act.* This act said it was against the law for anyone to criticize the government or the president. People who broke this law could go to prison.

American citizens were angry about the Sedition Act. They said the law seemed like something a king would do. Americans wanted the right to express their feelings about government.

The Kentucky Resolutions

Vice President Thomas Jefferson hated the Sedition Act. He wrote a statement against it. When the statement was adopted by the Kentucky legislature, it became known as the *Kentucky Resolutions.* The resolutions explained why the Sedition Act was wrong. It also said the states did not have to do what the federal government said.

The Kentucky legislature refused to obey the Sedition Act. The rest of the nation watched to see what would happen. But actually, very little happened. John Adams's term ended, and Thomas Jefferson became the new president. He immediately ended the Sedition Act.

The Kentucky Resolutions seemed to fade away, but one idea remained. That idea was called *states' rights.* It was the belief that states should have more power than the national government.

A Second Constitution

Not long after Kentucky became a state, many citizens were unhappy with the state constitution. Some hated slavery and wanted to *abolish* it. Others did not like that only electors could choose the governor. Delegates met once again and talked about these

The people of Kentucky supported Thomas Jefferson's Kentucky Resolutions.

What Do You Think ?

Do you think people should be allowed to criticize their leaders? Why or why not? Do you think state governments should have more power than the national government? Why or why not?

issues. Sometimes, the talking became arguing, but the delegates finally produced a new constitution.

The Issue of Slavery

Many delegates believed the state should help slave owners. They had spent a lot of money to buy their slaves. They believed slaves were property. If the government abolished slavery, slave owners felt they would be robbed of something they owned.

Many people in Kentucky were against slavery, but all the delegates except one were slave owners. The new constitution did not change slavery. In fact, it made the state's hold on slavery stronger than ever.

Electors

Though slavery did not change, the system of electors did. Instead of electors voting for the governor, now all white men were allowed to vote for him. This change pleased some Kentuckians. But the rest of the new constitution was nearly the same as the old one.

When slaves were moved from place to place, they usually had to walk. Only the overseers got to ride horses.

People traveled for hours to attend camp meetings where they learned about God.

The Great Revival

One of the most important things happening in Kentucky at this time had to do with religion. A religious change, called The Great Revival, began in central Kentucky.

In Cane Ridge, thousands of people listened to preachers talk about God. Other preachers traveled all across the state, telling people about God and the Bible. Many people heard these sermons and believed what the preachers said.

A lot of people joined the Baptist Church. It became the largest religion in the state. The Methodist Church came to Kentucky, too. The Catholic Church grew in Louisville and Bardstown. Later, enough Jewish people lived in Louisville that a *synagogue* was built there.

Religion and Slavery

The Great Revival caused important changes in Kentucky. Many preachers taught that slavery was a terrible sin. Some slave owners freed their slaves and began working to end slavery in our state.

Other slave owners believed the Bible taught that slavery was right. These slave owners hoped

The Kentucky Adventure

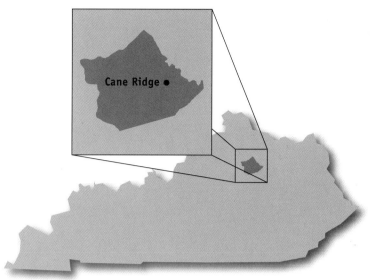

Cane Ridge

their slaves would also believe that was true.

Most enslaved people were very religious—but not the way their owners were. They did not believe the Bible said slavery was alright. They believed the Bible taught that people would be punished for their sins—and they believed slavery was a very big sin. They believed God would severely punish their owners someday.

Many slaves also learned Bible stories about a man named Moses. Moses was a slave to the Egyptian king. In the Bible, God showed Moses how to help his people escape. Many of Kentucky's slaves had faith that God would free

them, too. They sang songs called **spirituals** about Moses and freedom. One well-known spiritual went like this:

He delivered Daniel from de lion's den
Jonah from de belly of de whale
And de Hebrew children from de fiery furnace
So why not every man?

What Do You Think

What do you think the final line of this spiritual means? What were enslaved people asking?

The
SHAKERS
of South Union and Pleasant Hill

One religious group that came to Kentucky during the Great Revival was the Shakers. The Shakers were very devoted to God. They became so excited when they worshiped that they wiggled and shook. That is how they got the name "Shakers."

The Shakers loved to sing and dance. They also line danced and twirled about. They believed that singing, dancing, and working hard were the best ways to show God they loved him.

Ann Lee

Ann Lee started the Shaker religion. She set up the first Shaker community in Maine. *Missionaries* from Maine came to Kentucky and set up Shaker communities here. One was in South Union. The other was in Pleasant Hill.

Family Life

Shakers did not believe in marriage or having children. When a family joined the Shakers, the parents were no longer married. Shaker men and women lived together in large houses, but they had little contact. Men lived on one side of the house, and women lived on the other. Men and women did not even eat meals together.

Some Shaker children came with families who joined the faith. Others were orphans who were adopted by the Shakers. When children turned 21, they had to decide if they wanted to stay with the Shakers. If they didn't, the Shakers gave them some money and wished them well.

The Community

When people joined the Shakers, they gave everything they owned to the community. Because of this, the Shakers soon owned thousands of acres of rich Kentucky farmland.

Each community had many buildings. There was a meeting house, a dairy, a blacksmith shop, a smoke shop, a *tannery,* and even a woodworking shop. The Shakers grew their own food, made their own clothes, built their own homes, and took care of their ill. They had little contact with the outside world.

Buying and Selling Goods

The Shakers worked hard and became very successful. They

Many blacks joined the Shakers because they were treated fairly. The Shakers did not believe in slavery. They believed everyone— man, woman, black, or white— was equal.

made almost everything they needed. But they did not make glass, sugar, metal, and cotton. The Shakers earned the money to buy these things by raising silkworms and making fine silk cloth. They also raised herbs and made strong medicines. The Shakers were talented gardeners and sold good, healthy seeds. They also became famous for their well-made furniture.

Linking the Past to the Present

The Shaker community at South Union is now called Shakertown. The one at Pleasant Hill is called Shaker Village. If you visit these places, you can watch wool being spun into thread. You can watch a blacksmith make horseshoes. You can listen to Shaker music and see a Shaker dance. You can see Shaker buildings, furniture, clothes, dishes, and tools. You can even eat Shaker food at the restaurants!

3 MEMORY MASTER

1. What did the Pinckney Treaty do for Kentuckians?
2. What did the Sedition Act make illegal?
3. What was the Great Revival?
4. How did the Shakers get their name?

PEOPLE TO KNOW

John Adair
William Clark
Henry Clay
Andrew Jackson
Thomas Jefferson
Meriwether Lewis
Tecumseh

PLACES TO LOCATE

Camp Dubois
Fort Kaskaskia
Fort Massac
Harpers Ferry
Louisiana Territory
Louisville
Philadelphia
Pittsburgh
St. Louis
Tippecanoe
Washington, D.C.

WORDS TO UNDERSTAND

ally
duel
impressment
Louisiana Purchase

The Louisiana Purchase

The early 1800s was an important time for Kentucky. President Thomas Jefferson bought the Louisiana Territory from France. This land, known as the **Louisiana Purchase,** nearly doubled the size of the United States. It was a great thing for our country, but it changed Kentucky's place in the nation. Kentucky was no longer "the West".

The United States now owned both sides of the Mississippi River. Kentuckians would always be able to use the river. People were so excited that they threw huge parties. They shouted, cheered, sang, and danced!

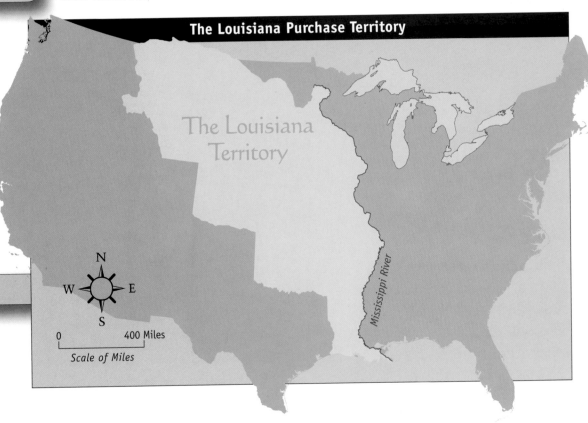

The Louisiana Purchase Territory

The Louisiana Territory

Mississippi River

N
W   E
S

0   400 Miles
Scale of Miles

Lewis & Clark

Thomas Jefferson wanted to know more about the land in the Louisiana Territory. He chose Captain Meriwether Lewis to explore the area and tell him about it. Captain Lewis's most important task was to find the region's rivers and waterways. Jefferson hoped to find a river that led to the Pacific Ocean.

Building a Team

Lewis had a big job ahead of him. He needed help. Exploring millions of acres of wilderness would take a long time. It would be dangerous. Lewis asked a Kentuckian, William Clark, to help him lead the journey. Clark was a skilled explorer, boatman, and map-maker.

Clark's first job was to find the right men to join the team. He traveled to Louisville and Clarksville. Eight Kentuckians joined the group and traveled with Lewis and Clark from the very beginning. These brave men (along with Clark) became known as the "Nine Young Men from Kentucky".

Activity

How Do You Spell . . . ?

Are you a good speller? William Clark was a poor speller. For example, Clark met a group of Indians called the Sioux (pronounced sue). In his journal, William Clark spelled Sioux 27 different ways. Can you think of 27 ways to spell a word that sounds like sue? Number a paper from 1 to 27. Then use your imagination to spell Sioux 27 different ways.

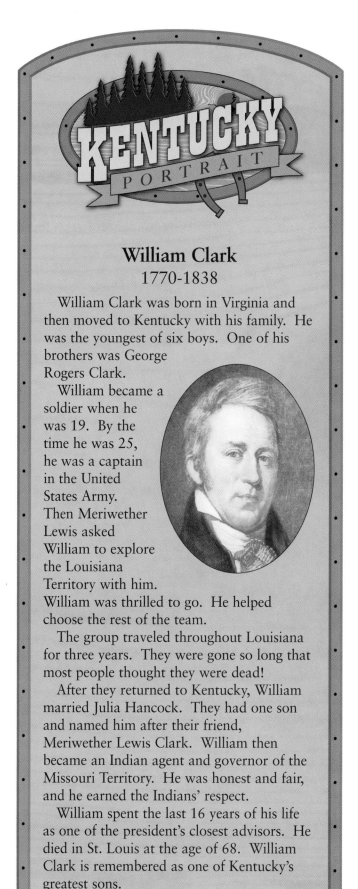

KENTUCKY PORTRAIT

William Clark
1770-1838

William Clark was born in Virginia and then moved to Kentucky with his family. He was the youngest of six boys. One of his brothers was George Rogers Clark.

William became a soldier when he was 19. By the time he was 25, he was a captain in the United States Army. Then Meriwether Lewis asked William to explore the Louisiana Territory with him. William was thrilled to go. He helped choose the rest of the team.

The group traveled throughout Louisiana for three years. They were gone so long that most people thought they were dead!

After they returned to Kentucky, William married Julia Hancock. They had one son and named him after their friend, Meriwether Lewis Clark. William then became an Indian agent and governor of the Missouri Territory. He was honest and fair, and he earned the Indians' respect.

William spent the last 16 years of his life as one of the president's closest advisors. He died in St. Louis at the age of 68. William Clark is remembered as one of Kentucky's greatest sons.

The Eastern Legacy

The Lewis and Clark journey began with the Eastern Legacy. Beginning in Washington, D.C., the Eastern Legacy turned out to be an adventure before the adventure! Here are all the stops Lewis and Clark made before they began their journey through the Louisiana Territory:

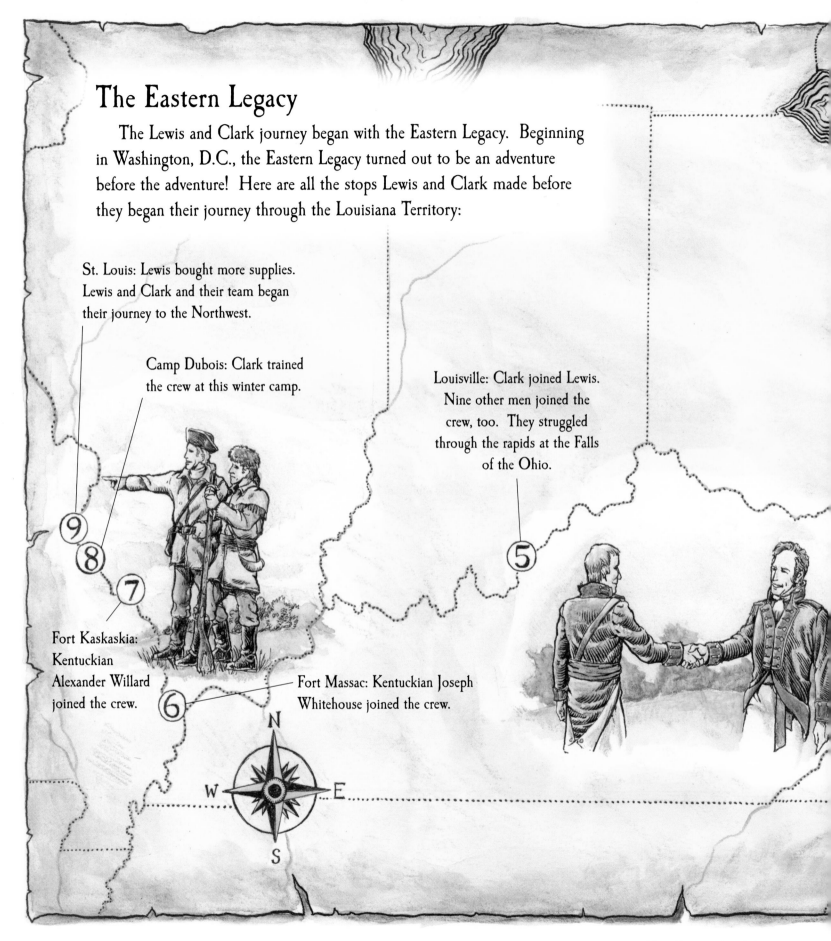

St. Louis: Lewis bought more supplies. Lewis and Clark and their team began their journey to the Northwest.

Camp Dubois: Clark trained the crew at this winter camp.

Louisville: Clark joined Lewis. Nine other men joined the crew, too. They struggled through the rapids at the Falls of the Ohio.

Fort Kaskaskia: Kentuckian Alexander Willard joined the crew.

Fort Massac: Kentuckian Joseph Whitehouse joined the crew.

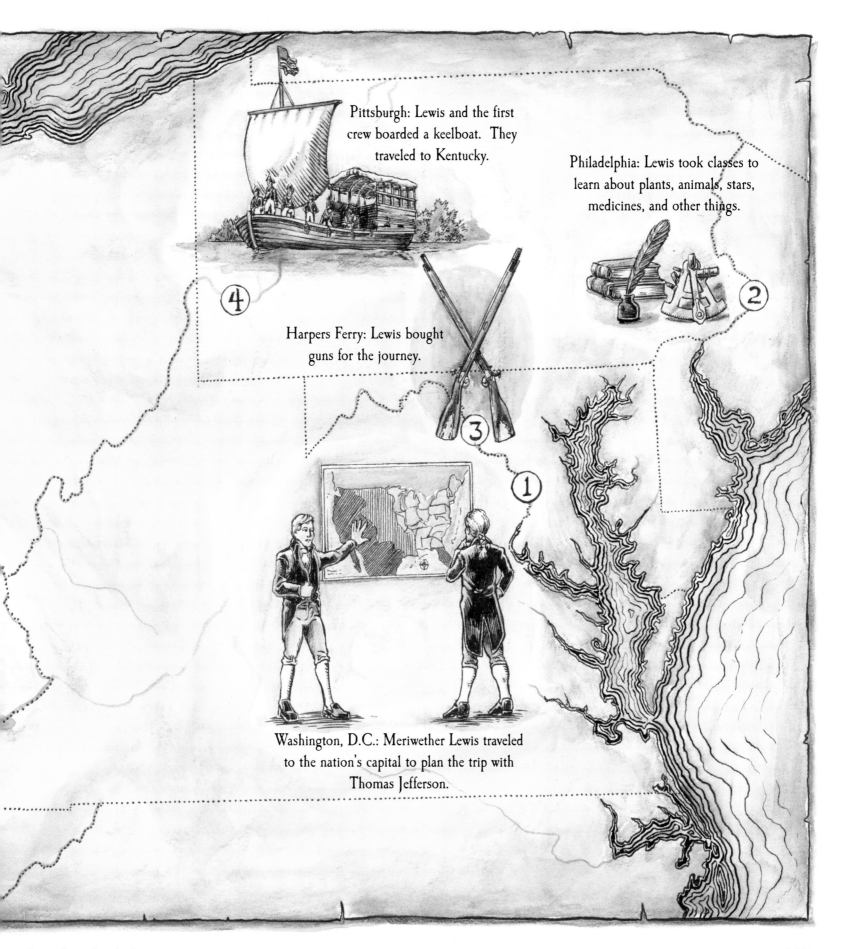

Pittsburgh: Lewis and the first crew boarded a keelboat. They traveled to Kentucky.

④

Philadelphia: Lewis took classes to learn about plants, animals, stars, medicines, and other things.

②

Harpers Ferry: Lewis bought guns for the journey.

③

①

Washington, D.C.: Meriwether Lewis traveled to the nation's capital to plan the trip with Thomas Jefferson.

Many people believe the Battle of Tippecanoe was the first battle of the War of 1812.

The War of 1812

England did not respect the American government. English ships often stopped American ships and forced U.S. sailors to work for them. This was called *impressment.* Americans grew angry and called for war.

The Battle of Tippecanoe

As more and more settlers moved into the Northwest, the number of Indian wars increased, too. Many Native American nations had established new homes in the Louisiana Territory. Now settlers were pushing them out again. After the army attacked a Native American village at Tippecanoe, Shawnee Chief Tecumseh joined his warriors with the British.

Henry Clay

Kentuckian Henry Clay was a powerful lawyer from Lexington. He served in the U.S. Congress for many years. Clay told Congress that the conflict with Native Americans was getting much worse. He said the British were talking to the Indians and making them

Linking the Past to the Present

The War of 1812 was the last time the United States and England went to war. Since then, the two countries have become friendly. Today, England is one of our greatest *allies.*

Henry Clay's feelings about politics were so strong that he once fought a *duel* to win an argument! He and the other man were both wounded.

The Kentucky Adventure

angry with the settlers. Clay pushed Congress to declare war on England.

Kentuckians in the War of 1812

Once again, Kentuckians were quick to join the fight. At a fierce battle in New Orleans, Kentuckian John Adair helped lead the United States to a victory over the British. The United States won the war, but nearly two out of every three soldiers who died were from Kentucky. More than 25,000 Kentuckians fought in the War of 1812.

The Jackson Purchase

After the War of 1812, the shape of Kentucky changed again. Isaac Shelby and General Andrew Jackson signed a treaty with the Chickasaw for nearly 8,000 square miles of land. The Chickasaw received $300,000 for the land. Kentucky got some of the land, and so did Tennessee. In Kentucky, this new region was called the Jackson Purchase.

The Jackson Purchase

4 MEMORY MASTER

1. What nearly doubled the size of the United States?
2. Where were Lewis and Clark exploring?
3. Who was Tecumseh?
4. Why is the Jackson Purchase named for Andrew Jackson?

Tecumseh
1768-1813

Tecumseh was born in Ohio, but he was very important to the Shawnee in Kentucky. As a child, Tecumseh saw many battles between the Shawnee and white settlers. He was afraid Indians would soon have no place to live. He wanted to find a way to stop the white settlers from taking all the land.

Tecumseh and his brother wanted all the Native American nations to work together to stop the settlers. The brothers traveled hundreds of miles, talking to different nations. They gathered Native Americans from Canada all the way to Kentucky. At one point, Tecumseh left his group to try to get more tribes to join them. While he was gone, U.S. soldiers attacked his camp. There were not enough warriors to fight. So many Indians died that Tecumseh's plan failed.

Tecumseh then joined with the British to fight the Americans. He was a brilliant war chief, but he died in a battle in Canada. Tecumseh's death changed history for all Native Americans. When he died, his dream seemed to die with him. Now there appeared to be no way to stop settlers from taking all the land.

Major General Sir Isaac Brock said about him, "A more . . . [fearless] Warrior does not, I believe, exist."

Chapter 7 Review

What's the Point?

Kentucky becomes the 15th state on June 1, 1792. The new state constitution protects slavery. Isaac Shelby is the first governor, and the capital city is Frankfort. Kentucky struggles with slavery, disease, and floods, but the economy and the population increase. The Louisiana Purchase, the Pinckney Treaty, and the Jackson Purchase change the geography of Kentucky and the rest of the United States. Many Kentuckians die in the War of 1812. Religion and education become more important.

Becoming Better Readers: Solving Problems

Now that Kentucky has become a state, do you think the problems will end? Pick one of the themes in the list to the right. Research the theme in this chapter and past chapters. How many times has Kentucky had to deal with this problem? Remember, you can use the timelines, chapter reviews, and index in your research.

Now imagine you are the new governor of Kentucky. Plan a solution to the problem you researched. Can you predict how it will be solved? As you read and study the rest of this textbook, you will learn if your predictions were correct.

Themes:
- Wars
- Conflict over land
- Slavery
- Fights with Indians
- Disease

Our Amazing Geography: Settling America

How many maps are in this chapter? Why do we study maps as part of history? Go back to the map of the Louisiana Purchase. Tell how the Louisiana Purchase changed life for Kentuckians. Tell how other parts of the United States changed. Can you use the map to tell why people settled Kentucky? Make a list of reasons why. Can you use the map to tell why people settled America? Make a list of reasons why. Now compare the two lists. Circle the reasons that are the same.

Mental Map

This chapter tells about a lot of changes for Kentucky. As each change happens, you probably have been able to make a mental map. Draw your mental map of where things are in Kentucky during these years. Label what you remember about where landforms, cities, or forts are. Label what you remember about where groups of people lived. When your mental map is drawn, trade with a partner. How do the maps compare? Did your partner remember some of the same things you did? To extend this activity, look up an actual map of Kentucky around 1819. You could use an encyclopedia, history book, or the Internet. How does your mental map compare?

Studying Portraits

Why is Matthew Jouett important to Kentucky history? Two Jouett portraits appear in this chapter. The one to the right is Asa Blanchard, the silversmith. Blanchard was the silversmith who crafted the beautiful candlesticks pictured on page 183. These candlesticks were for Governor Isaac Shelby. You can see Shelby's portrait on this chapter's timeline and also on page 176. Jouett painted the portrait of Shelby, too! Study the two portraits carefully. Compare them. Then make a list of three things in the portraits that are alike and three things that are different.

What do these portraits help you know about culture during this time? Look at clothing, background, facial expression, and shape. Include possible reasons why Jouett painted them. How would these paintings be different if they were painted today?

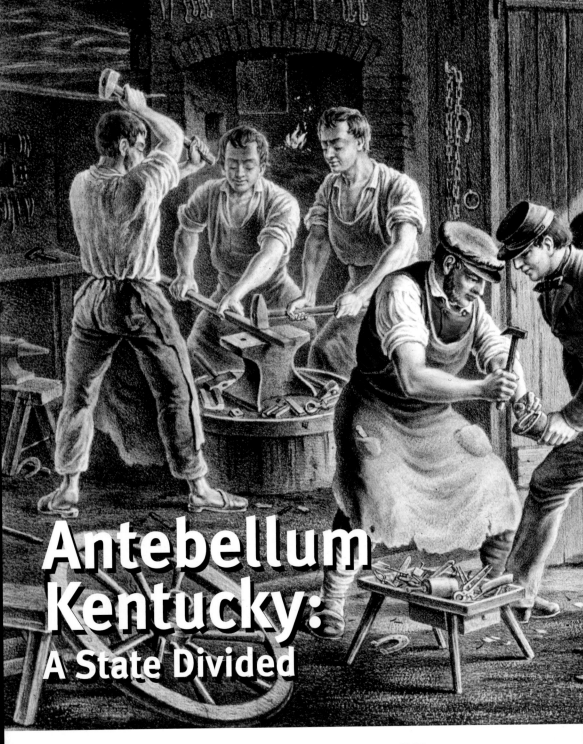

"*An oppressed people are [allowed] whenever they can to rise and break their [chains].*"

—*Henry Clay*

Antebellum Kentucky:
A State Divided

Timeline of Events

1819
The Panic of 1819 begins.

1828
The first horse track in Kentucky is built in Lexington.

1820	1825	1830

1820
Henry Clay proposes the Missouri Compromise.

1833
A cholera epidemic sweeps through Kentucky.

Chapter 8

People in the United States needed things from Kentucky. Our state grew wealthy by breeding horses and growing hemp and tobacco. Not everyone grew rich, however.

Enslaved people worked long hours without pay, planting and harvesting crops. Many poor farmers still owned no land. They had to work other people's land. The gap between the rich and the poor in Kentucky grew wider and wider.

By the middle of the Antebellum period, Kentuckians raised more horses than any other state.

1840
Kentucky is the top horse breeding state in the nation.

1844
Delia Webster is arrested for helping slaves escape on the Underground Railroad.

1850
Kentucky's third constitution is adopted.

1855
The Know-Nothings take control of the Kentucky legislature.

1835 1840 1845 1850 1855

1838
Native Americans pass through Kentucky on the Trail of Tears.

1846-48
The Mexican War

201

PEOPLE TO KNOW

John Adair
Henry Clay
Joseph Desha
Andrew Jackson
Robert Wickliffe

PLACES TO LOCATE

Harrison County
Maine
Missouri

WORDS TO UNDERSTAND

antebellum
creditor
debtor
Democrat
economic panic
free state
Missouri Compromise
political party
slave state
Whig

Henry Clay's beautiful home, Ashland, was built during Kentucky's antebellum period.

Antebellum Kentucky

The years after the War of 1812 and before the Civil War were good years for many Kentuckians. This time is called the antebellum period. *Antebellum* is a Latin word that means before the War.

One of the reasons it was a good time was because some Kentuckians became rich. Farms and plantations produced healthy crops, and businesses in the state grew. Kentucky goods were sold all over the United States.

Not all Kentuckians were happy, however. The "best poor man's land" was gone. And slavery reached its peak during the antebellum years. That means there were more slaves in Kentucky than ever before.

The Panic of 1819

Whenever a country goes to war, businesses in that country sell more goods. It takes a lot of weapons, tools, uniforms, and food to fight another country. That is what happened in Kentucky during the War of 1812.

During the Panic of 1819, storekeepers had many debts that worried them.

After the war ended, Americans did not need so many products from Kentucky. There were also problems with banks, so less money was available. Farmers and business owners in Kentucky began to struggle.

This struggle with money is called the Panic of 1819. Kentucky had a few wealthy land and business owners, but there were many more people who were poor. The rich and the poor argued about how to end the panic.

An ***economic panic*** is a time when there is very little money.

What Should the Government Do?

Most of the arguing was about what the state government should do to help poor people. Many poor people had borrowed money from banks and wealthy people. These people were called ***debtors.*** The people who loaned money were called ***creditors.***

The debtors wanted the state government to make laws that would give them more time to pay back the money they owed to creditors. The creditors did not want the state to help debtors. The creditors wanted their money back.

What Do You Think?

Do you think the government should help debtors pay the money they owe? Why or why not?

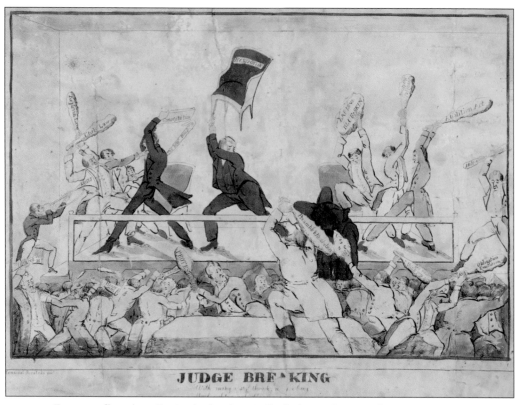

JUDGE BREAKING

Tempers flared as Kentucky leaders talked about the state's court system.

Old Court-New Court

About this time, John Adair became governor. He wanted to help debtors. He helped pass special laws that protected debtors and poor farmers from their debts. Creditors thought the new laws were unfair.

The Relief Party

Creditors took the new laws to court. The court decided they were not legal. Debtors had to start paying back the money they owed. Hundreds of debtors across Kentucky grew very angry. They formed a *political party* called the Relief Party.

Members of the Relief Party wanted a new court system that would make laws to protect debtors again. Creditors did not think the courts should be changed. State officials in Frankfort argued for weeks. Some of them, like Joseph Desha, supported the debtors. Others, like Robert Wickliffe, supported the creditors. Finally, the legislature set up a new court. The new court's judges were members of the Relief Party. They wanted to help the debtors. Wickliffe and the other creditors were furious.

Choosing Sides

People in the state of Kentucky began choosing sides. The judges in the old court had refused to step down, so Kentucky now had two court systems. Creditors and wealthy people liked the old court, but debtors and farmers liked the new court. For two years, no one was certain which court had the power to rule on cases. Finally, the old court system won. Debtors had to obey the laws set by the old courts.

Political Parties

Kentuckians weren't the only ones choosing sides. All across the nation, people split into political parties. The people who joined the *Democrats* did not want a large central government. They wanted strong state governments. The leader of the Democrats was Andrew Jackson.

The people who joined the *Whigs* wanted the United States to become a stronger country. They believed our nation should have a strong federal government. The Whigs were led by Kentuckian Henry Clay.

Activity

Judge Breaking

Political cartoons are a way to poke fun at problems while showing a need to fix them. Study the political cartoon "Judge Breaking" on the opposite page. Cover half of the cartoon with a piece of paper so you can study one section very closely. Then move the paper so you can study another section of the cartoon. Then answer the following questions:

- What is funny about the cartoon?
- Who are the two main people in the cartoon?
- Why are they in a boxing ring?
- Why did the artist pick a boxing ring instead of a circus ring?
- What problem in Kentucky does this cartoon show?
- How does the artist want you to feel about the problem?

Find one sentence on this page that you would use to explain this cartoon to your class.

Kentucky Portrait

Joseph Desha
1768-1842

Joseph Desha was born in Pennsylvania. He and his wife moved to Kentucky when he was in his mid-20s. Joseph joined the Kentucky militia and fought in the Indian wars and the War of 1812.

Joseph then turned to politics. He served in the Kentucky legislature. He also ran for governor. The first time he ran, he lost the election to John Adair. In the next election, he won as a member of the Relief Party.

Joseph Desha wanted a new court. On Christmas Eve, he talked to the legislature for hours and hours, which was against the law. State officials finally passed a law that set up a new court system. People all across the state were upset with Governor Desha.

When his term as governor ended, Joseph retired to his farm in Harrison County. He died there at the age of 74.

Henry Clay
1777-1852

Henry Clay was a lawyer from Lexington who became a powerful politician. Clay was elected to the U.S. House of Representatives, where he became Speaker of the House. He also became secretary of state under John Quincy Adams. Clay ran for president three times, but he never won.

The American System

Henry Clay's American System was a belief that the government should do things to help business. Clay's beliefs fit well with the Whigs, who supported a strong federal government.

The Missouri Compromise

The American System made Clay famous, but people remember him most for his help in delaying the war between the North and the South. The territory of Missouri wanted to become a state. But, whenever a new state joined the country, it had to decide whether it was a slave state or a free state. *Slave states* allowed slavery. *Free states* did not allow slavery. Missouri wanted to be a slave state.

Politicians from the North did not want another slave state because it would upset the balance of votes in Congress. There would be more representatives from slave states than from free states. That sounded like a good idea to southern politicians, but northern politicians would not allow it.

Finally, Henry Clay stepped in with a plan called the *Missouri Compromise.* Clay's plan added two states, Missouri and Maine, instead of just one. Missouri joined as a slave state, and Maine joined as a free state. That kept the number of free states and slave states equal.

The plan also created an imaginary line across the United States. States north of the line were free states. Those states south of the line were slave states. Politicians from both the North and the South voted to accept the plan.

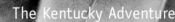

Clay's plan earned him a nickname, "The Great Compromiser".

Henry Clay is considered one of the most important leaders in the history of the United States.

Celebrating Henry Clay

People all across the nation thanked Henry Clay for saving the nation from war. Many people hoped he would become president. He served in government for 31 more years. Abraham Lincoln once said of him, "He was my . . . ideal . . . statesman."

Henry Clay died in 1852. He is buried in Lexington.

What Do You Think?

Clay was famous for saying, "I'd rather be right than president." What do you think he meant by this?

Linking the Past to the Present

Many counties in the United States are named for Henry Clay. There is a Clay County in each of the following states: Alabama, Florida, Georgia, Illinois, Indiana, Iowa, Kansas, Minnesota, Mississippi, Missouri, Nebraska, South Dakota, Tennessee, Texas, West Virginia, and Wisconsin.

1 MEMORY MASTER

1. What was the Panic of 1819?
2. Which governor helped pass the special laws that helped protect debtors?
3. Name two major political parties that held power at this time.
4. What was the Missouri Compromise?

PEOPLE TO KNOW

John and Henry Churchill
Meriwether Lewis Clark Jr.
Andrew Jackson
W.H. Thomas

PLACES TO LOCATE

Falls of the Ohio
Mexico
Texas

WORDS TO UNDERSTAND

canal
cholera
epidemic
lock
turnpike

Cholera Epidemics

During the Antebellum years, a deadly disease called *cholera* began killing thousands of people in Kentucky and the rest of the United States. When many people become ill with the same disease, it is called an *epidemic.* Doctors did not know what caused cholera. They also did not know how to cure the disease.

As soon as one person became ill, lots of other people quickly got sick, too. One epidemic killed 10 percent of the people in Lexington in just a few weeks. Another outbreak of cholera some years later killed thousands in south-central Kentucky.

Doctors tried to figure out what caused the disease. Some thought the cause was from dirty living conditions. Others thought it was from eating raw fruits and vegetables. A few even thought the disease was caused by sin!

Finally, doctors learned cholera was spread through water. Most towns got their drinking water from wells or springs. Rainwater washed the germs from garbage in sink holes into the wells and springs. People could not see, smell, or taste the germs, but they were there. Anyone who drank the germs got sick with cholera.

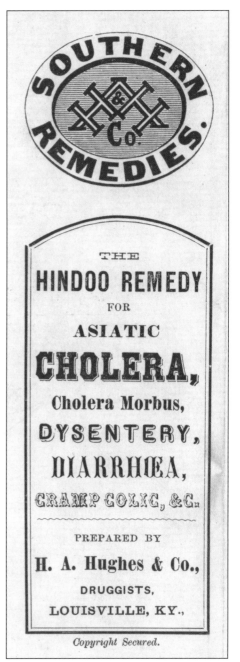

Local drug stores made and sold remedies for cholera.

The Trail of Tears

After Andrew Jackson became president of the United States, he decided to remove the Indians from all the southern states. Jackson wanted to make room for more white settlers. He had made agreements with the Indians about keeping their lands, but he did not keep his promises. He signed the Indian Removal Act, which forced Native Americans in the South to leave their homes.

Over a period of ten years, 70,000 Indians were forced to move to the West. Their journey was long and hard. It took many months. Some traveled by boat, but most traveled by land. Only a few had wagons. The Indians walked through snow in the middle of winter. Some of them did not have shoes.

Can you imagine walking for five or six months? Your whole body is cold, especially your feet. When you stop for the night, you have very little shelter. You don't have enough food to eat, so you keep getting sick. People around you, even your family members, are dying of cholera and other diseases. Supplies are running out, and the grain is spoiled.

There was much suffering along the way. Thousands of Indians died. Family members shed tears for their lost loved ones. This journey is called the Trail of Tears.

The Trail of Tears in Kentucky

After the United States won the Mexican War, Texas became the 28th state.

The Mexican War

For several years, the United States and Mexico had been arguing about control of land in the Southwest—including Texas. The United States did not want to lose Texas, so it finally declared war on Mexico.

Kentucky Volunteers

Only four days into the war, the federal government asked Kentuckians to help with the fighting. The men of Kentucky had fought in many wars before. They were strong, brave, and skilled with guns. Kentuckians were so eager to join the war that 105 companies of soldiers volunteered to fight. The government had asked for only 30. Our soldiers fought bravely until the war ended in a victory for the United States.

A Third Constitution

For many years, Kentuckians had been talking about the state constitution. Even though a second one had been written, people still didn't like it. After the war was over, people began calling for a third constitution.

Slavery

At the third constitutional convention, delegates for and against slavery battled for power. They both wanted the new constitution to protect the things that were important to them.

More than half of the delegates wanted slavery to continue in Kentucky. They argued until they won. When the third constitution was finished, it still protected slavery.

Public Education

The issue of slavery was not the only reason people wanted a new constitution. Kentuckians were also concerned that there were no schools paid for by taxes. For the first time, a school fund was set up, but very little money was put into it. Schools were so rare that few students could attend.

Duel!

When delegates at the convention became angry with one another, they sometimes challenged one another to a duel. A duel was a special fight with guns or swords. Even though it was against the law, many duels were held in public as people watched.

A duel started with two people holding their weapons up in the air. Then, when a third person counted to ten, the two men began fighting. Many government leaders were killed or wounded in duels.

Linking the Past to the Present

Kentucky's second constitution required elected leaders to swear that they never had and never would duel with anyone. The third constitution required the same thing. Today, when governors take office, they still swear not to duel!

Some duels were fought with guns like this one. Other duels were fought with long, sharp swords.

Transportation

As time passed, Kentuckians needed better ways to travel across the land. More people and goods were moving from place to place, and travel was very difficult.

Better Roads

The first roads in Kentucky were just trails through the woods. The next roads were made of dirt. When it rained or snowed, wagons and stagecoaches often got stuck in thick mud.

To make better roads, companies built turnpikes with hard surfaces. *Turnpikes* were roads that went from town to town or from river to river. People had to pay tolls to use them.

Bridges

Kentucky has many rivers and streams, so workers had to build lots of bridges. Many bridges built in the 1800s had roofs and walls. The covers kept travelers from slipping off during wet weather. A few of these covered bridges are still standing today. Have you ever seen an old covered bridge?

Steamboats

Rivers have always been useful for moving goods and people. At first, people used simple boats and barges that floated along as the water moved. Then steamboats were invented. They had engines that moved boats faster. Steamboats could go up or down a river instead of only in the direction of the water's flow.

Steamboats were powered by steam engines. The steam from boiling water moved the engine parts and turned a paddle wheel. The turning wheel pushed the boat through the water.

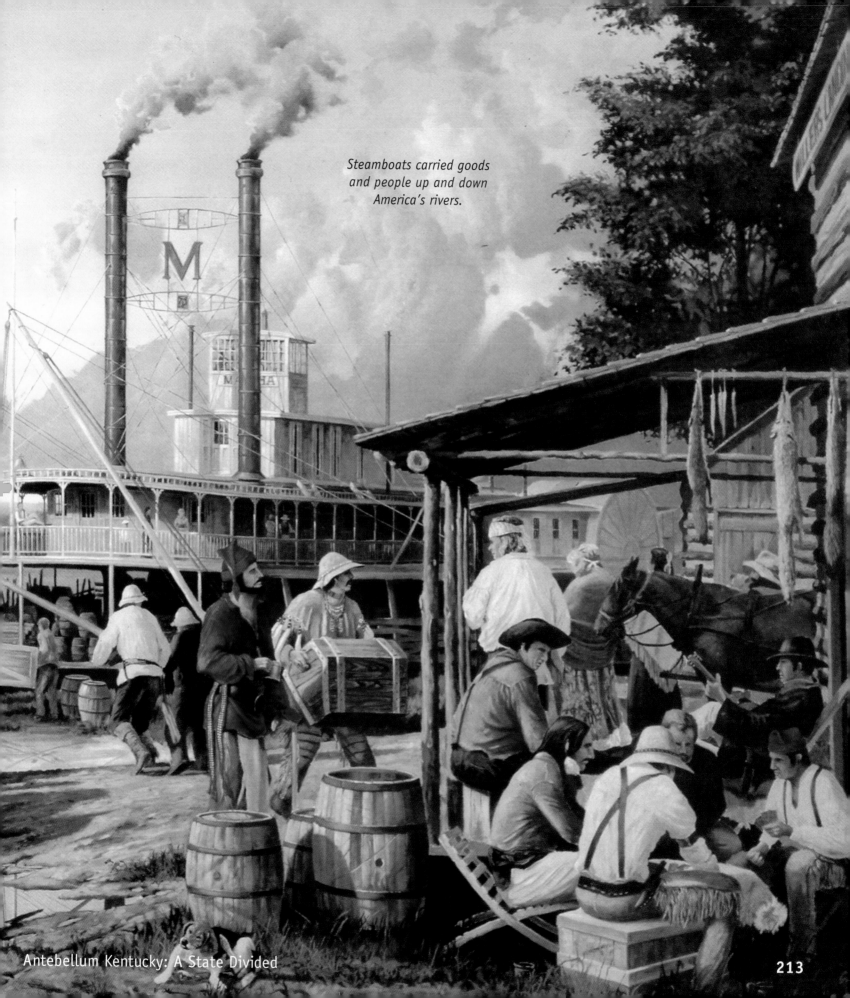

Steamboats carried goods
and people up and down
America's rivers.

Workers used horses and mules to haul away the dirt dug out of the canal beds.

Canals

Canals were another way to connect places. A *canal* is a waterway made by people. At this time, it was easier to transport goods on the water than across the land. However, the rivers didn't always flow where people needed them to. Kentuckians also built canals to make water travel safer.

For years, travel through the Falls of the Ohio was very dangerous. This was a two-mile section of rapids on the Ohio River. The water was choppy and risky to travel. Boats often overturned, and people sometimes drowned. A series of canals and *locks* called the Louisville and Portland Canal was built at the Falls of the Ohio. The water in the canal was smooth and calm. Finally, people traveling up or down the Ohio River had a safe route.

Railroads

Trains were the newest type of transportation. Workers began building railroad tracks by laying heavy iron rails. Then they pounded the rails into place with spikes. Hour after hour, men worked in all kinds of weather for very low pay.

The geography of Kentucky made the work even harder. Some mountains were just too steep for railroads. Workers had to dig tunnels through them. When they came to rivers, they had to build bridges.

How Canal Locks Work

1. High water: a boat enters the lock.
2. Back gates close. Water is let out of front gates.
3. Water level gets lower and lower.
4. Front gates open, and boat leaves the lock on a lower level.

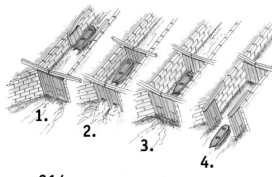

The Kentucky Adventure

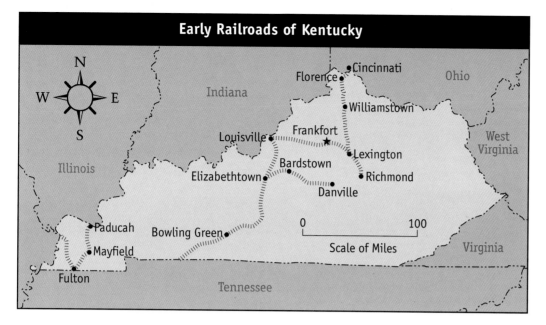

Early Railroads of Kentucky

Ohio · Cincinnati
Florence ·
Indiana
Williamstown ·
Frankfort
Louisville · ★ West Virginia
Lexington ·
Bardstown
Elizabethtown · · Richmond
Danville ·
Illinois
0   100
Scale of Miles
Paducah ·
Bowling Green · Virginia
Mayfield ·
Fulton ·
Tennessee

The L&N

The first railroad to run through Kentucky was the Lexington-Louisville line. Several years later, the most powerful company in the state was the Louisville & Nashville Railroad. Railroads became the country's first big companies. In fact, during these years, no business in Kentucky was as rich and powerful as the L & N.

Activity

Plan a Trip

Plan a trip from where you live to some landmark in Kentucky. Figure out the fastest way to get there using only the transportation discussed in this lesson (horses, carriages, turnpikes, bridges, canals, steamboats, or trains). Then figure out the fastest way to get there using modern transportation (highways, buses, cars, or airplanes). Which way is faster? How much faster?

What Do You Think

When trains first appeared, people called the huge steam engines "iron horses." Why do you think people called them that? Do you think trains are like iron horses? Why or why not?

Horseracing in the Bluegrass

Did you know that the beautiful Bluegrass region has more horse farms than any other place in the world? The grass, soil, and spring water of the Bluegrass provide exactly the right minerals to raise strong, fast horses. Horses became so popular in Kentucky that nine out of ten Kentuckians owned at least one horse during the Antebellum years.

Kentucky's first horse track was built in Lexington by the Kentucky Association for the Improvements of Breeds of Stock. Within a few years, horse breeders in Louisville were growing

"Horses are raised in great numbers, and of the noblest kinds. A handsome horse is the highest pride of a Kentuckian."

—Timothy Flint

concerned. Louisville, the largest city in the state, still didn't have a good horse track.

Churchill Downs

Louisville horse breeders met with Meriwether Lewis Clark Jr., the grandson of General William Clark. They sent him to Europe to study horse races, such as Ascot and the Epsom Derby. Clark came back to Kentucky with plans to build a grand horse track in Louisville. It would be modeled after the finest race tracks in Europe.

Clark met with his uncles, John and Henry Churchill, and they agreed to provide the money and land for the new track. The horse track was called Churchill Downs. The big race there was the Kentucky Derby!

At the first Kentucky Derby, a small, red colt named Aristides set a new world record. The crowd cheered wildly. Everyone agreed that the Kentucky Derby was a huge success.

The Grandstand

Building the track cost so much that Clark couldn't afford to build a grandstand. A wealthy Louisville businessman named W.H. Thomas paid for a small, wooden grandstand on the east side of the track. But the grandstand had a problem. The setting sun shined brightly in fans' eyes. It wasn't until 20 years later that the new grandstand, with two tall spires, was built on the west side of the track.

② MEMORY MASTER

1. How was cholera spread?
2. What was the Indian Removal Act?
3. Name three types of new transportation during this time.
4. Which region in Kentucky has more horse farms than any other place in the world?

PEOPLE TO KNOW

Cassius Marcellus Clay
John Gregg Fee
Margaret Garner
Sarah Frances Shaw Graves
Delia Ann Webster

PLACES TO LOCATE

Berea
Covington
Johnson County
Woodford County

WORDS TO UNDERSTAND

abolitionist
bondage
conductor
immigrant
Know-Nothing
station
Underground Railroad

Slavery in Kentucky

In the years before the war, Kentucky's rich farmland produced more hemp than any other state in the nation. Our state was also the nation's second highest producer of corn and tobacco. Planting, tending, and growing these crops took a lot of hard work. That work was done mostly by slaves.

One of every five people living in Kentucky at this time was an African American slave. Not all blacks were slaves, however. Some had been given their freedom or had purchased it. These people were known as free blacks.

In many parts of the state, there were few slaves. Slaves were less than one percent of the residents in Johnson County. But in other areas, such as Woodford County, slavery was a way of life. In regions like these, there were more enslaved people than whites.

What Do You Think

Why do you think there were more enslaved people in central Kentucky than in other parts of the state?

Woodford County●
Johnson County●

THE SALE.

Cheapside

Enslaved people were considered property. They were bought and sold, like horses or land. Slave traders took men, women, and children to public auctions, where they were sold to the highest bidders. The people who worked at the auctions did not think about the enslaved people's feelings. Elderly or injured slaves were sold for lower prices in an area to the side of the regular auction platform in Lexington. People soon began calling that area "Cheapside."

Slaves at Work

Slaves did all kinds of work. On farms and plantations, they worked from sunup to sundown. They planted seeds, took care of the fields and animals, and harvested the crops. They also cleaned their owners' homes, cooked their owners' meals, and took care of their owners' children. Some slaves became carpenters and blacksmiths. They had to give a share of their earnings to their owners.

Cruel Treatment

If a slave family was lucky, all the family members lived near each other. But at any moment an owner could sell a slave to someone who lived hundreds of miles away. Families were split up time after time. Often, children never saw their parents again.

My name is Sarah Frances Shaw Graves . . . I was born . . . in Kentucky somewhere near Louisville. I was brought to Missouri when I was six months old with my Mamma who was a slave owned by a man named Shaw . . . We left my Papa in Kentucky as he belonged to another man. My Papa never knew where my Mamma and me went and Mamma and me never knew where my Papa went.

This was not the only cruelty slaves faced. Owners could abuse slaves at any time. Enslaved people were beaten for not working hard enough, for breaking things, or sometimes for no reason at all.

THE PARTING "Buy us too"

Slaves often begged their owners not to sell them to far away places.

Sometimes, slaves escaped and returned to their loved ones. When they were discovered, they were punished and taken away again.

Fighting Back

Slaves were forced to live under these conditions, but they sometimes found ways to fight back. A few escaped to freedom in the North. Some worked very slowly. Others destroyed crops or livestock. Some told jokes or stories or sang songs that made fun of their owners.

What Do You Think ?

Can you think of other ways slaves could fight back without their owners knowing it?

Antebellum Kentucky: A State Divided

Underground Railroad A Way to Freedom

Roads to Freedom

CANADA

Boston
Detroit
Buffalo
Chicago
New York
Wheeling
Cincinnati
Parkersburg
Alexandria
St. Louis

Memphis
Charleston

Atlantic
Ocean

Houston
New Orleans

Gulf of Mexico
THE
BAHAMAS

Legend

MEXICO
General routes of escape
Slave state—slavery permitted
Free state—slavery prohibited

CUBA

Enslaved people hated living in **bondage.** They wanted freedom to choose how to live. In Kentucky, many slaves chose to risk their lives by attempting to escape.

These slaves followed routes to the North on the **Underground Railroad.** The Underground Railroad was not really underground, and it was not really a railroad. It was a secret system run by whites and free blacks who joined together to help slaves escape.

The journey to freedom on the Underground Railroad was long and dangerous. Sometimes owners chased runaway slaves. If the runaways were caught, the slave owners punished them. Some slaves were whipped. A few were even beaten to death. Others went to jail. Sometimes, owners sold runaway slaves away from their families.

Conductors and Secret Codes

Men called "patrollers" roamed about the countryside looking for runaways, so slaves had to travel mostly at night. The runaways used the moon and stars, especially the North Star, to guide them. They also looked for secret codes in songs people sang, quilt patterns, and special signals. The codes helped them know where to go. The codes also warned of danger.

During the day, slaves hid in the forests or the homes of people who wanted to help them escape. These people were called **conductors.** The conductors hid runaway slaves in safe places called **stations.** Many stations had secret passageways, hidden staircases, or underground rooms. Over a period of about 60 years, nearly 100,000 slaves escaped by using the Underground Railroad.

The Underground Railroad in Kentucky

Most of Kentucky's northern border was shared with free states. Kentucky is also bordered on three sides by rivers. As a result, our state became important to slaves on the run.

Helping slaves escape was against the law, but many Kentuckians did it anyway. There were Underground Railroad stations in Maysville, Covington, Newport, and Trimble County. Just across the Ohio border, there were several anti-slavery communities. Hundreds of Kentuckians helped slaves escape to these places.

Activity

Finding Freedom Road

In groups, choose a place in your community that would make a good "safe house" for the Underground Railroad. Keep it a secret from the other groups. Half of your group should write a song or chant that contains clues on how to get to the safe house. The other half of the group should draw a path showing directions to the safe house. Now, exchange songs but NOT drawings with another group. After reading another group's song, draw a path to where you think their safe house is. When you are done, switch back. Did you figure out the path and the safe house?

Delia Ann Webster
1817-1876

Delia Ann Webster was born in Vermont. She became a teacher and moved to Lexington. While living there, Delia noticed the terrible treatment of slaves. She once said that slavery was, "a system as bad as the Devil and wicked men can make it." She wanted to free as many slaves as she could.

When Delia returned from a short trip, police arrested her. They accused her of helping three slaves escape to Ohio.

Later, Delia bought land in Trimble County, Kentucky. She hired free blacks to work for her. The free blacks worked in the fields, but they also helped her run a station on the Underground Railroad! When slaves in the area began to disappear, the police came after her again.

After the Civil War, Delia was forced to leave our state. Former slave owners burned and destroyed her home, four barns, and 17 other buildings on her property. She did not have enough money to repair them, so she never came back to Kentucky. She taught school in Indiana until her death at the age of 59.

BELOVED

On a cold January night, 17 runaway slaves from Kentucky crossed the frozen Ohio River at Covington. Among them were Robert and Margaret Garner and their four children. They hid overnight in the home of a freeman named Elijah Kite.

The next morning, Kite's house was surrounded by slave owners, patrollers, and police officers. They stormed the house, but the slaves fought back. As the men burst through the door, Margaret Garner killed her 3-year-old daughter. She then tried to kill her other children and herself. She later said that she would rather her children were dead than slaves.

Margaret did not die that day. Instead, she went to jail. She stood trial for two weeks. At the trial, many people talked about the horrors of slavery. A woman named Lucy Stone Blackwell said:

With my own teeth would I tear open my veins and let the earth drink my blood, rather than to wear the chains of slavery. How then could I blame her for wishing her child to find freedom with God and the angels, where no chains are?

The judge said he was sorry but he had to obey the laws of the state of Kentucky. Margaret had to remain a slave.

Margaret and her family boarded a steamboat bound for Kentucky. As they were traveling, the boat got into an accident. Margaret and her baby boy fell into the river. The baby drowned, but Margaret lived. She was not sad that another of her children was dead. Rather, she was glad the baby had escaped a life in slavery.

After the trip back to Kentucky, there is no record of Margaret Garner. Even today, no one is sure what happened to her. More than 100 years later, Toni Morrison wrote a book based on the life of Margaret Garner. The title of the book is *Beloved*. A few years later, *Beloved* was made into a movie starring Oprah Winfrey.

What Do You Think

Do you think Margaret Garner was a good parent? Do you think she should have gone to prison for killing her child? Why do you think someone would rather kill her children than see them live as slaves?

Working to End Slavery

People who worked to end slavery were called **abolitionists.**
They were men and women, black and white, young and old. Some
abolitionists were freed slaves. They gave speeches and wrote in
newspapers and books. Abolitionists wanted everyone to learn
about the horrors of slavery. They believed that if more people
knew about slavery, they would work harder to outlaw it.

Cassius Marcellus Clay
1810-1903

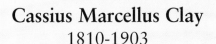

Cassius Marcellus Clay was born in Madison County, Kentucky. He
attended public school, was tutored at home, and then went to St. Joseph's
College, Transylvania University, and finally, Yale. He returned to Kentucky
and graduated from Transylvania with a law degree.

Cassius was an abolitionist who hated slavery. Because he served in state
government, he often got into arguments with politicians who supported
slavery. He once even fought in a duel. Another time, a man tried to shoot
him.

Cassius Clay helped his cousin, Henry Clay, run for president. Then he
started an antislavery newspaper called the *Lexington True American*. Many
Kentuckians hated the paper and organized a committee to get rid of it. One of
the members of this committee was Cassius's son, James!

The group did not stop Cassius Clay. He just moved
the paper to Cincinnati.

Cassius worked hard to help Abraham Lincoln
get elected, and the two men became good friends.
Cassius later helped Lincoln with a document that
tried to free the slaves in the southern states.

Cassius Clay was one of the greatest abolitionists
our state has ever known. He lived to be 93 years
old. He is buried in Richmond.

Linking the Past to the Present

In 1942, almost 40 years after Cassius Marcellus Clay died, a black
family in Louisville named their baby Cassius Marcellus Clay. The
second Cassius Clay became even more famous than the first. Do
you know who he is? (Hint: He is known today as Muhammad Ali.)
Why do you think his parents named him Cassius Clay?

The Know-Nothings

Slavery was not the only thing dividing people in Kentucky and the rest of the country. Several politicians formed a new political party that quickly gained control of the state government. This party, called the **Know-Nothings,** believed people who were different were dangerous.

The Know-Nothings hated Catholics and people from other countries. Many **immigrants** had moved to Louisville, and the Know-Nothings wanted them to leave. One night, a large group of Know-Nothings raided some areas of Louisville. They killed at least 19 Irish and German immigrants.

The Know-Nothings did not hold political power for very long. Their rage showed how angry and divided Kentucky and the rest of the United States had become. It would not be long until brother turned against brother. Our country would soon be torn apart by an angry, bloody war.

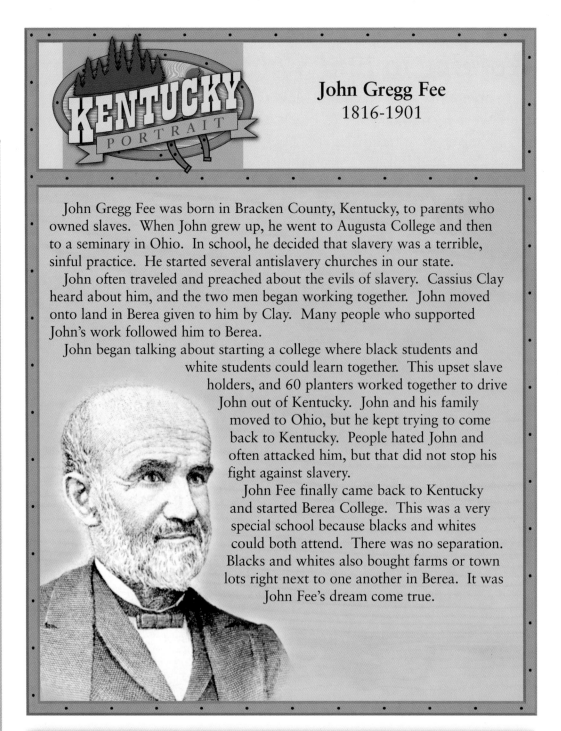

KENTUCKY PORTRAIT

John Gregg Fee
1816-1901

John Gregg Fee was born in Bracken County, Kentucky, to parents who owned slaves. When John grew up, he went to Augusta College and then to a seminary in Ohio. In school, he decided that slavery was a terrible, sinful practice. He started several antislavery churches in our state.

John often traveled and preached about the evils of slavery. Cassius Clay heard about him, and the two men began working together. John moved onto land in Berea given to him by Clay. Many people who supported John's work followed him to Berea.

John began talking about starting a college where black students and white students could learn together. This upset slave holders, and 60 planters worked together to drive John out of Kentucky. John and his family moved to Ohio, but he kept trying to come back to Kentucky. People hated John and often attacked him, but that did not stop his fight against slavery.

John Fee finally came back to Kentucky and started Berea College. This was a very special school because blacks and whites could both attend. There was no separation. Blacks and whites also bought farms or town lots right next to one another in Berea. It was John Fee's dream come true.

③ MEMORY MASTER

1. What are two important Kentucky crops?
2. What was the secret system of moving slaves to free states called?
3. What is an abolitionist? Name one.
4. What was special about Berea College?

Chapter  8 Review

What's the Point?

After the War of 1812, Kentucky faced many challenges, including an economic panic, a cholera epidemic, the Mexican War, and very little money for public education. Kentucky's third constitution kept slavery legal. Great improvements were made in transportation, including the invention of the steamboat. Horse tracks were built, and crops continued to do well. Kentucky had more slaves than ever before, and abolitionists protested. Many slaves gained freedom through the Underground Railroad. The issue of slavery pushed the nation toward war.

Becoming Better Readers: Kentucky's Horse Tracks

Do you remember what year the first horse track was built in Kentucky? (Hint: look at this chapter's timeline.) How did the horse track affect Kentucky's economy? To find out, do some extra reading.

First, go to the index of this textbook. See where you can find information about horses or horse tracks in other chapters. Then, use the library or Internet sites recommended by your teacher to find more information. Look for sources that will tell you the history of Churchill Downs and the Kentucky Derby. Take notes as you read. Then discuss with your class what you have learned about Kentucky's horse track economy.

Our Amazing Geography: Augusta, Kentucky

Locate Augusta, Kentucky on a map. What do you notice about its location? Look at Kentucky's northern border on the map. Do you see how the Ohio River borders Ohio and Kentucky? Remember that at this time, Kentucky was a slave state, and Ohio was a free state. There were safe houses, or Underground Railroad stops, in Augusta. Some of these were the General Payne Home, White Hall, Shockey Hideaway, and "Echo Hall" (now known as Augusta Female College dormitory). These safe houses were all near the river. Why was Augusta's location both a problem and a solution for freeing slaves through the Underground Railroad?

"*Kentucky has not seceded, and I believe never will. She loves the Union and will cling to it as long as possible . . . God knows what is to be the end.*"

—Kentucky Senator
John J. Crittenden

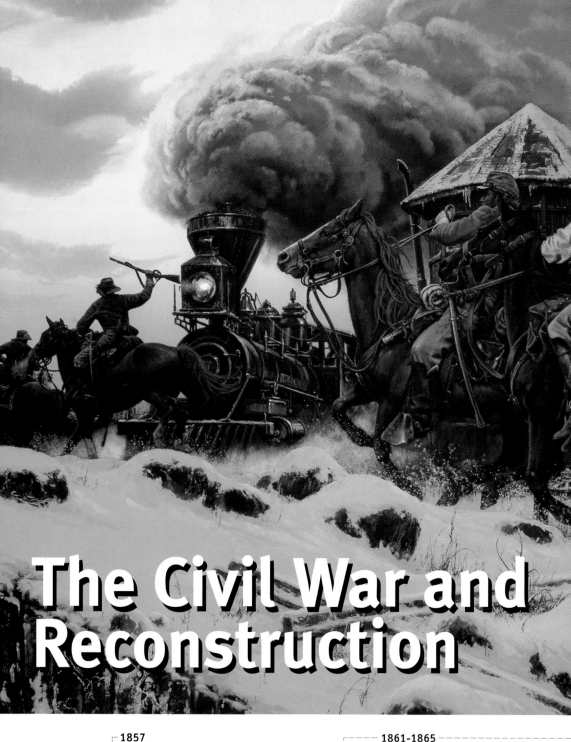

The Civil War and Reconstruction

Timeline of Events

1856	1858	1860	1862	1864

1857
The U.S. Supreme Court decides in *Dred Scott* that African Americans have no constitutional rights.

1861-1865
The Civil War

1862
The John Hunt Morgan raids begin.

1863
Abraham Lincoln issues the Emancipation Proclamation.

1859
The first Louisville and Nashville (L&N) Railroad line opens.

1861
Kentucky refuses to join either the North or the South in the Civil War.

1865
Abraham Lincoln is assassinated. The Thirteenth Amendment outlaws slavery in all states.

Many Kentuckians had become rich, but there was a cloud of doom over the state. That cloud was the issue of slavery. In every state, people talked about what should be done.

Some Kentuckians wanted to keep slaves. Others wanted to free them. As people took sides, the issue of slavery split the state. Then it split the entire nation.

Kentuckian John Hunt Morgan and his Confederate soldiers attacked Union trains in Kentucky. They stopped many shipments of supplies from reaching Union troops.

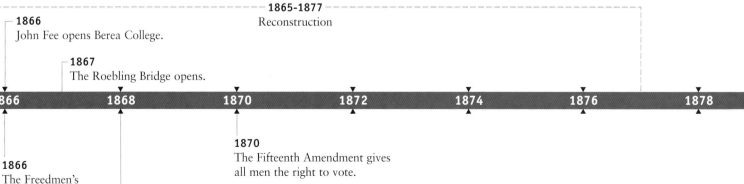

1865-1877
Reconstruction

1866
John Fee opens Berea College.

1867
The Roebling Bridge opens.

1866	1868	1870	1872	1874	1876	1878

1866
The Freedmen's Bureau begins helping people in Kentucky.

1868
The Fourteenth Amendment makes anyone born in the United States a citizen.

1870
The Fifteenth Amendment gives all men the right to vote.

PEOPLE TO KNOW

Jefferson Davis
Abraham Lincoln
Dred Scott

PLACES TO LOCATE

Biloxi, Mississippi
Gettysburg, Pennsylvania
Hodgenville
Mississippi River
New Orleans, Louisiana
The North
Richmond, Virginia
The South
Western Territories

WORDS TO UNDERSTAND

border state
Confederacy
debate
laborer
neutral
secede
Union

What Do You Think?

Why do you think there were more farms in the southern states than in the northern states?

Different Ways of Life

Life was different for people living in different parts of the United States. Because of this, the North and the South wanted different things from government. The North wanted help with business and industry. The South wanted laws that protected slavery.

The North and the South

In the North, there were many factories, railways, and mills. Towns grew into big cities. Many people still farmed, but they did not own slaves. Northerners felt workers should be free to choose where they worked.

228

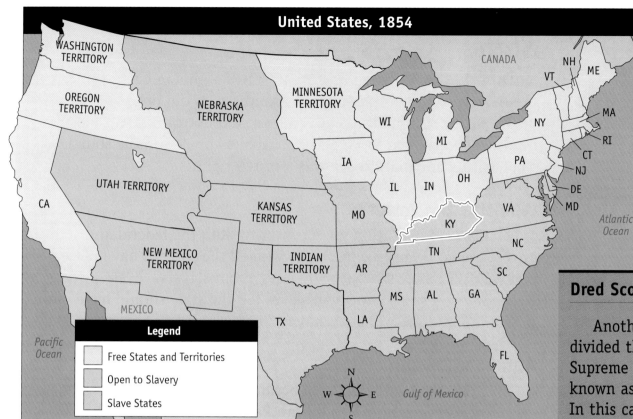

United States, 1854

Legend
- Free States and Territories
- Open to Slavery
- Slave States

In the South, farming was still the most important part of the economy. Cotton, tobacco, sugar, and rice were the main crops. Powerful people owned plantations and used slaves as *laborers*. Four million enslaved people lived and worked in the South. Many southern landowners felt they would not be able to run their farms or plantations without slave labor.

The Western Territories

As people moved into the territories west of the Mississippi River, the debate grew. Northern states did not want slavery to be legal in the western territories. This did not mean all northerners hated slavery. Some just did not think it was good for business.

The southern states worried that the North would try to abolish slavery. Americans felt so deeply about slavery that many people began to feel we were no longer one nation, but two.

Dred Scott

Dred Scott

Another event that divided the nation was a Supreme Court decision known as the *Dred Scott* case. In this case, the Supreme Court ruled that blacks—free or slave—were not citizens and thus had no rights.

The Declaration of Independence says that "all men are created equal." But one of the justices who helped make the *Dred Scott* decision wrote, "The general words seem to embrace the whole human family . . . but it is too clear . . . that the enslaved African race were not intended to be included."

The Supreme Court's decision on *Dred Scott* hurt and angered many people. Yet slave owners thought it was right. Northerners felt they had to take action. If they didn't, slavery would keep growing.

States' Rights

Do you remember reading about states' rights in Chapter 7? The U.S. government was passing laws southerners did not like. Many people in the South felt the government did not care about their needs. They wanted more power to make choices on the state level. They felt having that power was a state's right.

Who Has the Power?

The U.S. Constitution gives power to both the federal and state governments. Many Kentuckians wanted the state to have more control over its laws—especially laws about slavery. Even Kentuckians who did not own slaves felt the state should have more power than the federal government.

Abraham Lincoln

By 1860, the southern states became deeply worried that a president from the new Republican Party would end slavery. The Republican candidate that year was Kentucky-born Abraham Lincoln. During the campaign, Lincoln said, "A house divided against itself cannot stand." That meant the United States could no longer be half slave and half free.

Lincoln promised not to change slavery in the South. But he said he would not allow slavery in any new states. He said the nation needed to prepare for the end of slavery in all states.

What Do You Think?

Do you think state governments know our needs better than the federal government? Do you think state governments should have more power than the federal government? Why or why not?

When Abe was a young man, he took a load of cargo down the Mississippi River to New Orleans. While there, he saw a slave auction. It upset him terribly. He said, "If I ever get a chance to hit that thing [slavery], I'll hit it hard." His later life proved those words to be true.

Abraham Lincoln
1809-1865

KENTUCKY PORTRAIT

Perhaps the most famous person ever born in Kentucky was Abraham Lincoln. He was born near Hodgenville, but his family moved to Indiana when he was 7 years old. After Abe's mother died, his father remarried. Nine-year-old Abe became so attached to his new mother that he called her "angel mother".

Abe grew tall and strong. By the time he was 19, he had reached his full height of 6 feet, 4 inches! He had long arms and big hands. Abe became so skilled with an axe that he could split a rail with one blow. Later in life, politicians nicknamed him "The Railsplitter".

Abe had less than one year of classroom education, but he was very bright. He read and studied whenever he could.

There weren't very many books on the frontier, so he read the Bible and books people loaned him.

Abe married a woman from Lexington named Mary Todd. They had four sons, but all except the first one died before they became adults.

Abe became interested in politics and *debate.* He joined the Whigs and tried to model himself after Henry Clay. Abe then decided to run for a position in the Illinois state government. After losing his first election, Abe ran again. This time he won. He was reelected four times. During these years, Abe was studying to become a lawyer.

Abe was an excellent lawyer and became well known in Illinois. He often spoke out about slavery. He served one term as a U.S. Congressman and then worked as a lawyer for the next ten years. In 1860, Abraham Lincoln became president of the United States.

One of Abe's most famous speeches was given in Gettysburg, Pennsylvania, at a Civil War battle site where many men had died. The speech is now known as the Gettysburg Address. In it, Abe said, " . . . we here highly resolve that these dead shall not have died in vain, that this nation, under God, shall have a new birth of freedom, and . . . government of the people, by the people, for the people, shall not perish from the earth."

Many people believe Abraham Lincoln did more for America than anyone in history. He will always be remembered as the man who dedicated his life to mending a broken country.

The South Leaves the Union

Across the South, people decided they did not want to be a part of this country anymore. One by one, the southern states *seceded,* or broke away, from the United States. They formed their own government and called themselves the Confederate States of America, or the *Confederacy.* The northern states remained part of the United States. They were called the *Union.*

The Confederacy was a separate country from the United States. It had its own government and its own capital (Richmond, Virginia). It had its own president, Kentuckian Jefferson Davis. The Confederacy even had its own money.

The Civil War is also called the war between the North and the South.

KENTUCKY PORTRAIT

Jefferson Davis
1808-1889

Jefferson Davis, the first and only president of the Confederate States of America, was born in Christian (now Todd) County, Kentucky. He attended both the U.S. Military Academy and Transylvania University. Jefferson then served in the army for seven years, but he had to quit due to poor health.

For the next ten years, Jefferson lived in Mississippi and worked as a planter. After the Mexican War, Jefferson became a U.S. senator. He strongly supported slavery and states' rights. Eventually, he became the main spokesman for the entire South. He did not want the South to leave the Union, but he wanted the national government to have less power. When Mississippi seceded, Davis left the U.S. Senate.

That same year, Jefferson Davis was elected by Confederates to serve as their president. He had great faith in the cause, and southerners loved him. But Jefferson's dedication was not enough to win the war. He could not raise enough money for supplies. He could not convince other countries to recognize the Confederacy as a separate country. He could not get state and local leaders to support his decisions.

After four years of fighting, the South lost the war. Union soldiers captured Jefferson and charged him with treason. He spent the next two years in prison. Finally, the U.S. government dropped the charges, and Jefferson was released. He then tried to become a businessman, but he was never successful. Jefferson Davis spent his last years at Beauvoir, his home in Biloxi, Mississippi.

Linking the Past to the Present

In the late summer of 2005, Jefferson Davis's 153-year-old home, Beauvoir, was damaged by Hurricane Katrina. Before the hurricane, the home and other buildings had been restored and turned into a museum. The storm destroyed several buildings, and many priceless artifacts were lost.

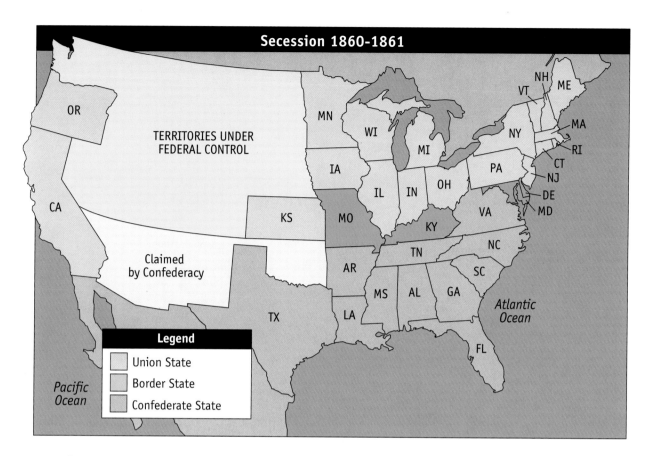

Secession 1860-1861

TERRITORIES UNDER FEDERAL CONTROL

Claimed by Confederacy

Atlantic Ocean

Pacific Ocean

Legend
- Union State
- Border State
- Confederate State

Border States

Kentucky was one of four southern states that were not sure what to do. These states, called ***border states,*** wanted to keep slaves, but they did not want to leave the Union. They also did not want to fight the South.

Some Kentuckians wanted to join the Confederacy. Most of these people lived in the central part of the state, where there were many slaves. Other Kentuckians wanted to remain in the Union. They lived in areas where there were fewer slaves.

Finally, state officials in Frankfort declared Kentucky was ***neutral.*** That meant the state was not part of the Union or the Confederacy. It remained separate from both.

"You might as well put two game-roosters in the same pen and tell 'em not to fight as to start up a war between the North and the South and tell Kentucky to keep out of it."

—"Aunt Jane" from the works of Eliza Calvert Hall

1 MEMORY MASTER

1. How did the economies of the North and the South differ?
2. What did Lincoln want to do about slavery?
3. Who was the president of the Confederacy?
4. What did it mean for Kentucky to be neutral?

LESSON 2 The Civil War

PEOPLE TO KNOW

Sister Mary Lucy Dosh
Thomas Edison
James A. Garfield
Ulysses S. Grant
George Johnson
Robert E. Lee
Julia Ann Marcum
John Hunt Morgan

PLACES TO LOCATE

Bowling Green
Columbus
Nazareth
Perryville

WORDS TO UNDERSTAND

civil war
Emancipation Proclamation
hardtack
honor guard
pension
sacrifice
swindle
telegraph

The War Begins

In April of 1861, the Civil War began. A *civil war* is a war between two regions of one country. Both the Union and the Confederacy wanted Kentucky. The Ohio River and the L&N Railroad were important for moving soldiers and goods between the North and the South. Many battles took place in our state as the North and South fought for control.

The Confederates Move In

Only six months after the war began, Confederate soldiers took control of Columbus, Kentucky. Then they formed a new state government in Bowling Green. The Confederacy chose George Johnson to be Kentucky's new governor. But Johnson was not governor of the entire state. He had power only in the regions controlled by the Confederates. A few months after he became governor, George Johnson died from a battle wound.

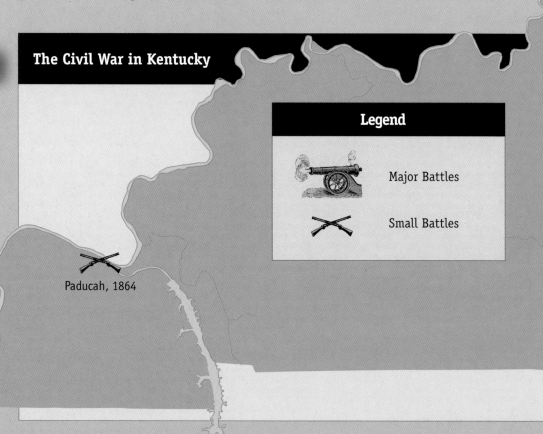

The Civil War in Kentucky

Paducah, 1864

Legend

Major Battles

Small Battles

Union General Ulysses S. Grant fought to take Columbus back. He also took back Bowling Green. President Lincoln was so impressed with Grant's work in Kentucky that he later made Grant commander of the entire Union army. Years later, Grant became president of the United States. Another future president, James A. Garfield, led Union troops in eastern Kentucky.

"There are great armies of both sides . . . in Kentucky. The final issue is very doubtful. Both sides think they will be the winner."

—Ellen McGoughy Wallace, 1862

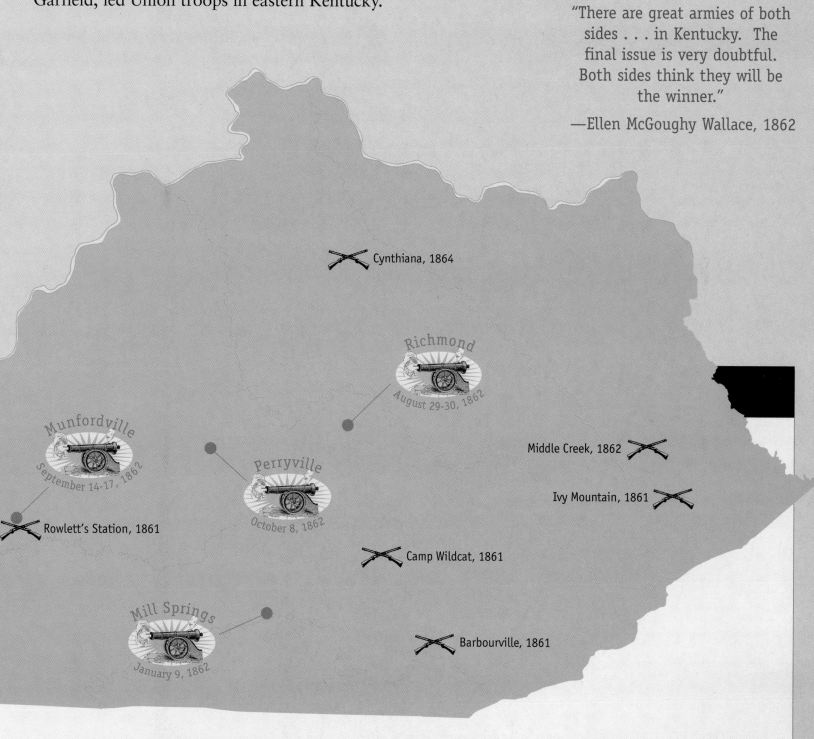

Cynthiana, 1864

Richmond
August 29-30, 1862

Munfordville
September 14-17, 1862

Middle Creek, 1862

Perryville
October 8, 1862

Ivy Mountain, 1861

Rowlett's Station, 1861

Camp Wildcat, 1861

Mill Springs
January 9, 1862

Barbourville, 1861

John Hunt Morgan

John Hunt Morgan was a Kentuckian who supported the Confederacy. Even before he joined the Confederate army, he began raiding Union troops. After he joined the Confederates, he quickly became an important leader.

Morgan's raids were different from regular battles. His raiders formed small groups and raced about the countryside. They stopped trains, destroyed goods, blocked communication, and kept Union soldiers from traveling across the land.

Raid on the L & N

John Hunt Morgan led raids all over Kentucky and Tennessee. He and his men once burned tunnels on the Louisville & Nashville Railroad. This stopped the flow of supplies to Union troops. Because they had no supplies, the Union army had to delay one attack for more than three months!

The Christmas Raid

Later, John Hunt Morgan led a ten-day raid in south-central Kentucky. Union leaders sent more than 20,000 soldiers to stop him. Morgan and his men captured a huge wagon filled with holiday foods and treats. These treats were on their way to a Christmas party for Union soldiers. The next day, Morgan's men destroyed a train bridge. Once again, supplies to Union soldiers were cut off.

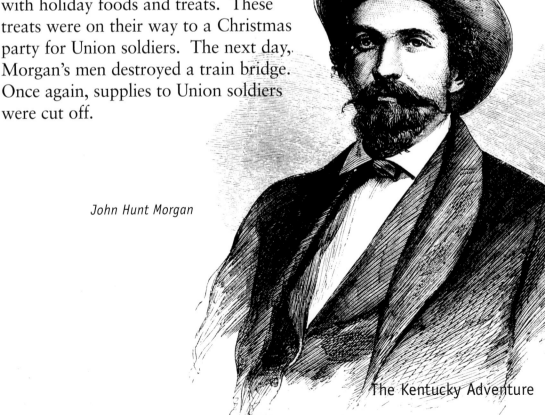

John Hunt Morgan

Linking the Past to the Present

Today, there is a statue of John Hunt Morgan in Lexington. Some people do not like it. They don't think it is right to celebrate Confederate soldiers. What do you think? Should we celebrate the efforts of Confederate soldiers? Why or why not?

A Message Through a Wire

One of the things John Hunt Morgan and his raiders did was block communication between Union soldiers and their leaders. Think of all the ways we communicate with one another today. In addition to writing letters or calling by telephone, we also use cell phones, text and instant messages, and email.

Just 100 years ago, things were very different. The easiest way to send messages back then was over the telegraph. The **telegraph** used a system of clicks over an electric wire. Different clicks stood for different letters. People on each end of the wire, "read" the messages. Telegraph wires were strung for hundreds of miles between towns.

One of the people who ran the telegraph was Thomas Edison, who lived in Louisville. He was very skilled, but he thought the telegraph was flawed. He soon started thinking of ways to make things better. Edison later moved to New Jersey, where he became one of the world's greatest inventors. His most famous invention is the light bulb.

The Battle of Perryville

The largest and deadliest Civil War battle in Kentucky took place in Perryville. Sixteen thousand Confederate troops fought against nearly 58,000 Union soldiers. When it was over, more than 8,000 soldiers were dead, wounded, or missing.

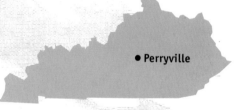

The Battle of Perryville ended in a Union victory.

A Soldier's Life

More than 30,000 Kentuckians joined the Confederate army, while nearly 60,000 joined the Union. Twenty thousand of those Union soldiers were black. That was the second-highest number of black soldiers among all the states.

In Garrard County, the Union set up Camp Dick Robinson to find and train soldiers. These soldiers were proud to fight for President Lincoln, so they called themselves "Lincoln Guns". Soldiers on both sides of the struggle thought the war would not last long or be very hard, but they were wrong. The war lasted four terrible years.

"Camp Misery"

Thousands of soldiers were wounded in Civil War battles. Doctors and nurses did the best they could, but they worked under harsh conditions and had poor supplies. Wartime hospitals were scenes of terrible suffering. Simple wounds often became so infected that arms and legs had to be removed. Some soldiers called the hospitals "Camp Misery".

Life in Camp

Soldiers did not fight in battles all the time. In fact, they spent most of their time in camp. They set up camp in one place for a while. Then they marched to another place and set up camp there.

In camp, soldiers drilled and learned how to march. Sometimes they played cards. Some soldiers played games, while others played musical instruments, like fiddles and flutes. They often

What Do You Think?

If you were a Civil War soldier and had to leave home, who would you miss the most?

got homesick. They wrote letters to their friends and family—especially their girlfriends or wives.

Hot and Cold

Being a soldier was often miserable. Can you imagine walking through sticky mud carrying a heavy pack on your back? Imagine bugs and mosquitoes buzzing around you as you try to sleep. It was very hot in the summer, and soldiers wore heavy uniforms. Winters were cold, rainy, and often snowy.

Sometimes, two soldiers tied their tents together and slept next to each other. This kept them warmer during chilly nights. Soldiers often got sick and died. In fact, more soldiers died from sickness than from battle wounds. Their shoes wore out, and there was little food. Many soldiers had nothing to eat except a very hard cracker called *hardtack*.

This is the 1st U.S. Colored Infantry.

African American Soldiers

During the war, blacks were still enslaved. Some were forced to build forts or drive wagons for the Confederate army. Others left the South to fight for the North.

The Union set up special training camps for black soldiers. One was Camp Nelson in Jessamine County. Although black soldiers were no longer slaves, they were separated from white soldiers. Black soldiers had to wear worn-out uniforms. They received little or no money. They were free, but they were not treated as equals.

Some white men did not believe black men could fight. They were wrong. Black men were brave soldiers. One white officer said black soldiers fought better than white soldiers because they had a stronger purpose. They were fighting for their freedom and for the freedom of the people they loved.

Life on the Homefront

Even though most Civil War battles were fought outside Kentucky, things were hard for people here, too. Men left their families to fight while most wives and mothers stayed behind to run the farms and plantations. The women had to do all the men's work plus their own.

Struggles for Poor Farmers

The farmers who did not own slaves or care very much about government had to make sacrifices for the war, too. To *sacrifice* means to give up something. Every man who served in the army had to sacrifice living at home and spending time with his family.

Slaves wanted to know what was happening with the war, but most could not read. One enslaved man hid under his owner's house and listened to him read the newspaper to his wife. Then the man told others what he had heard.

What Do You Think

Have you ever given up something that was important to you? How did you feel? How do you think the people who did not believe in the war felt about losing their belongings?

The Great Hog Swindle

Toward the end of the war, the U.S. government needed food for the Union army. The Union (Republican) officer in charge of Kentucky said all hog farmers in our state could only sell their hogs to the government. Even though other buyers would have paid more than the government did, Kentucky farmers had no choice. If they did not obey, they could be arrested. Hog farmers in our state lost thousands of dollars.

The Union officer also made agreements with a few meat-packing plants in Louisville. A plant is like a factory. While some plants stayed busy, others sat empty. This hurt all Kentuckians working in the hog business.

Finally, President Lincoln put an end to all the rules about buying and selling hogs in Kentucky. Kentuckians were glad the hog business was fair again, but they still disliked the Republican Party. They blamed the Republicans for all the money they had lost.

To **swindle** people means to cheat them.

The war hurt our state's poor farmers. When prices went up, only wealthy people could afford to buy the things they needed. Then the government asked farmers to plant more wheat, beans, and corn to help feed soldiers. Without crops of their own or money to buy food, poor families sometimes went hungry.

Most of our state's poor farmers were proud to be soldiers. They believed they were fighting for a good cause. Others thought the war was wrong and unfair. They said it was "a rich man's war and a poor man's fight".

Women Help the War Effort

Across the state, women's groups helped the war effort. They collected food and clothing, set up hospitals, and raised money. They gathered flax or wool from their farms and turned it into cloth to make uniforms. They helped make weapons and ammunition. They organized social events to raise money, and they sent boxes of supplies to the troops.

This woman took her three children to the army camp so her family could stay together.

Julia Ann Marcum
1844-1936

Julia Ann Marcum was born and raised in Tennessee. During the Civil War, Julia and her family supported the Union. This choice made them targets for attacks by Confederate troops.

During one of these attacks, teenaged Julia grabbed an ax and fought with a soldier. She injured him, and then her father shot him. Julia lost an eye and a finger in the struggle, but that was not the last attack on the family. The Marcums finally left Tennessee and made their home in Kentucky.

After the war, Julia tried to teach school. However, her wounds made that impossible. Julia felt the government owed her a *pension* since she helped fight the Confederacy. She worked hard to get leaders to listen to her. Finally, the government recognized her as a Civil War hero and granted her the pension.

Julia returned to Kentucky, where she lived for another 50 years. At her funeral, she received full military honors. By granting her the pension, the U. S. government had admitted her to the Grand Army of the Republic. Julia Ann Marcum was the only female member.

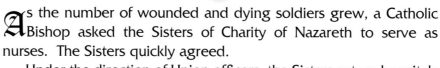

the Sisters of Charity of Nazareth

As the number of wounded and dying soldiers grew, a Catholic Bishop asked the Sisters of Charity of Nazareth to serve as nurses. The Sisters quickly agreed.

Under the direction of Union officers, the Sisters set up hospitals in Paducah, Louisville, Bardstown, Uniontown, and Lexington. They bathed, fed, and cared for hundreds of ill and wounded soldiers from the North and the South.

Angels of the Battlefield

Most of the soldiers were lonely and homesick. Sometimes, the Sisters sat near these men and just listened as they talked about their families. A few of the wounded were very young drummer boys. These boys dearly missed their mothers. One dying boy asked a Sister to place her head near his. Another asked a Sister to hold him as he died. He said, "I'll try to believe you are my mother."

Not all the Sisters survived the war. Several died from illnesses. When Sister Mary Lucy Dosh died, both armies stopped fighting so they could give her a quiet and respectful military funeral. Her **honor guards** were 12 officers, six in Union blue and six in Confederate gray. Union and Confederate soldiers alike wept for their 22-year-old "Angel of the Battlefield".

Showing Thanks

People all across the United States were thankful to the Sisters for their work. Do you remember reading about John Hunt Morgan? Morgan's mother was so grateful to the Sisters for their help that she made new uniforms for all of them. Doctors, generals, government leaders, and even President Abraham Lincoln sent letters of thanks to the Sisters.

Losing Loved Ones

When great battles were fought, the names of those who died were sent home by telegraph. The lists were posted on a wall, and townspeople gathered to see if they knew anyone on the list. Many people could not read, so sometimes a person read the names aloud.

Almost 11,000 soldiers from Kentucky died during the Civil War. This was about one out of every seven men who served. Women lost their sons, husbands, brothers, and fathers. Children lost their brothers, fathers, and grandfathers.

Linking the Past to the Present

Have you ever seen the Vietnam Memorial in Washington, D.C.? It is a long, black wall that bears the name of every American soldier who died in the Vietnam War. There are nearly 58,000 names on that wall. If a wall today listed the names of all who died in the Civil War, it would have nearly 600,000 names. The Civil War remains the deadliest war ever fought on American soil.

Nearly every family in Kentucky lost someone in the Civil War.

The Emancipation Proclamation

On January 1, 1863, President Abraham Lincoln issued the *Emancipation Proclamation.* It said that all slaves in southern states were free. In reality, it freed only a few slaves.

In the proclamation, Lincoln wrote that the slaves who lived in Confederate states were free. But the Confederate states did not recognize Lincoln as their president, so they did not obey. Since border states, like Kentucky, were not in the Confederacy, Lincoln's proclamation did not apply to them either! The only slaves who were actually freed were runaways hiding in the North whose owners could no longer come after them.

African Americans did not lose hope, however. The Emancipation Proclamation was a bold step. It was the first time an American president had tried to free slaves. The war was no longer just about keeping the Union together. It had become a struggle to rid the nation of slavery once and for all.

The War Ends

After four years of war, the Confederate army was worn out. The South knew it could not win, so Confederate General Robert E. Lee surrendered in Virginia. Kentucky would never be the same. Much of the state had been destroyed. It would take years to rebuild it.

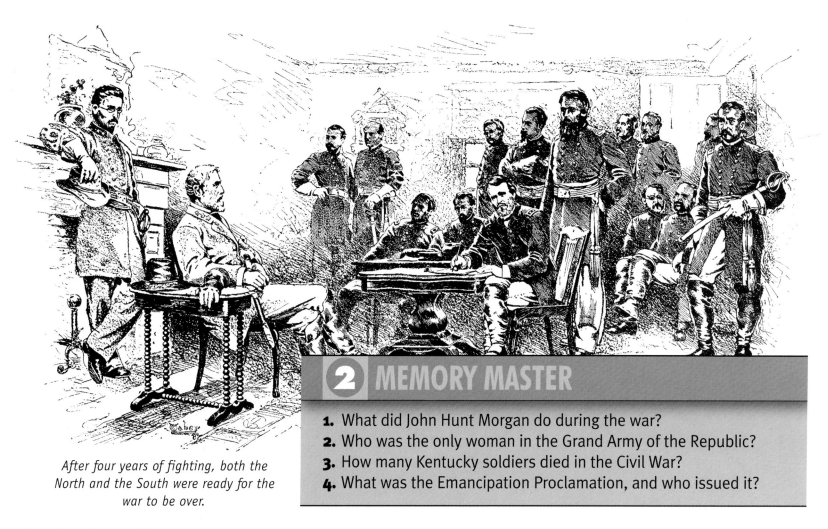

After four years of fighting, both the North and the South were ready for the war to be over.

2 MEMORY MASTER

1. What did John Hunt Morgan do during the war?
2. Who was the only woman in the Grand Army of the Republic?
3. How many Kentucky soldiers died in the Civil War?
4. What was the Emancipation Proclamation, and who issued it?

Free at Last!

After the war ended, slave owners in the Commonwealth did not want to release their slaves. Then Congress passed the Thirteenth Amendment, which freed all slaves. The Kentucky legislature refused to ratify the amendment. The legislature's decision didn't matter, however. The amendment was ratified by enough states that it became part of the Constitution. Kentucky's slaves were free at last!

The Assassination of Abraham Lincoln

Abraham Lincoln had a plan to help the country recover from the damage caused by the war. His plan was called *Reconstruction,* which means rebuilding.

Lincoln never had a chance to use his plan. Just after the war ended, Lincoln and his wife went to a theater in Washington, D.C. They were watching a play when a man fired a gun at the newly reelected president. Early the next morning, Lincoln died. Andrew Johnson became president.

Most Kentuckians did not like Abraham Lincoln while he was president. But years later, people realized how much he had done to keep the country together and to end slavery. Now he is one of Kentucky's greatest heroes.

The North Takes Control

Since the South lost the Civil War, the North was in control. Many northerners felt southerners should be punished. Northerners also felt former slaves should be given the same rights whites had. Southerners did not agree. After the war ended, the Union army had to stay in the South to protect former slaves from abuse.

The Reconstruction years were bloody and difficult. Many southerners had a hard time accepting that slavery was over. All Americans had questions. How would the South adjust to life without slavery? Would Union and Confederate neighbors be able to get along? How would former slaves be treated? What kind of state would Kentucky become?

The Lost Cause

During the Civil War, Confederates believed the South was a new country, entirely separate from the United States. After the Confederates lost the war, many southerners remained proud that they had fought so long and hard. They believed a smaller country (the Confederacy) had the right to protect itself from a larger one (the Union). This idea became known as the "lost cause" because the Confederates lost the war.

For generations, many southerners have honored the "lost cause". They celebrate former Confederate leaders and soldiers, and they role-play Civil War battles. Tourists travel to the South every year to watch these **reenactments.**

Activity

A Reconstruction Political Cartoon

This cartoon was drawn after the end of the Civil War. Look at it closely to answer these questions:

1. What is the title of the cartoon?
2. What does the kettle stand for?
3. The kettle is leaking. What do you think that means?
4. The woman is a symbol for the United States. The baby stands for the Thirteenth Amendment. Why do you think the woman is holding the baby?
5. The man is President Andrew Johnson. What do you think the cartoon says about him?

COLUMBIA—." Now, Andy, I wish you and your boys would hurry up that job, because I want to use that kettle right away. You are all talking too much about it."

MENDING THE FAMILY KETTLE.

The Freedmen's Bureau

The U.S. government wanted to help former slaves in Kentucky and other states, so it set up the *Freedmen's Bureau.* The Freedmen's Bureau gave food, shelter, and medicine to African Americans in need. It also helped poor whites.

Some former slaves chose to keep working for their former owners. Bureau workers helped them make work agreements. Now blacks were paid for their work. Workers also had the freedom to leave one place and work at another if they wanted to.

White Kentuckians had always believed owning land was the best symbol of freedom. Now that many blacks were free, they hoped for land of their own, too. The Freedmen's Bureau helped former slaves rent or buy land, so they could build homes and plant crops.

Sharecropping

Since they could no longer own slaves, wealthy landowners needed workers. People who didn't own land needed a way to make a living, so they became sharecroppers.

A *sharecropper* was a farmer who signed a contract to work on land owned by someone else. In return, a landowner agreed to give the sharecropper a house, tools, and some of the crop. If a sharecropper owned a mule or farm tools, the landowner did not have to provide these things. Then the sharecropper got a bigger share of the crop. Some sharecroppers sold the crops for money and paid rent to the landowner.

Sharecropping did not pay well, so most sharecroppers went into *debt.* They traded their share of the crop for the things they needed, but their share was never enough. They had to borrow money to buy the rest. Each year, sharecroppers went deeper and deeper into debt.

Schools for African Americans

Most former slaves did not know how to read or write. After they were freed, they had a hard time finding jobs.

The Freedmen's Bureau helped blacks become educated. It built schools and hired teachers. Most of the teachers were African American women. People who did not think blacks should be educated made threats and sometimes even attacked the brave teachers.

But threats did not stop teachers from teaching or former slaves from learning. They knew education was the key to a better future. Kentucky's first black students were so dedicated that they often risked their lives to attend school. Only three years after the war, there were nearly 10,000 black students in Kentucky.

After the war, the Freedmen's Bureau built more than 250 schools for Kentucky's black students.

The Civil War and Reconstruction

The Fifteenth Amendment allowed many freedmen to vote for the first time— but they didn't get to keep that right for long.

New Amendments

Besides the amendment that ended slavery, the federal government added two more amendments to the U.S. Constitution. Once again, the Kentucky legislature refused to ratify them.

The Fourteenth Amendment

The Fourteenth Amendment said that anyone born in the United States was a citizen. That meant anyone born to slave parents in the United States was now a citizen. The amendment also says that every citizen is equal. Do you remember that the *Dred Scott* case said African Americans were not citizens? The Fourteenth Amendment changed that. Now blacks had the same rights whites had.

The Republicans supported the amendment, but the Democrats didn't. They said it was another attack on states' rights. Even though the South was part of the United States again, many Kentuckians still did not trust the federal government. They continued to believe state government should have more power.

The Fifteenth Amendment

When Congress passed the Fifteenth Amendment, Kentucky leaders grew even more upset. This amendment says the right to vote can not be denied because of race. Many white men in Kentucky were so angry that they refused to vote. Then they passed laws that denied voting rights for other reasons. Most blacks in the South still could not vote.

Still Divided

In the next election for governor, the Democratic candidate, John Helm, won. The Democrats did not support fair treatment of blacks, but they won most of the positions in the legislature. It was clear that most Kentuckians had not changed their ways of thinking.

Ku Klux Klan

Some angry whites and former slave owners joined a violent group called the **Ku Klux Klan,** or KKK. KKK members did not think blacks should have the same rights as whites. They did not want blacks to vote or become government leaders.

Klan members dressed up in hoods and white gowns. They broke into African American homes and attacked families. They beat students and set fire to schools, churches, and entire neighborhoods. Sometimes they killed former slaves. They also hurt whites who helped blacks. The federal government had to send a general to Elizabethtown to protect citizens against Klan violence.

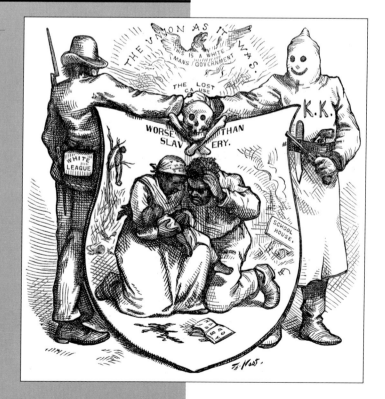

The Roebling Suspension Bridge

During Reconstruction, something very exciting happened in Kentucky. One of the nation's first **suspension** bridges was built. It spanned the Ohio River. The bridge allowed trains to travel from Cincinnati to Covington. When it opened, it was the longest suspension bridge in the world.

Have you ever wondered how a suspension bridge works? This kind of bridge has two long cables that hang from tall towers. The cables stretch from one end of the bridge to the other and are held in place by enormous concrete blocks. The roadway hangs from smaller cables attached to the main cables.

The Covington-Cincinnati Bridge was designed by John August Roebling. He was a German engineer who later designed the Brooklyn Bridge in New York City. In 1983, the bridge in Kentucky was renamed for its German designer. It is known today as the Roebling Suspension Bridge.

3 MEMORY MASTER

1. Did the Kentucky legislature ratify the Thirteenth Amendment? Why or why not?
2. What new kind of bridge was built in Kentucky after the Civil War?
3. How did the Freedmen's Bureau help people?
4. What do the Fourteenth and Fifteenth Amendments say?

Have you ever gone to a Cincinnati Reds or Bengals game? If so, you have probably seen the Roebling Bridge.

Chapter 9 Review

What's the Point?

The issue of slavery splits the nation. President Lincoln wants the country to stay united, but the southern states secede. They form the Confederate States of America. Even though Kentucky declares neutrality, several Civil War battles are fought here. The war causes many problems in Kentucky. Lincoln issues the Emancipation Proclamation. The North wins the war. The U.S. Congress passes three new amendments. Reconstruction is a time to rebuild the South after the Civil War. It is a time of conflict and unfair treatment of blacks. Former slaves struggle to find jobs, become educated, and gain equal rights.

Becoming Better Readers: Amendments

The Thirteenth, Fourteenth, and Fifteenth Amendments were made to the U.S. Constitution between 1865 and 1870. Find a copy of these amendments, and read them. One place you can find them is at www.usconstitution.net. Write down any words you don't know, and look them up. Now rewrite them in your own words. As you reread these three amendments, ask yourself what each one says that is different from the other two.

Our Amazing Geography: Difficult Travel

Do you remember which river the Roebling Suspension bridge crosses? While the river made travel easy for boats, it was difficult for horses and carriages to cross. Think of a landform in Kentucky that is hard to cross. It could be a river, lake, hill, or someplace far away from a road. Design a way to cross this landform without using an airplane. Draw a picture of your design. Talk to your classmates. Does anyone think it might be built some day?

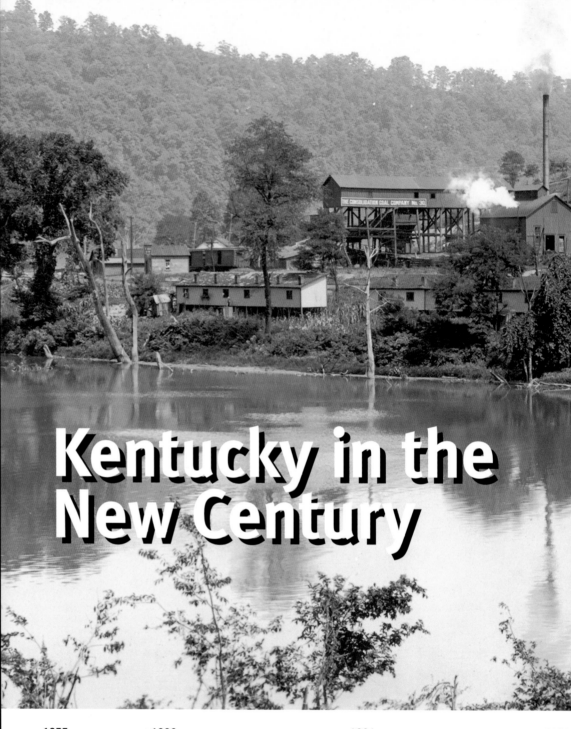

"The harder we worked, the less we had."

—Tenant farmer J.T. Strand

Many cities in Kentucky began as mining towns. Do you know how your city began?

Kentucky in the New Century

Timeline of Events

1880

1885

1890

1895

1900

1877
Kentucky's first telephone is installed.

1882
The feud between the Hatfields and the McCoys begins.

1891
Kentucky's fourth constitution is adopted.

1904
The Day Law takes effect.

1887
The State Normal School for Colored Persons opens in Frankfort.

1888
Laura Clay organizes the Kentucky Equal Rights Association.
"Honest Dick" Tate steals most of the money in the state treasury.

1896
The Tollgate Wars

1900
Governor William Goebel is assassinated.

Chapter 10

The years between 1880 and 1940 were hard, violent years in Kentucky. Poor Kentuckians grew even poorer. Many children worked to help support their families, so they did not go to school. Our state also struggled with growing racial tension.

The coal industry produced great wealth but also brought loss, sadness, and death. The violence in Kentucky during these years caught the world's attention. People began believing things about Kentuckians that were not always true.

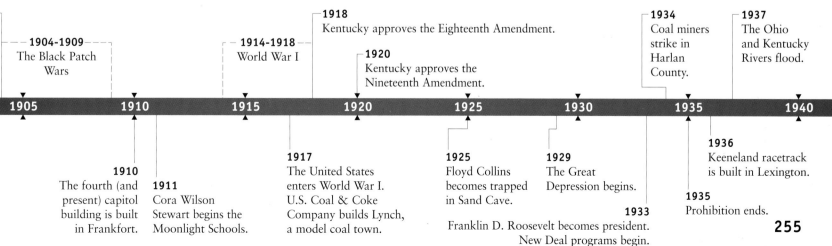

1904-1909
The Black Patch Wars

1910
The fourth (and present) capitol building is built in Frankfort.

1911
Cora Wilson Stewart begins the Moonlight Schools.

1914-1918
World War I

1917
The United States enters World War I. U.S. Coal & Coke Company builds Lynch, a model coal town.

1918
Kentucky approves the Eighteenth Amendment.

1920
Kentucky approves the Nineteenth Amendment.

1925
Floyd Collins becomes trapped in Sand Cave.

1929
The Great Depression begins.

1933
Franklin D. Roosevelt becomes president. New Deal programs begin.

1934
Coal miners strike in Harlan County.

1935
Prohibition ends.

1936
Keeneland racetrack is built in Lexington.

1937
The Ohio and Kentucky Rivers flood.

1905   1910   1915   1920   1925   1930   1935   1940

Family Feuds

Kentucky was a very different place in 1900 than it was in 1800. The ways people used the land had changed. The places people lived had changed. The Civil War and Reconstruction were over, but anger and violence continued for many more years. One form of violence our state became famous for was called feuding. A *feud* is an argument that goes on for a very long time. Some families feuded for generations.

The Tollgate Wars

Much of the violence in Kentucky during this time had nothing to do with boundaries or land. People were still upset about toll roads and bridges.

A few Kentuckians decided they were tired of paying tolls. They began burning tollhouses and destroying tollgates. One gatekeeper was seriously hurt. In some counties, nearly every tollgate was destroyed. Even though the violent acts were against the law, they worked. Within a few years, every tollgate company was gone. Poor Kentuckians could travel across the land for free.

This tollgate in Bath County was run by the Chafin family. What do you think happened if a traveler didn't have enough money to pay the toll?

The Hatfields and the McCoys

The Hatfields and the McCoys were two families who lived near the border between Kentucky and West Virginia. The McCoy family lived in Kentucky, and the Hatfield family lived mainly in West Virginia.

Bad feelings between the two families began when a McCoy accused a Hatfield of stealing a hog. As the years went by, other events caused the families to grow angry with one another. When three McCoys killed a Hatfield, the feud was on! There were other, more deadly, feuds in Kentucky. But newspapers carried stories about the Hatfields and the McCoys. That made their feud the most famous one of all.

What Do You Think ?

The tollgate wars ended tolls, but do you think violence is a good way to solve problems? What could people have done instead?

RATES OF TOLL
ON THE
Louisville and Shep-
herdsville Turnpike Road.

For every 20 head of sheep, one cent per mile.
For every 20 head of hogs, two cents per mile.
For each head of cattle, two cents every five miles.
For every horse, mule, ass, jenny, or other animal of the large kind, with a rider, one cent per mile.
For same, without rider, three cents per five miles.
For each pleasure carriage drawn by one horse, mule, ass or jenny, two cents per mile.
For same, with two horses, mules, &c., three cents per mile.
For same, with more than two horses, &c., one cent per mile for each additional horse, mule, &c.
For each public stage, hack or omnibus, drawn by two horses, mules, &c., conveying more than four passengers, five cents per mile.
For same, drawn by four horses, &c., eight cents per mile.
For each cart, wagon, or other conveyance, drawn by one horse, mule, &c., or two oxen, two cents per mile.
For same, drawn by two horses, mules, &c., or two yoke of oxen, three cents per mile.
For same, by three horses, &c., four cents per mile.
For same, by four horses, &c., five cents per mile.
For same, by five horses, &c., six cents per mile.
For same, by six horses, &c., seven cents per mile.
For each cart, wagon, &c., as above, on return trip, when empty, one half the above rates.

E. D. STANDIFORD, Prest.
E. G. MINOY, Sec.

The State Normal School for Colored Persons

The state government was corrupt, but not everything it did was bad. One good thing the state government did was establish a training school for black teachers. When the school opened, it was called the State Normal School for Colored Persons. Teachers could learn spelling, penmanship, math, history, and even how to sing!

Over the years, the school grew and changed its name many times. Finally, it became a university and changed its name for the last time. Do you know which school this is? It's Kentucky State University!

Corruption

Another problem in Kentucky after Reconstruction was *corruption.* At every level of government—state, county, and local—political leaders were dishonest.

James W. "Honest Dick" Tate

One such leader was the state *treasurer,* James W. Tate. A treasurer's job is to manage the state's money. Tate was so famous for his honesty that his nickname was "Honest Dick." But Tate was not really honest.

He left on a short trip to Cincinnati and was never seen in Kentucky again. Shortly after Tate left, officials in Frankfort discovered that almost all the money in the state treasury was missing! Most people believed "Honest Dick" had taken it, but the police never found Tate or the money. This money could have been used to build better roads and schools, but now the old ones had to do. All Kentuckians suffered because of what "Honest Dick" did.

Corruption in Louisville

The state's largest city, Louisville, had become corrupt—especially during city elections. Corrupt officials paid *repeaters* to vote more than once in city elections. These officials also scared away voters who planned to vote for candidates the officials did not like. One city election was so corrupt that the courts threw out all the results and held a new election.

A Fourth Constitution

Kentucky was changing and growing, but the government still worked under the old state constitution, which supported slavery. Once again, Kentuckians began calling for a new constitution. They knew Kentucky could not become a modern state under the old one. One hundred delegates went to Frankfort to begin work on the state's fourth constitution.

Changes to the Constitution

The delegates knew many changes needed to be made. Experiences with past leaders, like "Honest Dick" Tate, made them afraid to give too much power to one person. The delegates wanted

The Kentucky Adventure

to make sure leaders would not be able to stay in office for too long. They also worried about the power of big businesses, especially the Louisville and Nashville (L&N) Railroad.

The new constitution made rules that helped keep the state government from becoming corrupt. For example, it limited the governor's time in office to one four-year term. It finally outlawed slavery in Kentucky.

Election Laws

Because of the problems with past elections, the delegates changed voting laws, too. Louisville became the first city in the United States to use a secret *ballot.* Voters cast their votes in private. The new constitution required the secret ballot throughout the entire state. The delegates also made it possible to *amend,* or change, the constitution.

Linking the Past to the Present

The constitution approved in 1891 still governs Kentucky today. Kentuckians have amended it several times, but they have not voted to write a new one. One amendment changed the term limit for the governor. Today, the governor of Kentucky can run for reelection.

A Fourth Capitol Building

The state government had grown, and the capitol building in Frankfort was too small. State leaders wondered if they should move the capitol to another city. They talked about it for two years. Finally, leaders bought a piece of land in South Frankfort and began work on a larger building. Five years later, the new building opened. This building is still our state capitol today.

What Do You Think

Our state capitol building is nearly 100 years old. Have you ever been there? Do you think we need a new one? Why or why not?

Activity

Our State Constitution

How long has today's state constitution been around? Do you think things have changed since 1891? Do you think the constitution is fine as it is, or should it be updated to fit changing times? You can become a historian by studying two sections from our state constitution. Think about how you understand these words today. Also think about how lawmakers understood them over 100 years ago. Discuss your answers with the class.

Section 177—Commonwealth not to lend credit, nor become stockholder in corporation, nor build railroad or highway. The credit of the Commonwealth shall not be given . . . nor shall the Commonwealth construct railroad or other highway.

Section 239—Disqualification from office for presenting or accepting challenge to duel. Any person who shall, after the adoption of this Constitution . . . give, accept or knowingly carry a challenge to any person or persons to fight in single combat, with a citizen of this State, with a deadly weapon, either in or out of the State, shall be deprived of the right to hold any office of honor or profit in this Commonwealth. . . .

During the dispute, Governor Taylor called out the militia to try to keep peace.

Governor William Goebel

One of the men who helped write the new constitution was William Goebel. Almost ten years after the constitution was finished, he ran for governor against Republican William Taylor. The election results were very close, but Taylor was declared the winner.

The people who helped Goebel did not believe Taylor won. They said the Republicans had cheated. Hundreds of men from all over the state went to Frankfort to support Taylor. Hundreds of others went to support Goebel. Most of these men brought weapons with them. The city became a battle zone.

Gunned Down

As Goebel walked toward the capitol building one day, someone shot him. Over the next few days, his helpers worked to change the election results. Goebel became the governor, took the oath of office, and then died.

The shooting caused the feuding between Democrats and Republicans to flare up again. William Taylor had to flee the state, and John C.W. Beckham became governor. Goebel's death added to the image of Kentucky as a violent state.

To this day, no one knows who shot William Goebel.

The Kentucky Adventure

The Telephone Comes to Kentucky

The telegraph had been used in Kentucky for years. But communication was much easier when people could talk to one another. A new invention called the telephone allowed people to do that.

Two years after the first phone came to our state, workers ran telephone lines across the Roebling Bridge. Now, people in Kentucky could talk to people in Ohio! Within three years, there were 132 telephones in Kentucky.

When telephones were first invented, it was hard for workers to run telephone lines in the hills. Most Kentuckians did not have phones until many years later.

African Americans and Segregation

The new constitution outlawed slavery forever, but as time went on, tension between blacks and whites grew worse. It especially showed up in schools. Berea College was the only school in Kentucky that allowed both blacks and whites. All other schools were **segregated.** That means there were separate schools for blacks and whites.

More than half the students who graduated from Berea were black. That angered some of the lawmakers in Frankfort. Carl Day proposed a new law that would keep whites and blacks from

Schools, restrooms, restaurants, and other services for blacks were always in much poorer condition than those for whites.

Violence in Corbin

Even though the law said blacks and whites were equal, life for Kentucky's African Americans continued to be unfair. Angry mobs of people attacked black men, women, and children. One of the most violent places was Corbin.

In many parts of the South, jobs were hard to find. Sometimes black men got good-paying jobs. This made white men angry. In Corbin, white men were enraged when African Americans began working for the railroad. Finally, white mobs forced all of Corbin's black citizens onto trains. The men in the mobs said they would beat or kill anyone who did not leave the city.

Lynching, or killing people violently, was common during this time. Corbin's African Americans knew they had to leave. More than 60 years passed before blacks returned to Corbin.

The Kentucky Adventure

attending the same schools—including Berea. The *Day Law* passed. For the next 50 years, it kept Kentucky's schools segregated.

"Separate but Equal"

Several people tried to challenge the Day Law in court, but the U.S. Supreme Court said segregation was legal. Then a black man in another state was forced off a train because he tried to ride in a "Whites Only" car. In this case, the Supreme Court said *facilities* for blacks and whites should be "separate but equal." In truth, facilities were never equal.

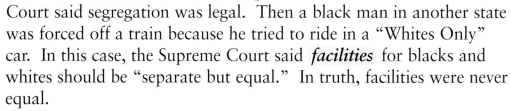

John Marshall Harlan
1833-1911

John Marshall Harlan was one of nine children. His father wanted him to become a lawyer, so he named John after John Marshall, a famous Supreme Court justice. Young John graduated from Transylvania University Law School and became a lawyer—just like his father wanted.

A few years later John became a county judge. He then opened a private law firm. He traveled across the state making speeches and encouraging people to support the Union. When the Civil War began, John gathered a company and became a leader in the Union army. He even fought against John Hunt Morgan and his men.

After the war, John became *attorney general* for the state of Kentucky. He ran for governor two times, but he didn't win. When President Rutherford B. Hayes named him to the U.S. Supreme Court, he was only 44 years old.

John served on the Supreme Court for 34 years. He became famous for casting *dissenting* votes on important issues—especially on rights for blacks. To dissent means to disagree. Because of this, other leaders began calling him "the Great Dissenter."

John thought blacks deserved fairer treatment. He once wrote that the Constitution should be "color blind." At the time, few judges or politicians agreed with him. Later, John Harlan was considered one of the greatest justices ever to serve on the Supreme Court.

What Do You Think?

What do you think John Harlan meant when he said the Constitution should be color blind? What does it mean to be color blind? Is the Constitution color blind today? How?

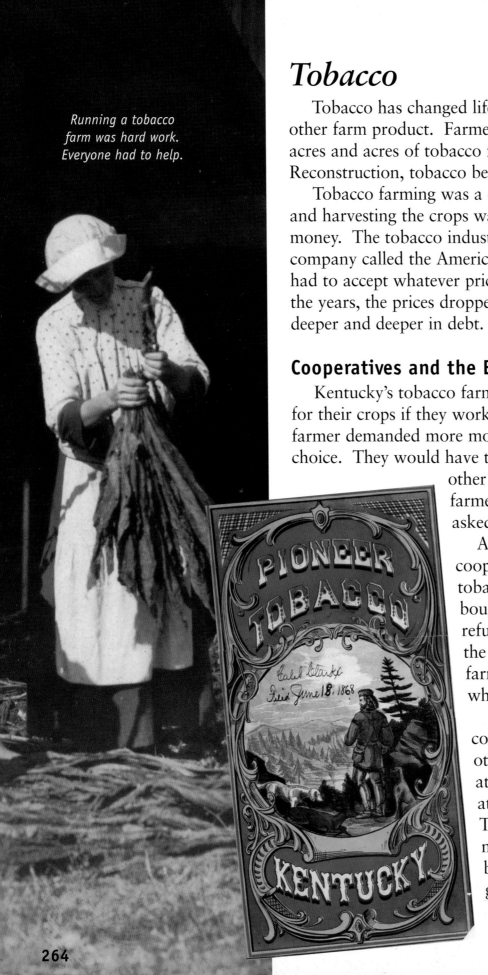

Running a tobacco farm was hard work. Everyone had to help.

Tobacco

Tobacco has changed life for Kentucky farmers more than any other farm product. Farmers in central and western Kentucky grew acres and acres of tobacco for cigarettes and cigars. After Reconstruction, tobacco became Kentucky's largest cash crop.

Tobacco farming was a difficult way of life. Planting, growing, and harvesting the crops was hard work, and it usually brought little money. The tobacco industry was controlled by a powerful company called the American Tobacco Company. Tobacco farmers had to accept whatever prices the tobacco company offered. Over the years, the prices dropped lower and lower, so farmers sank deeper and deeper in debt.

Cooperatives and the Black Patch Wars

Kentucky's tobacco farmers believed they could get higher prices for their crops if they worked together. The idea was that if every farmer demanded more money, the tobacco company would have no choice. They would have to pay more because there would be no other place for them to buy tobacco. These farmers joined together in *cooperatives* and asked for more money.

A few farmers refused to join the cooperatives. They continued to sell their tobacco for less, so the tobacco company bought all they had. The tobacco company refused to pay the higher prices charged by the farmers in the cooperatives. These farmers became very angry with the farmers who would not join.

Some of the angry farmers wore costumes, rode horses, and tried to scare the other farmers into joining. The men who attacked were called *night riders.* The attacks were called the *Black Patch Wars.* The worst attack was when hundreds of night riders rode into Hopkinsville. They burned several tobacco warehouses to the ground.

Strike!

Wherever tobacco was grown, farmers fought back. In central Kentucky, burley tobacco farmers stored their harvest in warehouses and refused to sell it. Then they went on *strike.* Over 30,000 farmers refused to plant tobacco until they received the prices they wanted.

By the end of that year, the tobacco company paid the higher prices the farmers demanded. Many farmers thought they would not have to fight for more money again. They thought the tobacco company would keep paying the higher prices. But it didn't. When the cooperatives failed a few years later, the prices for tobacco dropped once again.

The wars between tobacco farmers were called Black Patch Wars because some tobacco fields look like big, black patches.

1 MEMORY MASTER

1. Which two families were involved in the most famous Kentucky feud?
2. In what way were some Kentucky leaders corrupt?
3. What was the school for black teachers called when it first opened? What is it called today?
4. Who fought in the Black Patch Wars? Why did they fight?

This is one of the warehouses where farmers stored tobacco during the Black Patch Wars.

PEOPLE TO KNOW

Madeline Breckinridge
Laura Clay
Cora Wilson Stewart

PLACES TO LOCATE

Europe

WORDS TO UNDERSTAND

Prohibition
revenuer
suffrage

Kentucky Schools

Many historians believe education has been the biggest problem in the history of Kentucky. For years, the state spent less than half the amount of money on education that most other states spent. Every county had to have at least one school, but only half the children in our state went to the schools.

The Schoolhouse

Most students went to one-room schoolhouses. In the early days, these buildings were made of logs. During wet weather, the roofs leaked, and wind blew through the cracks in the walls and floors. These early schools did not have yards, fences, or even outhouses.

Later, whitewashed buildings replaced the log schools, but there were still problems. There was no running water, and the schools had very few supplies. One potbellied stove had to heat the entire room. Sometimes, supplies for the whole year included only chalkboard erasers, a box of chalk, a bucket for coal, a mop, and floor oil.

This photograph shows a school for white children.

This photograph shows a school for black children.

Teachers

Despite the challenges, Kentucky teachers were dedicated. They received very little pay, but that did not stop them from caring about their students. They wanted students to succeed. When there were too many students for one teacher, the teacher urged the students to help one another. A few Kentucky students studied hard and became well-educated. But most lagged far behind the rest of the nation.

Cora Wilson Stewart

Moonlight Schools

Many adults in our state had never learned to read or write. This was mostly because as children their families had needed them to work. They did not have time to go to school. One woman decided grown men and women who had not gone to school deserved a chance to learn.

Cora Wilson Stewart arranged for 50 schoolhouses in Rowan County to be used at night to teach adults. On the first night of classes, Cora expected 150 students to attend. She was very surprised when more than 1,200 men and women appeared at the Moonlight Schools. The youngest student was 18. The oldest was 86!

One problem the Moonlight Schools faced was that textbooks were written for children. They were about things like animals and toys. Reading stories for children made adult students feel silly. Cora began writing a simple newspaper called *The Moonlighter*. It contained real news about people and events in Kentucky. The adults were glad they could read about things that were important to them. Cora also wrote books for adult students.

The Moonlight Schools helped people so much that word spread quickly. Soon, they were in almost every part of the state. Then Moonlight Schools began popping up in other states, such as Tennessee and West Virginia. Almost all of these schools used reading materials Cora had written.

Linking the Past to the Present

Today, adults all across the United States attend night classes. These classes give people who work during the day a chance to go to school at night.

Cars driving up creek beds often got stuck and had to be pulled out by mules.

Kentucky Roads

If you could go back in time, you would be shocked at the condition of Kentucky's roads. They were so bad that it was almost as easy to cross the entire United States as it was to go from Pikeville to Paducah!

People still traveled by wagon or horse on dirt roads. When it rained or snowed, the dirt turned to thick, sticky mud, and people often got stuck. Kentucky's poorly maintained roads became even more of a problem after cars were invented. People traveling from state to state often went out of their way to avoid going through Kentucky because of the terrible roads.

State leaders started thinking more about the roads in Kentucky. They built new highways and repaired damaged roads. This helped our state become more modern.

What Do You Think ?

Some people think better roads and highways have been the most important development in the entire history of Kentucky—even more important than electricity, telephones, and air conditioning! What do you think was the most important development? Why?

World War I

In 1914, a terrible war broke out in Europe. It involved so many countries that it was called a world war. At first, the United States wanted to stay out of the war. But when German submarines killed some American travelers, Congress decided the United States should join the war after all.

Kentucky Does Its Part

As usual, Kentuckians were quick to respond to the military call to serve. Nearly 100,000 soldiers from Kentucky fought in World War I. Close to 2,500 of them died.

The men who served in the war had to leave their jobs, but the work still had to be done. Women began working in new ways to try to help. They worked in factories, as telephone operators, and on streetcars and railroads.

Women's clubs made bandages and knit socks. Families had "Fireless" Mondays, "Meatless" Tuesdays, and "Wheatless" Wednesdays so they used less fuel and food. If families used less, the government could send more food overseas to help the soldiers. Kentuckians also planted "victory gardens" to grow more food at home. They turned off their lights earlier, so they could save fuel.

News that the United States had declared war on Germany spread quickly.

This poster is trying to get families to use less wheat. If they could save one loaf of bread a week, that wheat could be sent to feed the soldiers.

Scenes like this one were common at the beginning of Prohibition.

Prohibition

While the war raged in Europe, several groups in Kentucky began talking about the dangers of alcohol. These people wanted to outlaw making, buying, and selling alcoholic beverages. This idea was called **Prohibition.** The people who wanted Prohibition traveled around the state giving speeches. They also worked to help pass laws against alcohol.

The people against Prohibition talked about the money that came into the state through the whiskey business. If Prohibition passed, all that money would be gone. The two groups argued for years. In the end, the people who wanted Prohibition won. Kentucky outlawed the production and sale of alcohol a year before the rest of the nation did.

Revenuers and sheriffs pose next to stills they gathered during a raid in Catlettsburg.

Revenuers

Fifty years before the amendment passed, whiskey-making had become a growing problem in Kentucky. Making world-famous Kentucky corn whiskey was a way of life for many mountain families. Then the government passed tax laws on whiskey made in home stills. Most whiskey-makers refused to pay them. When government officials called *revenuers* tried to collect the taxes, they were often met by a gun.

The End of Prohibition

Eventually, the U.S. government found it could not stop people from making, selling, or drinking alcohol. The Twenty-first Amendment passed 13 years later. It made alcohol legal once again.

"Bootlegging" Kentucky "Moonshine"

Even though it was against the law, many Kentuckians went right on making whiskey. In fact, requests for homemade whiskey rose because people couldn't buy alcohol in stores. Some whiskey-makers hid their stills up in the mountains. Others hid them down in hollows. They covered them with branches and leaves during the day and ran them only at night. Whiskey made by the light of the moon was called "moonshine".

Moving the whiskey from the stills to customers was tricky. The police often searched cars, trucks, wagons, and even people on horseback, looking for moonshine. The people carrying the whiskey from place to place had to be very sneaky. Sometimes they hid bottles of moonshine in their boots. That is how they came to be known as "bootleggers".

Voting Rights for Women

After the war was over, the soldiers came home. Women went back to working in their homes. They had been allowed to help during the war, but life had not changed for them. They still couldn't attend many schools, hold many jobs, or earn even half as much as men. Most importantly, however, they still couldn't vote.

Women all across the United States demanded greater rights, including *suffrage,* or the right to vote. In the fight for this right, several women from Kentucky led the way. Two of these women were Laura Clay, founder and first president of the Kentucky Equal Rights Association (KERA), and Madeline "Madge" Breckinridge, KERA's second president.

Madeline Breckinridge

Breckinridge wanted the government to help poor Kentuckians, but every time she asked, government leaders said no. Breckinridge came to believe that Kentucky would not get leaders who cared

Laura Clay led this group of women in a march at a political meeting in St. Louis, Missouri. Laura Clay is in the middle holding up an umbrella.

Governor Edwin Morrow signs the amendment that gives the right to vote to women in Kentucky.

Laura Clay
1849-1941

Laura Clay, the daughter of Cassius Clay, was born near Richmond. She attended a small public school until she was 14. Then she went to the Sayre Female Institute in Lexington. At Sayre, she realized she was smarter than many boys she knew. Laura grew frustrated that she would never have the same rights as these boys.

When Laura's parents divorced, her mother lost everything. Laura became concerned that Kentucky laws did not protect women. Laura wanted to change that. She and her sisters fought for the right to vote.

Laura Clay organized the Kentucky Equal Rights Association. This group forced the legislature to make new laws. Laura also gave speeches all across America. People listened to her, and women slowly began to gain more rights.

Laura Clay died when she was 92. She had spent her life fighting for women's rights.

about people until women could help choose them. She decided women had to have the right to vote. Breckinridge was Henry Clay's great-granddaughter. Many said she had his talent for speaking. When she spoke, people listened.

Breckinridge gave speeches while women across the nation handed out flyers, marched with signs, and talked to lawmakers. Some women even refused to eat until leaders allowed them to vote. These actions finally worked. In 1920, Congress passed the Nineteenth Amendment, which gave women the right to vote.

2 MEMORY MASTER

1. How are schools today different from one-room schoolhouses?
2. What were Moonlight Schools? Who started them?
3. How did Kentuckians help during World War I?
4. What is suffrage? Which amendment is about women's suffrage?

PEOPLE TO KNOW

John L. Lewis
John C.C. Mayo

PLACES TO LOCATE

Eastern Coal Field
Harlan County
Lynch
Western Coal Field

WORDS TO UNDERSTAND

black lung
boom
broad form deed
coal tipple
cribbing
deep-shaft mining
labor union
legacy
scatter tag
scrip
strikebreaker
strip mining

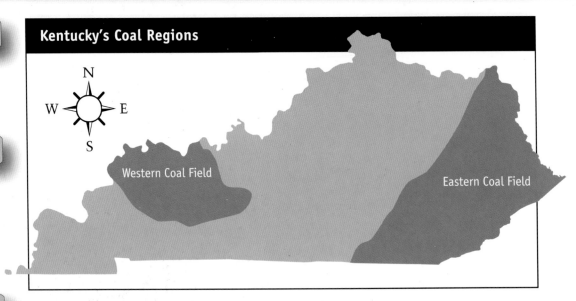

Kentucky's Coal Regions

Western Coal Field

Eastern Coal Field

King Coal

Perhaps the most important change in Kentucky during this period was the rise of the coal mining industry. In earlier chapters of this book, you learned about the rich stores of coal that lie in the Eastern and Western Coal Field Regions. As companies across the world realized the many uses of coal, the history of Kentucky changed forever.

Activity

Histori-Coal Names

Because coal was such an exciting and important resource, people made up fun nicknames for it. Can you tell which of the nicknames in the list below were really used? Can you tell which ones were not? Go through the list and decide which five nicknames are real. Then make up your own nickname for coal.

King Coal   Black Diamonds
Black Dust   Pop Rocks
King of the Mountains   Snow Shadow
Ancient Sunshine   Black Gold

Many families were left with ruined land and no money after they signed broad form deeds.

Broad Form Deeds

In the 1880s, coal buyers came to Kentucky looking for underground deposits of coal. When they found it, the buyers asked land owners to sign *broad form deeds.* These deeds allowed land owners to keep the land above ground while the coal companies had rights to the coal below ground.

For many years, broad form deeds allowed mining companies to earn millions of dollars while they destroyed the land. Many land owners claimed they never signed broad form deeds. But that did not stop the coal companies. Hundreds of Kentuckians lost their land.

What Do You Think

Do you think broad form deeds were fair? Should state leaders have stepped in to make sure eastern Kentuckians knew what they were signing? Why or why not?

Linking the Past to the Present

Today, coal is still an important source of energy in the United States. More than half of the electricity used in our country comes from coal. Can you guess how much of Kentucky's electricity comes from coal? It is 96%, more than any other state in the USA!

KENTUCKY PORTRAIT

John C.C. Mayo
1864-1914

One of the most important people in the coal industry in Kentucky was John Caldwell Calhoun Mayo. Born in 1864 in Pike County, John became one of the wealthiest men in Kentucky.

Young John was smart. He read every book he could find and became a schoolteacher at the age of 16. While he was in college, he learned about the deposits of coal under the ground in eastern Kentucky. John hired a lawyer to write broad form deeds. He used these deeds to purchase coal rights to thousands of acres of land. Most land owners did not understand how much they were losing when they signed the deeds.

John told many wealthy men about his plans. They bought huge amounts of land, too. Soon, John had great wealth and political power. His plan made a few people rich, but thousands remained very poor. Kentucky would never be the same.

Coal miners pose at the entrance of a deep-shaft mine.

Methods of Mining

There is more than one way to mine coal. One method is called **deep-shaft mining**. Another is called **strip mining**.

Deep-Shaft Mining

In deep-shaft mining, workers had to go down into Earth through a narrow hole. When a miner went deep into the ground, he entered a dangerous world. It was pitch black, and the only light he had was a coal oil lantern, usually connected to his helmet.

The mine roof was supported by timber **cribbing**. The cribbing and roofs often collapsed and injured or killed miners. Little fresh air made its way into the mine, so miners got sick from underground gases. In the early days, miners put a canary in a cage and lowered it into a mine. Then they pulled the cage back up. If the canary was alive, it was safe for workers to go into the mine. If the canary was dead, workers knew poisonous gases were there.

Coal dust is damaging to people's lungs, but coal miners breathed it day after day, year after year. Many developed an illness called **black lung**. When a miner got black lung, he lost his job. His family was left with no income. Because of that, many ill coal miners pretended they were well and kept working in the mines. They got sicker and sicker every year until they died.

Activity

Reading a Graph

Use the graph to answer the following questions:

1. How many miners were killed between 1900 and 1909?
2. During which years did the most miners die?
3. During which years did the fewest miners die?
4. How many years does the graph cover?
5. Why do you think so many miners died between 1920 and 1949?

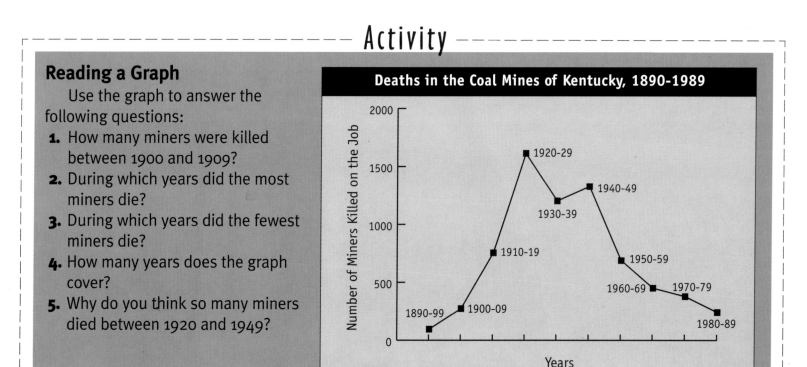

Deaths in the Coal Mines of Kentucky, 1890-1989

Number of Miners Killed on the Job

2000

1500 — 1920-29

1000 — 1940-49 / 1930-39

500 — 1910-19 / 1950-59

1890-99 / 1900-09 / 1960-69 / 1970-79

0 — 1980-89

Years

Strip Mining

Mining changed after large mining machines were invented. Giant tractors and dirt haulers removed whole mountaintops to uncover the coal. This is called strip mining because it strips the land. It is much safer than deep-shaft mining. It also requires fewer miners, but it leaves deep scars on the land. Have you ever seen a mountain that has been strip mined?

When an area is strip mined, the spot where earth is removed is called "the cut".

This miner's shack in Four Mile was over 50 years old when this picture was taken. Coal companies rarely repaired homes, but there were few choices for poor mining families. They had to make the best of what they had.

The Kentucky Adventure

Company Towns

Many coal companies built towns for their workers. The houses in the towns were usually small and poorly built. In fact, they were called shacks. If you were a coal miner, your address might be Shack #24, Seco, Kentucky. Each month, rent for the shacks was taken out of workers' paychecks. Most coal companies hired guards to patrol the towns.

This is Red Ash. It was built as a mining town around 1880.

The Company Store

In most company towns, mine owners built and controlled all the schools, churches, and stores. Sometimes the coal companies paid mine workers in *scrip* instead of money. Scrip was only good at the company store, so miners and their families had to shop there. People living in company towns didn't have choices about where to live, where to shop, or even where to go to church.

Kentucky coal miners felt trapped. The harder they worked, the less they had. Miners didn't earn enough to take care of their families. Each month, families had to charge goods at the company store. Then the coal company took rent and the store debt out of each miner's paycheck. After that, there was nothing left for the family. In the early days, the coal companies didn't even pay for mining supplies. A sign in one company store read, "All explosives, tools, and supplies to the mining of coal shall be furnished by the mine worker."

This was the company store in Lejunior in 1946.

For people living in the mountains, there were few jobs besides mining. One miner said: "I didn't have any choice but to work in the mines. I had a family. They had to eat."

Country-western singer Merle Travis wrote a song about life as a Kentucky coal miner. Here are some of the words:

You load sixteen tons, what do you get?
Another day older and deeper in debt.
Saint Peter don't you call me 'cause I can't go
I owe my soul to the company store.

Each mining company had its own **scatter tags.** These round, metal disks were thrown into the coal cars with the freshly mined coal. When a company received a shipment of coal, the scatter tags told them which company had mined the coal.

Lynch, Kentucky

The most famous company town in Kentucky was Lynch in Harlan County. It was built by the U.S. Coal & Coke Company. At one point, almost 10,000 miners and their families lived there.

Lynch was designed to be a model for other company towns. It had a company store, post office, theater, hotel, hospital, churches, and schools. It even had an Olympic-size swimming pool. Lynch also had the largest **coal tipple** in the world, which held 15,000 tons of coal. The world record for the most coal mined in a single shift was set in Lynch. On that day, miners loaded 256 train cars with coal in only nine hours.

The citizens of Lynch had access to good medical care, housing, education, wages, and even recreation. But it was still a community controlled by one man, the owner of the coal company. He made all the decisions for the town. No one who lived there had a say. Lynch remained under U.S. Coal & Coke's control for many years. Then it became an independent town.

Strikes and Labor Unions

Some of Kentucky's worst problems in the new century were caused by poor working conditions and low wages. Workers had no power, so the coal companies ignored their complaints. Things started to get better after the labor unions came to Kentucky. A *labor union* is a group of workers who work together to get more pay, fairer treatment, and a safer place to work.

The UMWA

One of the largest labor unions was the United Mine Workers of America (UMWA). It started strikes to try to force mining companies to make changes. Workers refused to work until they got what they wanted. The mining companies did not want workers to strike. They forced workers to sign papers saying they wouldn't join unions.

Striking miners blocked a road in Harlan County. They wanted to stop people from getting to the mine.

John L. Lewis
1880-1969

John Lewis was born in Iowa. In the 7th grade, he left school to work in the coal mines. Years later, John worked for the UMWA. During that time, he pushed the coal companies until he won higher wages for miners.

When coal sales later dropped, the coal companies tried to cut miners' pay. But John would not let that happen. Under his direction, coal miners went on strike. After five months, the strike worked! Even though the companies were selling less coal, the miners got the same pay.

A few years later, workers began leaving the UMWA. John gave speeches, put up signs, and passed around flyers that said, "The President wants you to join the union!" Three months later, almost all of Kentucky's coal miners had joined unions.

John gave speeches and helped make important changes in the coal mining industry. Miners were so grateful for the things he did that he became a folk hero. Many coal mining families even hung his picture in their homes.

John continued to fight for the rights of mine workers until the day he died. During his last years, he won better medical care and yearly pay raises for coal miners. He helped make the coal mining industry what it is today.

John Lewis is on the right in this photograph. He is talking with a congressman at the U.S. capitol.

"Bloody Harlan"

Sometimes, when unions held strikes, the coal companies fought back. That is what happened in Harlan County. There were so many strikes and so much violence that the county became known as "Bloody Harlan."

In Harlan County, coal companies hired "gun thugs" to protect company officials and strikebreakers from angry miners. *Strikebreakers* are workers who refused to strike. They kept working so the mine didn't have to shut down. Mining companies loved strikebreakers because they kept mining coal and making money for the company. Striking coal miners hated strikebreakers because they helped the mine keep running. As long as people were working, company leaders didn't have to meet strikers' demands.

The violence in Harlan lasted about five years. During that time, six miners and five company men were killed. In addition, 13 miners and five company men were injured. People who lived through this time called it "Hell in Harlan."

This strikebreaker looks happy that soldiers are protecting him.

Coal mining continues to be a way of life for many Kentuckians.

A Way of Life That Continues

The coal industry was good for some people. Those who owned the rights to the coal fields and mines earned millions of dollars. During *boom* periods, companies built towns and paid workers fairly well. Even in the bad times, the coal mines gave families a way to survive. During the peak years, more than 60,000 workers earned their livings in the Kentucky coal mines.

The story of the early coal mines and the people who worked in them is one that Kentuckians hold dear. For over 100 years, the coal mines have left scars on the land and scars on people's lives. The *legacy* of the early mines will never be forgotten. It lives on in company towns, museums, and the memories of people whose lives have been forever changed by that rich, black mineral lying deep within the Kentucky hills.

Linking the Past to the Present

Today, people still argue about the best ways to mine and use coal. They also talk about the best ways to protect workers.

What Do You Think

Kentucky is a land of great mineral riches. Can you think of other areas around the world that have huge deposits of minerals? Are these places powerful? Are the people who live there rich or poor? Why?

③ MEMORY MASTER

1. How much of Kentucky's electricity comes from coal?
2. Name two ways to mine coal. How are they different?
3. Why did coal mining companies build company towns? Who lived in them?
4. What is a labor union?

Taking a Break

Life in our state was often hard, but Kentuckians took time to play whenever they could. What do you like to do for fun? You might be surprised to learn that nearly 100 years ago, people had fun doing many of the same things you do today.

Sports

In the late 1800s, there was no television or even radio. People enjoyed going to sporting events, such as baseball or football games. In 1921, Kentuckians celebrated a great football victory. Centre

Keeneland

During this period, horse racing was still a favorite pastime. Churchill Downs was not the only horse track in Kentucky. Lexington's Keeneland Race Course opened, too. The big race held every spring at Keeneland is called the Blue Grass Stakes.

Keeneland was special in many ways. There were hundreds of beautiful trees, and there was no **loudspeaker.** The people who managed the track did not get any money from it. All the money was paid out in winnings, donated to charities, or used to maintain the track. Today, none of these things has changed—except there is a loudspeaker now.

Keeneland is still important to horse buyers, too. Every July, buyers from all over the world travel to Lexington to purchase winning thoroughbreds at the Keeneland yearling sales. The world-record price for a horse was set at Keeneland. It was $13.1 million!

This photo of a race at Keeneland was taken during the track's first year.

The Kentucky Adventure

College beat mighty Harvard, which was one of the best teams in the nation! No one expected a small state college to win. When it did, there were parties and celebrations all over the state.

Around this same time, girls' basketball was popular. Few teams were as well-known as the Ashland girls' basketball team, which won five state tournaments.

Radio

After radios were invented, families gathered around to listen to radio programs. The radio brought stories, music, and news from across the world. In Kentucky, people listened to country or bluegrass music shows, like "The Grand Ole Opry." They also listened to comedies, like "Amos 'n' Andy." Families tuned into the Renfro Valley Barn Dance on the radio to hear "Red" Foley and "Slim Miller."

In the past, radio was as popular as television is today.

Trapped!

Touring caves was another thing people liked to do. On a cold January day in 1925, Floyd Collins crawled into a narrow passage in Sand Cave. He had explored hundreds of miles in other caves. He was considered the greatest caver of his time.

Floyd was only 120 feet from the cave entrance when a 27-pound rock shifted and trapped his foot. Floyd tried to push it off, but the more he tried, the more rocks fell on him. He was stuck tight. He had only one light and hadn't told anyone where he was going. Floyd wondered how long he would be stuck in the cave.

A night and day passed before Floyd's family noticed he was missing. Once they found him, they tried to get him out, but they couldn't. Rescuers worked for days, but they couldn't free Floyd's foot from the rock that pinned it.

Floyd's story was covered on the radio news and splashed on the front page of newspapers. Crowds of people came to watch the rescue effort. For two weeks, the entire nation worried as Floyd Collins suffered in the cold, wet, underground passage.

The rescuers talked to Floyd and sent food down to him. At first, he was cheerful and certain he would be rescued. But then part of the narrow passage above him collapsed. There was no way to get more food down to him. Floyd died a few days later. Three months after he died, workers brought Floyd's lifeless body to the surface and gave it a proper burial.

Floyd Collins

The Great Depression

A *depression* is a time when many people can't make enough money to take care of their families. They want to work, but they can't find jobs. A terrible depression took place in the 1930s. It was the worst one the United States has ever known. It is called the Great Depression.

The Great Depression dealt a hard blow to Kentuckians. The prices farmers could get for their goods were nearly the lowest in the nation. The price for tobacco dropped so low that it set a record. Prohibition had destroyed many companies that made whiskey. Worst of all, people across the nation were buying much less coal.

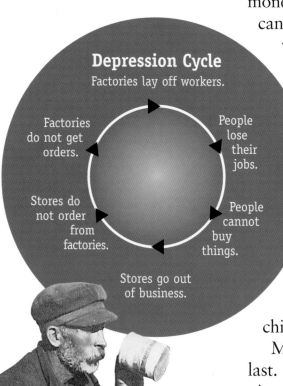

Depression Cycle
Factories lay off workers.

People lose their jobs.

People cannot buy things.

Stores go out of business.

Stores do not order from factories.

Factories do not get orders.

People who lived in the streets were grateful for even bread and water.

Working to Survive

Families had to work together to survive such hard times. Some families lost their homes. When that happened, several families often lived together in one house. Then several children slept together in one bed.

Mothers mended old clothes again and again to try to make them last. Families grew gardens in their backyards. Fathers placed pieces of cardboard in their shoes because the soles were worn through.

Poor people stood in long lines to get free soup and bread. Local police and firemen collected food and gave it to families who had no money. People tried to help each other as much as they could.

The New Deal

Americans began to wonder if the depression would ever end. They worried that life would just keep getting worse. Then they elected a new president, Franklin D. Roosevelt. He had a plan for ending the depression.

Roosevelt called his plan the *New Deal.* In it, the government hired people to fill all kinds of jobs. Thousands of people finally went to work. Here are a few of the New Deal programs in Kentucky:

- **WPA (Works Progress Administration)**—This was a program that hired workers to build schools, roads, and bridges. It also gave jobs to artists who painted murals or writers who wrote books and plays.

- **TVA (Tennessee Valley Authority)**—This was a huge system of dams built throughout the South. The dams controlled flooding, produced electricity, and provided thousands of jobs. In western Kentucky, the TVA created the Land Between the Lakes.
- **CCC (Civilian Conservation Corps)**—This program gave jobs to nearly 80,000 young Kentuckians. They helped clean up forests and streams and plant trees.

A Lasting Image

The New Deal did not end the Great Depression, but it gave people jobs and hope for a better future. Many New Deal programs are still with us today.

Sadly, the image of Kentucky as a "backward" state is still with us, too. The newspapers and radios in every state carried stories about the feuds, tobacco wars, and bloody coal strikes. Americans heard about the thousands of poor people who lived here. People began to think all Kentuckians were poor and violent. That wasn't true, but it was all people heard. Would our state ever be able to change its poor image? The next years would answer that question.

This picture, taken shortly before the Kentucky Dam was completed, shows the lock operator's office. Would you like to be a lock operator?

Activity

The Tennessee Valley Authority

Did you know workers began building the Kentucky Reservoir in 1938? They did not finish until 1944. The dam was built by the TVA as a New Deal project. Over 5,000 men worked on it. The finished dam formed the Kentucky Reservoir and over 2,000 miles of shoreline!

To learn more about it, go to http://www.tva.gov/sites/kentucky.htm and kentuckylake.com. Then answer the following questions:

- How is the Kentucky Reservoir used today?
- Do you think it was helpful to Kentucky's economy? How?

Now, write a paragraph about another TVA project. You can learn more about TVA projects by searching online or going to the library.

This is Louisville during the Flood of 1937.

The Flood of 1937

Kentucky is sometimes flooded by pouring rains. Yet few storms caused as much misery as the Flood of 1937. In the midst of the Great Depression, the January rains began to fall. They fell, and they fell, and they fell. In fact, the amount of rain that fell that month set a record that still stands today. The Ohio and Kentucky Rivers swelled and flooded towns all along their shores.

Half of Frankfort and almost all of Paducah were under water. The problems in Louisville were even worse. When the river spilled over its banks in Louisville, the water destroyed several electrical power plants. There was no electricity for more than two weeks. More than 230,000 people were homeless. Soldiers had to come in to keep the peace.

People in Maysville and other flooded cities started getting sick from germs in the water. They took medicine and hoped the water would quickly dry up. But it didn't. The flood waters stayed for more than a month. Once clean-up finally began, leaders began thinking of ways to protect their cities from future floods. Now, many cities along the Ohio River have floodwalls that keep water out. They also have pumps that move flood water to areas where people don't live.

4 MEMORY MASTER

1. What were some things people did for fun during this time?
2. Who was Floyd Collins?
3. What was life like during the Great Depression?
4. What caused the Flood of 1937?

Chapter 10 Review

What's the Point?

This period in history is very hard. Kentuckians deal with poverty, poor education, feuds, and corruption in government. Tobacco remains an important crop to the economy. Changes in the 20th century include World War I and new amendments to the U.S. Constitution. Kentucky's large deposits of coal bring wealth to a few while coal miners struggle with poverty and danger. The Great Depression affects the whole nation. Some people get jobs in President Roosevelt's New Deal programs. The Flood of 1937 causes great hardship. Kentuckians have to deal with a poor image.

Becoming Better Readers: A Summary

This chapter is full of stories about interesting people and events. Pick one section to re-read. As you re-read it, take notes. Now, use your notes to rewrite the story in your own words. This is called a summary. A summary is shorter than an original. After you have written your summary, trade it with a partner. Decide if your partner's summary is too long, too short, or just right.

Our Amazing Geography: World War I (WWI)

During World War I, two groups of countries fought. The United States formed a group with Great Britain, France, and Russia. Can you find these countries on a map? Can you find Kentucky on a world map? Most of the fighting in WWI took place in Europe. Which ocean did U.S. soldiers have to cross to get there? Which hemisphere was the fighting in?

Activity

Coal Debate

There are many ways to think about coal mining in Kentucky. Cut a piece of paper into ten strips. On five of the strips, write good things about coal mining. Use this chapter to help you. On the other five strips, write bad things about coal mining. In groups, put all your strips into two separate piles. Then read them all. Does coal mining seem more good or more bad?

"Let us learn from history but not dwell on the past . . . we can have a good future if only we [make the most] of the [chances] that are before us."

—Kentucky Governor
Paul Patton

Modern Kentucky

It took workers years to complete the Pikeville Cut-Through project. The project cut right through a mountain and changed the course of a river.

Timeline of Events

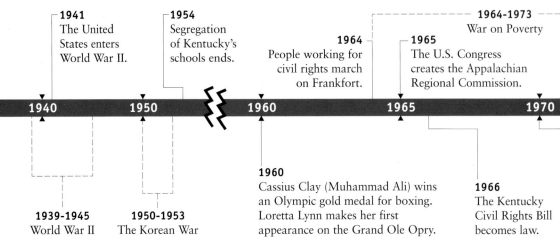

1941
The United States enters World War II.

1954
Segregation of Kentucky's schools ends.

1964
People working for civil rights march on Frankfort.

1964-1973
War on Poverty

1965
The U.S. Congress creates the Appalachian Regional Commission.

1940 1950 1960 1965 1970

1939-1945
World War II

1950-1953
The Korean War

1960
Cassius Clay (Muhammad Ali) wins an Olympic gold medal for boxing. Loretta Lynn makes her first appearance on the Grand Ole Opry.

1966
The Kentucky Civil Rights Bill becomes law.

Chapter 11

The second half of the 20th century brought both good times and hard times to Kentucky. The United States fought in more wars. African Americans struggled to gain equal rights and fair treatment. In Kentucky, people celebrated the things that had changed for the better—and grew concerned about the things that hadn't.

1975
Race riots break out in Louisville. The Vietnam War ends.

1977
U.S. President Jimmy Carter signs a national strip mining bill.

1990
The Gulf War
The Kentucky State Legislature passes the Kentucky Education Reform Act.

2003
War in Iraq begins.

1975   **1980**   **1985**   **1990**   **2000**   **2005**

April, 3, 1974
Kentucky suffers 26 tornadoes in 39 counties.

1983
Martha Layne Collins is elected Kentucky's first female governor.

1988
Broad form deeds are outlawed in Kentucky.

September 11, 2001
Terrorists attack the United States.

1970
People protesting the Vietnam War burn a building on the University of Kentucky campus.

The Japanese attack at Pearl Harbor took our country by surprise.

A Second World War

In the second half of the 20th century, another world war took place. It is called World War II. The United States was not involved in the war for the first two years. Then the Japanese bombed the U.S. naval base at Pearl Harbor, Hawaii. After that, the United States joined France, England, and the Soviet Union as part of the **Allied Powers.** Allied soldiers fought the **Axis Powers** of Germany, Italy, and Japan.

Helping the War Effort

About 300,000 men and women from Kentucky served in World War II. But the war required help from everyone at home, too. American families tried to use less food, electricity, and fuel—just as they had during World War I.

Thousands of Kentuckians also helped by making war goods. Some factories stopped making the products they usually made. They made supplies for the war instead. One such factory was the Louisville Slugger baseball bat factory in Louisville. Instead of making bats, workers began making parts for rifles.

Women Go to Work

World War II changed life for women, too. During the Great Depression, work was hard to find. Wives and mothers stayed home so men could have the few available jobs. When the war began, men left their jobs to go fight. Once again, women had to work outside their homes. In the factories, women pounded nails, drilled holes, and used heavy equipment.

America was proud of its hard-working women. The U.S. government gave them a nickname—"Rosie the Riveter." Rosie was a symbol of the hard work women did to make sure the Allied countries had enough war supplies. The efforts of these women helped win the war.

A "Rosie" from Kentucky

"Rosie the Riveter" was not a real person, but a real woman from Pulaski County played "Rosie" in a movie. The Kentucky woman's name was Rose Will Monroe.

Rose lost her husband and then moved with her two daughters to Michigan. There, she worked as a riveter in a factory that built war planes. When an actor from Hollywood came to the factory to film a movie, Rose caught his eye. She was strong, attractive, and perfect for the role of Rosie the Riveter.

The movie did not make Rose a star, however. After the war, she returned to Kentucky and lived near Louisville for the rest of her life.

These women worked as welders to support the Allied troops during World War II.

"Rosie the Riveter"

The End of World War II

The Allied Powers won the war, but 8,000 Kentuckians died in Europe and Asia. One of those who died was Franklin R. Sousley of Fleming County. You may not have heard of him, but he appears in one of the most famous statues in America. The statue shows Sousley and three other soldiers. They are raising the American flag after a terrible battle on the Japanese island of Iwo Jima.

This is the Iwo Jima Memorial in Washington, D.C. One of the soldiers in the statue is Kentuckian Franklin Sousley.

Fort Knox

Did you know that the Declaration of Independence and the U.S. Constitution were kept in Kentucky during World War II? In the 1930s, workers at Fort Knox built a special building to store the nation's gold supply. It is one of the safest places in the world. Government leaders wanted to make sure the Declaration and Constitution were safe during the war, so they sent them to the special building at Fort Knox. Today, you can see both documents at the National Archives in Washington, D.C.

The Kentucky Adventure

Vietnam

A third war in Asia caused people in our country to argue and *protest*. During the 1960s and 1970s, the United States sent more than 500,000 soldiers to fight in South Vietnam. Many Americans supported the war while others did not think our troops should be there.

Crowds of people protested. Some of the protests were in Kentucky. At the University of Kentucky, angry students burned down a building. The governor had to call out the National Guard to gain control.

After many years, the Vietnam War finally ended. Around 125,000 Kentuckians served, and over 1,000 of them were killed.

In Frankfort, there is a **memorial** *to the Kentuckians who died in Vietnam. It is a giant sundial. Each day, the sundial casts a shadow over the names of Kentucky's war dead.*

War on Poverty

While soldiers fought in Vietnam, the U.S. government talked about how to end *poverty* in eastern Kentucky. Eastern Kentucky is part of a large region called Appalachia. After U.S. President Lyndon B. Johnson visited the home of an unemployed coal miner, the government began a "War on Poverty." During the next year, it spent $54 million to improve the lives of poor Kentuckians. The money paid for schools and created the *Appalachian Regional Commission (ARC)*. Among other things, the ARC built roads in places where there were none.

Five years later, the government's "War on Poverty" was mostly over. It did not help Kentucky very much. Ten of the 25 poorest counties in the nation were still located in our state. There were still many problems with unemployment, health care, and education.

What Do You Think ?

What are the causes of poverty? Does the government have a responsibility to help the poor? Why or why not?

Do you know the difference between a tornado watch and a tornado warning?
A *tornado watch* means a tornado might occur.
A *tornado warning* means a tornado has been spotted.

• Brandenburg

A War with Wind

Have you ever seen *The Wizard of Oz*? Do you remember the tornado that carried Dorothy to Oz? That was an imaginary tornado, but tornadoes are very real. They are also very dangerous. People in Kentucky often have to protect themselves from these violent storms.

Many people will never forget the tornadoes that hit Kentucky on April 3, 1974. During the night, 26 tornadoes struck in 39 counties. The biggest tornado hit Brandenburg. It was one of the largest tornadoes ever recorded. Winds blowing at 260 miles per hour peeled bark off trees and tossed cars, trucks, and trains into the air.

The Brandenburg tornado killed 31 people. Across the rest of the state, 40 more people were killed, and over 1,000 were injured. Thousands lost their homes or businesses.

Linking the Past to the Present

The 1974 tornadoes hit without warning. Today, we have equipment that helps us know when tornadoes are coming. If people know a tornado is coming, they can try to get to a safe place.

Twin beams of light shine in tribute to the people who died at the World Trade Center on September 11.

Other Wars

Our country fought in other wars during this period, too. One war was in 1990 in the Middle Eastern country of Kuwait. It was called the Gulf War. Over 1,400 National Guardsmen from Kentucky served.

Then, on September 11, 2001, two planes crashed into the World Trade Center in New York City. Another plane crashed into the Pentagon in Washington, D.C. A fourth plane crashed in Pennsylvania. Almost 3,000 people were killed that day.

Within a few hours, Americans learned the crashes were caused by terrorist attacks. **Terrorists** are people who try to scare people into doing what they want. In every state, Americans were saddened and angry about the attacks. President George W. Bush declared a "war on terror". He sent troops to fight terrorists who had taken control of Afghanistan. Soldiers from Fort Campbell in Kentucky were among the first to go.

In 2003, yet another war began. This one started because some Americans believed leaders in the country of Iraq wanted to harm our country. To prevent this harm, our country declared war on Iraq. Some Americans believed the United States should not have done that. Others thought our soldiers should be there. The war in Iraq reminded some people of the war in Vietnam.

1 MEMORY MASTER

1. Why did the United States enter World War II?
2. Name two ways Kentuckians helped the World War II effort.
3. What was the Appalachian Regional Commission set up to do?
4. Name two wars besides World War II that you learned about in this lesson.

PEOPLE TO KNOW

Muhammad Ali
Edward T. Breathitt
Albert B. "Happy" Chandler
Lyman T. Johnson
Dr. Martin Luther King Jr.
Jackie Robinson

PLACES TO LOCATE

Frankfort
Louisville
Sturgis

WORDS TO UNDERSTAND

Civil Rights Movement
desegregate
editor
Kentucky Education Reform Act
   (KERA)
racism
reform
segregation
sit-in

The Civil Rights Movement

African Americans were among the soldiers who fought in World War II. In other countries, they had tried to stop unfair treatment. When they returned home, however, they were treated unfairly by people in their own country.

The unjust laws that began after Reconstruction were still in effect. For example, whites and African Americans still did not go to school together. Even public universities did not allow blacks to attend. African Americans struggled to be treated fairly. Groups of people began to work for equality. Their work became known as the *Civil Rights Movement.* Civil rights are the basic rights every citizen should have.

During the Civil Rights Movement, African Americans worked together to end unfair treatment.

Thousands of people gathered in Washington, D.C., to hear Dr. Martin Luther King Jr. speak about equal rights.

The End of Segregated Schools

Ending *segregation* of schools was one of the most important efforts of the Civil Rights Movement. Until this time, only whites could attend the University of Kentucky (UK). Lyman T. Johnson, a black teacher in Louisville, wanted to take classes at UK. The school said he could not attend because he was black. Johnson felt that was unfair, so he took the case to court. A federal judge finally decided that UK had to admit Johnson. Because of the judge's decision, people of all races could attend the University of Kentucky.

Five years later, the U.S. Supreme Court ended segregation in all public schools. Many white Kentuckians refused to obey. In Sturgis, people tried to stop black students from attending school. The National Guard went to Sturgis and made sure African Americans were allowed into the school.

National Guard troops protect a black student in Sturgis. Some students had to secretly slip out the back doors of their classrooms.

Busing

After schools *desegregated,* there was a new problem. Neighborhoods were still segregated. Since most of the children in a neighborhood went to the same school, schools were mostly white or mostly black. School boards were not happy about this. They wanted schools to have a mixture of black students and white students.

After schools desegregated, black students and white students had more chances to become friends.

The Kentucky Adventu

A few school boards convinced judges to order students to ride buses to schools miles away from their homes. This made students and parents angry. One day, whites in southwestern Louisville began arguing and fighting with one another. They also destroyed school buses. Once again, soldiers had to restore the peace. Nearly 50 people were injured in the riot.

Sit-Ins

Even though blacks went to school with whites, they were treated unfairly in other places. Hotels, restaurants, and even water fountains were separate for whites and blacks. Protesters in large cities fought this unfair treatment by holding sit-ins. A *sit-in* was something protesters did to try to change things. They sat peacefully in a public place and refused to leave until they were treated fairly.

When state leaders refused to guarantee equal rights to blacks, Dr. Martin Luther King Jr. came to Kentucky. He led Protesters on a march to the capitol in Frankfort. Dr. King wanted laws that guaranteed fair and equal treatment of all citizens. A year after the protest, Governor Edward T. Breathitt signed a new law that guaranteed equal treatment of all people in Kentucky.

More than 10,000 people gathered to listen to Martin Luther King Jr. speak in Frankfort.

Linking the Past to the Present

The fight for civil rights went on all across the nation. The *editors* of two Lexington newspapers, the *Herald* and the *Leader*, decided not to print stories about it. The editors thought people in Kentucky would stop protesting if they didn't know what was going on in other places. The two newspapers joined into one several years later.

In 2004, the *Herald-Leader* apologized for not covering stories about the Civil Rights Movement. They also printed articles about events that happened 40 years earlier.

What Do You Think

Do you think newspapers have a responsibility to tell the truth? Do you think a newspaper should hide information? Why or why not?

Albert B. "Happy" Chandler
1898-1991

Albert B. Chandler was born in Corydon, Kentucky. As a young man, he played baseball and football. Albert was fun-loving and always smiling, so his teammates began calling him "Happy." He served in the army, became a lawyer, and was elected governor of Kentucky. He then became a senator.

Albert became the Commissioner of Baseball during the last year of World War II. His job was to make sure all the baseball teams, or clubs, followed the rules. At this time, only whites could play professional baseball, but that soon changed.

The Brooklyn Dodgers wanted to sign a talented black player named Jackie Robinson. Albert had the power to make rules—even if no one agreed. That is exactly what he did. He allowed the Dodgers to sign Jackie Robinson.

After serving as baseball commissioner, Albert became the governor of Kentucky for a second time. He helped establish the University of Kentucky Medical Center. He also sent troops into Sturgis during the race riots. Albert Chandler died in Versailles in 1991.

Muhammad Ali (Cassius Marcellus Clay)
1942-

One of the most famous modern Kentuckians is Muhammad Ali. He was born in Louisville. His parents named him after antislavery activist Cassius Marcellus Clay. As a young man, Cassius was interested in boxing. He worked hard and finally won a gold medal at the 1960 Olympics. When he returned to Louisville, Cassius thought he would be treated fairly, but he wasn't. He was disappointed to learn that nothing—not even a gold medal—changed some people's unfair attitudes.

Young Cassius was very bright, and the *racism* in Louisville upset him. He began studying the teachings of a religious leader named Elijah Muhammad. After becoming the world boxing champion, Cassius announced his new name—Muhammad Ali. He said he would not join the army or fight in the Vietnam War. This made people angry, and they took away his championship title. He later won the right to fight again. He earned the title two more times.

Ali's struggle to fight racism made him a hero to millions of people all around the world. Today, Louisville honors Ali as one of its greatest citizens. There is even a museum in Louisville dedicated to Muhammad Ali, his struggles, and his many successes.

KERA built many new school buildings. Old buildings were worn and overcrowded.

Education Reform

Civil rights was not the only struggle during the last half of the 20th century. A movement to provide better education for every student in Kentucky was taking place, too. By the end of the century, our state led the nation in education reform. To *reform* something means to change it for the better.

The Kentucky Education Reform Act

Kentuckians who wanted better public education organized into groups. They studied the problems and then acted. People from more than 60 school districts filed lawsuits against the state of Kentucky. They claimed the public education system in Kentucky was unfair. The state constitution said that education for every child was supposed to be equal. But schools in areas with more money had higher-paid teachers and better books, buildings, and equipment. The state supreme court agreed with the lawsuits. Education in Kentucky had to become fairer. State leaders passed a law called the ***Kentucky Education Reform Act (KERA).***

KERA made schools more responsible. Since KERA, Kentucky's schools have improved, but much more needs to be done. Educational leaders in other states have copied KERA to improve their schools.

What Do You Think ?

Do you think Kentucky's schools need more improvements? Talk with your parents to see what they think should be done to improve education in our state.

2 MEMORY MASTER

1. What was the Civil Rights Movement?
2. What did Lyman T. Johnson do?
3. What is a sit-in, and what is it for?
4. What is education reform?

WORDS TO UNDERSTAND

Academy Award
aircraft
astronaut
diversity
etching
genetics
literary critic
mandolin
Nobel Prize
poet laureate
press aid
stroke

A Wealth of Peoples and Cultures

Do you remember what culture is? You first read about it in Chapter 1. Culture is the ways of life shared by a group of people. It includes the foods people eat, the clothes they wear, and the homes they live in. The music people make and the languages they speak are also part of their culture. People in different places develop different cultures, traditions, and ways of living. Parents teach these things to their children. This is how culture survives through the years.

One of the things that makes Kentucky strong is its mix of cultures. Many Kentuckians have shared their culture and talent with the world. They have written stories, made music, acted in movies and plays, painted pictures, played sports, and worked for better government, education, and science. Let's meet a few of them.

KENTUCKY PORTRAIT

Linking the Past to the Present

Several years after the new laws were passed, the state of Kentucky outlawed broad form deeds. Today, mining companies cannot take coal from people's land without their permission.

Ollie "Widow" Combs
(1905-1993)

One of Kentucky's heroes is a woman named Ollie Combs. Ollie lived near Clear Creek in Knott County. One Thanksgiving Day, she saw large bulldozers on her land. The bulldozers were ready to strip mine the coal under her property. Ollie did not want that to happen, so she did the only thing she could think of. She lay down in front of the bulldozer and refused to move. After a while, the police came and took her away.

When people learned what had happened, they grew angry at the coal company. They were glad Ollie had stopped the bulldozers. They began calling her "Widow" Combs. Kentucky Governor Edward T. Breathitt said he understood why Ollie did what she did. He knew hundreds of Kentuckians had seen their land ruined by coal companies. Soon, the Kentucky state government passed a new law that helped protect people's land.

President Jimmy Carter invited Ollie to join him at the White House. He was grateful to her for calling attention to a big problem. When President Carter signed a new strip mining law, the "Widow" Combs stood at his side.

HARRY CAUDILL
(1922–1990)

Harry Caudill was born in Long Branch. He went to the University of Kentucky and became a lawyer. Harry wrote an important book called *Night Comes to the Cumberlands*. In his book, Harry talked about the problems of poor people in Appalachia. Millions of Americans read the book. Government leaders read it, too. Soon, the government began helping people in Appalachia.

JESSE STUART
(1906–1984)

Jesse Stuart was born in W-Hollow and lived in Greenup most of his life. His family was very poor, and his father could not read. Unlike his father, Jesse went to school. His teachers found that he was a good writer. Jesse grew up and wrote many stories, poems, and books. In 1954, he became the *poet laureate* of Kentucky. Jesse knew education had changed his life.

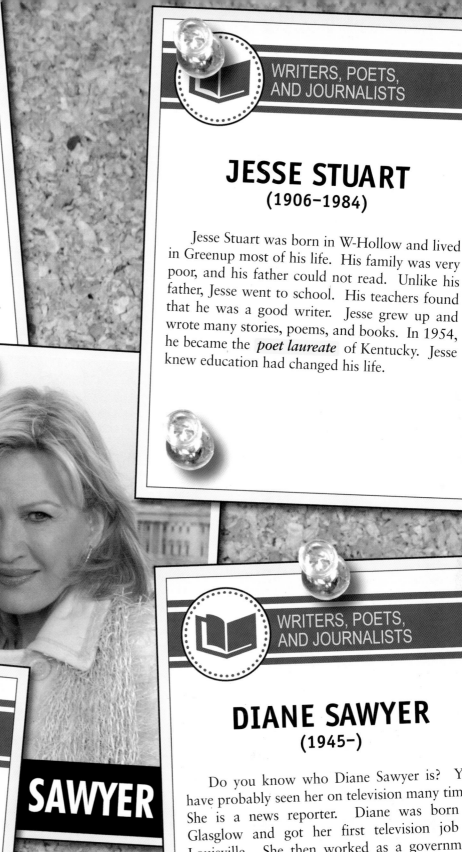

SAWYER

WENDELL BERRY
(1934–)

Wendell Berry was born in Henry County. He graduated from the University of Kentucky and then went to Stanford. He has written 25 books of poetry, 16 volumes of essays, and 11 novels.

DIANE SAWYER
(1945–)

Do you know who Diane Sawyer is? You have probably seen her on television many times. She is a news reporter. Diane was born in Glasglow and got her first television job in Louisville. She then worked as a government *press aid* and a television news reporter. Now, you can watch Diane every weekday morning on *Good Morning America*. She is one of America's most successful television news reporters.

WRITERS, POETS, AND JOURNALISTS

ROBERT PENN WARREN
(1905–1989)

Robert Penn Warren was born in Guthrie. He became a writer and a literary critic. A *literary critic* is a person who studies the way things are written. Robert wrote a book called *All the King's Men*. The book was about dishonesty in politics. It received the Pulitzer Prize, which is the highest award a book can receive. Robert taught English at Yale University and became our country's first poet laureate. He once said, "The urge to write poetry is like having an itch. When the itch becomes annoying enough, you scratch it."

MUSICIANS

LORETTA LYNN
(1935–)

Loretta Lynn was born in Butcher Hollow in Johnson County. Her father was a coal miner. Loretta got married when she was 13. She loved to sing and began writing songs. When Loretta hit it big in the 1960s, she sang about her Kentucky roots. Her most famous song, "Coal Miner's Daughter", was made into a movie. Loretta is a member of the Country Music Hall of Fame and was named Country Music's Entertainer of the Decade in 1980. She is often called the "First Lady of Country Music".

MUSICIANS

BILL MONROE
(1911–1996)

Music is one way people express their feelings. Some Kentucky musicians wrote the stories of their lives in songs. One such musician was Bill Monroe, who was born in Rosine. Bill sang in a high voice while he played a *mandolin*. He called his new style Bluegrass. Today, Bill is known as the "Father of Bluegrass Music". His most famous song is "Blue Moon of Kentucky". Bill is now honored in the Country Music Hall of Fame. He also received a Lifetime Achievement Award.

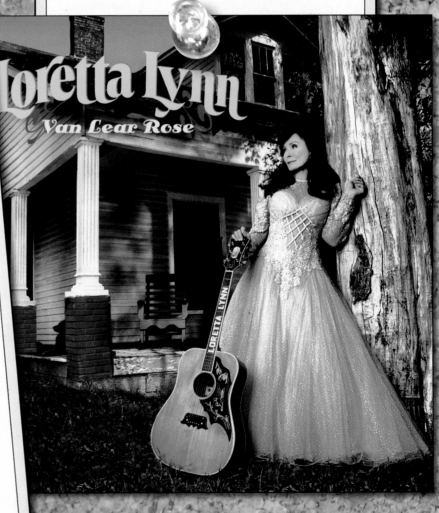

 ACTORS

JOHNNY DEPP
(1963–)

Have you seen the *Pirates of the Caribbean* movies? The actor who plays Jack Sparrow is Johnny Depp, from Owensboro. Johnny has starred in many other movies, too. He played Willy Wonka in the 2005 version of *Charlie and the Chocolate Factory*. Johnny starred in his first movie at the age of 19.

 MUSICIANS

THE JUDDS
(Naomi 1946–) (Wynnona 1964–)
(Ashley 1968–)

Naomi Judd was born in Ashland. Her first daughter's name was Christina, but the world knows her today as Wynnona. Naomi's second daughter, Ashley, is a famous movie actress. Wynnona wanted to be a singer. Naomi supported her daughter's dream by moving the family to Nashville. Soon, mother and daughter were singing together. They called themselves The Judds. Fourteen songs performed by The Judds have made it to number one on the country music charts. Naomi retired from singing, so Wynnona now sings by herself. The Judds remain one of the most successful musical groups in history.

 ACTORS

PATRICIA NEAL
(1926–)

Patricia Neal was born in Packard. She became a talented actress and even won an *Academy Award*. That is the highest award for an actor. One of her most famous movies is *Breakfast at Tiffany's*. Patricia was pregnant with her fifth child when she suffered several *strokes*. Recovering from the strokes was long, hard work, but she did not give up. Patricia began acting again and earned more awards. She has also worked to develop medical recovery centers throughout the southern Appalachian region.

ATHLETES

DARRELL GRIFFITH
(1958–)

Darrell Griffith was an All-American basketball player who led the University of Louisville to an NCAA championship. He was also named College Player of the Year. Darrell was picked by the Utah Jazz in the first round of the 1980 NBA Draft. He averaged 20 points per game in his first year in the NBA and was named Rookie of the Year.

ATHLETES

TAMARA McKINNEY
(1962–)

Tamara McKinney was born in Kentucky. Her mother was a ski instructor, so Tamara learned to ski when she was very young. She began racing in competitions and winning many of them. She became the first American to win the women's overall World Cup title. For eight years, she was the most successful skier on the women's World Cup tour.

DARRELL GRIFFITH

ATHLETES

ISAAC BURNS MURPHY
(1861–1896)

Isaac Burns Murphy was born in Fayette County to a former slave. As a young man, he was hired to exercise horses at Lexington Stables. Isaac got his first chance to ride in a race when he was 14. His horse won! Isaac won three Kentucky Derbies and 625 other races. In fact, he won almost half of the races he entered. Isaac Murphy was the first jockey voted into the Jockey Hall of Fame.

VALERIE STILL
(1961-)

Do you know who holds the record as the greatest scorer in the history of Kentucky Wildcat basketball? It is Valerie Still, who played four years and scored 2,763 points. Valerie is a member of the Kentucky Athletic Hall of Fame. She also began the Valerie Still Foundation. This organization helps young girls become successful by making the most of their talents.

Man O' War (1917-1947)

One of Kentucky's most beloved athletes did not have two legs; he had four. This athlete's name was Man O' War. He was one of the greatest racehorses ever. In fact, Man O' War won one race by 100 lengths! He lost only once. Man O' War was also known as "Big Red" because he was reddish in color. A life-sized statue of Man O' War now stands at Kentucky Horse Park.

ATHLETES

MICHAEL WALTRIP
(1963-)

Michael Waltrip was born in Owensboro. He and his brother Darrell began their stock car racing careers by racing go-karts. Michael won his first stock car race at the Kentucky Motor Speedway. After winning a race several years later, he drove his car backwards around the entire track. This was to pay respect to a driver who had died in an airplane crash a few days before the race. Michael won the Daytona 500 two times. In 2001, he joined the Dale Earnhardt Jr. racing team.

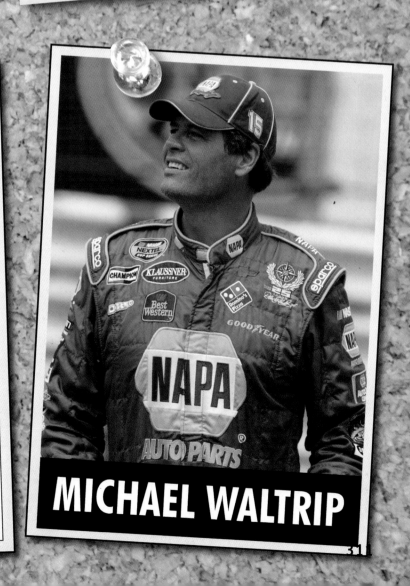

MICHAEL WALTRIP

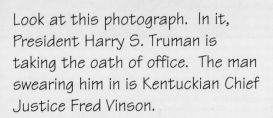

POLITICIANS

MARTHA LAYNE COLLINS
(1936–)

In 1983, Kentuckians elected their first female governor. Her name was Martha Layne Collins. She was once a schoolteacher. Martha worked hard to make Kentucky a better place to live. She convinced the Toyota Company to build a plant in Georgetown. Today, that plant provides jobs to thousands of Kentuckians.

Look at this photograph. In it, President Harry S. Truman is taking the oath of office. The man swearing him in is Kentuckian Chief Justice Fred Vinson.

What Do You Think?

Kentucky is one of the few states that has had a female governor. Do you think more states should? Why or why not? Do you think the United States will ever elect a female president?

Fancy Farm

Fancy Farm is in Graves County in western Kentucky. Every year, politicians meet there and give speeches. Kentuckians can listen, eat great food, and talk about politics. This yearly event reminds people in Kentucky of how politics used to be—friendly and personal. Meetings at Fancy Farm have been taking place for more than 125 years!

ARTISTS

JOHN JAMES AUDUBON
(1785–1851)

John James Audubon lived in Henderson and Louisville. He was a talented artist. John painted and drew pictures of hundreds of birds. He set a goal to draw every kind of bird in America. John studied for many years. Then he drew pictures for a set of four books called *Birds of America*. Over the next years, John wrote many more books filled with pictures of birds and other animals.

SCIENTISTS

THOMAS HUNT MORGAN
(1866–1945)

Thomas Hunt Morgan went to the State College, which is now the University of Kentucky. After graduating, he became important in the field of genetics. *Genetics* is the study of the development of human beings—especially how things pass from parents to children. Thomas even won a Nobel Prize. The *Nobel Prize* is given every year to a person who has made a great discovery.

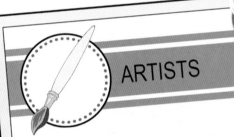

ARTISTS

PAUL SAWYIER
(1865–1917)

Paul Sawyier's family moved to Frankfort when he was five years old. Paul went to an art school and began drawing portraits of people. He then made *etchings* of a covered bridge. People loved the etchings, especially after the bridge closed. Paul bought a houseboat and lived on the Kentucky River for several years. He painted and etched many images of our state.

SCIENTISTS

FRANKLIN STORY MUSGRAVE
(1935–)

Story Musgrave was another graduate of the University of Kentucky. He learned to fly while he lived in Kentucky. In fact, Story flew more than 120 different kinds of *aircraft*. Then he went to work for NASA as a scientist and an *astronaut*. Story became one of the most successful astronauts in history. He helped develop the space shuttle program and flew on several shuttle missions.

Kentucky is home to people from countries and cultures all over the world. This Chinese New Year celebration is taking place at the First Presbyterian Church in Owensboro.

Diversity

Now you've met some of the talented people who have lived in Kentucky. They come from every region and every kind of background. Our state's *diversity* makes our lives rich and our state strong.

Some cultural groups hold festivals to share their traditions. Have you ever been to one? You can taste new foods, listen to new kinds of music, and sometimes even see special dances. Learning about people who have come from other places reminds us of the things that are good in our country. Our freedom and ways of life are treasures that people are willing to leave their homelands to find.

Do you know people in your school or community who are different from you? Do they speak different languages? Do they go to different churches? Do they wear clothes that are different from yours? Even though someone may look different, you probably have many things in common. Most people want a safe place to live, food and water, clothes to wear, good health, and an education.

What Do You Think ?

What challenges do people learning a new language face? What do you think it would be like to live in a place where no one speaks your language? Have you had to learn a new language?

③ MEMORY MASTER

1. What is culture?
2. Name two famous musicians, artists, or actors from Kentucky.
3. Name a famous athlete or politician from Kentucky. What did this person do?
4. What is diversity?

Chapter 11 Review

What's the Point?

The last half of the 20th century in Kentucky is marked by many kinds of wars: wars with other countries, war with weather, and the war on poverty. The Civil Rights Movement is successful in giving equal rights to African Americans. The government tries to improve education. The federal government creates the Appalachian Regional Commission, signs the Kentucky Civil Rights bill into law, and outlaws broad form deeds. The Kentucky Education Reform Act works to improve schools. Many cultures and talented people have made Kentucky what it is today.

Becoming Better Readers: Paraphrase

In Chapter 10, the reading activity was on writing a summary. For Chapter 11, you will write a paraphrase. A paraphrase is when you write a quote in your own words. A paraphrase is almost the same length as the original quote. Look through this chapter and choose one sentence that tells about something important in Kentucky history. Then copy it onto your own paper. Write the sentence in your own words. Go word by word so your paraphrase is almost the same length as the original sentence. How is a paraphrase different from a summary? When would you need to use a paraphrase?

Our Amazing Geography: Why Is It Important?

Look carefully at a map of the world. Using Lesson 1 and Lesson 2, locate the countries and cities from the "Places to Know" list. Then, on a map of Kentucky, locate all the Kentucky cities listed. As you find each country and each city, quiz yourself to see if you remember why this place is important in history. Which countries and cities do you think are most important to modern-day Kentuckians?

Activity

Cultural Multimedia Show

You have read about many talented people from Kentucky. They bring diversity to our state and show how rich our culture is. What about you? What are your talents? You have much to offer, too. For this activity, your class will put on a show. In small groups, decide what you will do. It can be a song, a poem, a painting, a play, an invention, a sport, a new law, or a story. When your group decides what it wants to do to celebrate Kentucky, work on the project together. After all the projects are ready, present or perform them. Then discuss what you have learned.

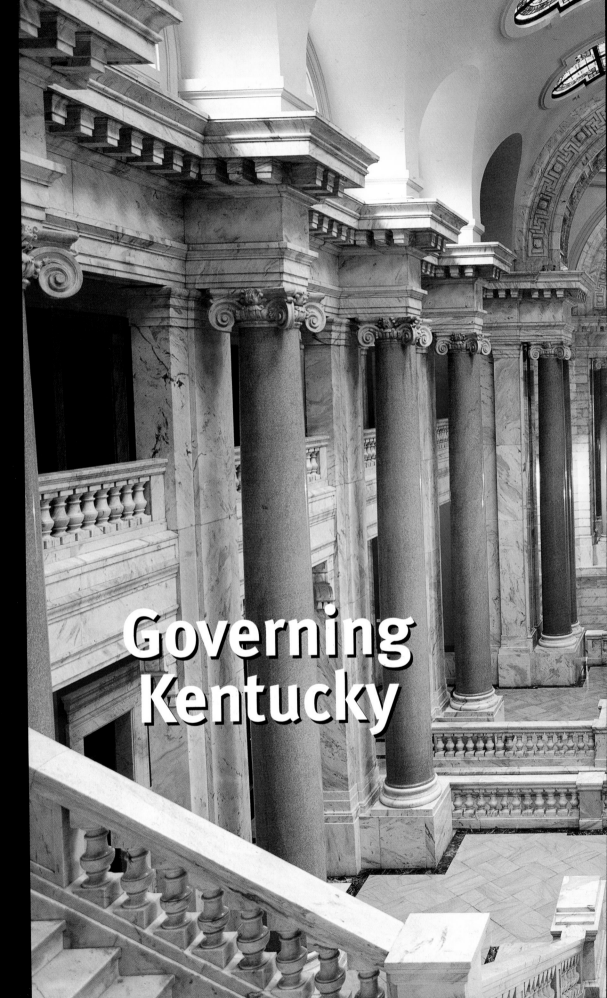

Governing Kentucky

Chapter 12

Our government began with the idea that people have rights and freedoms. The Constitution says the power comes from the people, not from a king or queen. Not only should government be "for the people", it should also be "by the people". That means every citizen—young or old—can make a difference in our government.

This is the inside of the state capitol building in Frankfort. How would you like to work here?

WORDS TO UNDERSTAND

amendment
graffiti
income
individual right
intersection
privacy
property right
responsibility
tariff

The government builds parks and then pays workers to keep them clean and nice.

The Purpose of Government

Did you know that government is part of your daily life? The last time you checked out a book at the library, went to a public school, or played in a city park, you were using a service provided by our government. Government is all around you.

Accomplish Common Goals

The state government is made up of people who live in Kentucky. Kentuckians share their goals and ideas with the people they have chosen to be their state leaders. Then the state leaders make- laws that support the goals of the people in the state.

For example, people in Kentucky want a safe society. Part of this goal is the need for safe roads. To keep the roads safe, the government uses our tax dollars to pay for road construction and repair. The government also pays for traffic signs to help people stay safe while driving. In this way, our government helps us achieve the goal of a safe society.

Establish and Maintain Order

What if there were no traffic lights or stop signs? What would happen if three cars came to an *intersection* at the same time? If no cars stopped, there would be an accident. How do we know whose turn it is to go through the intersection? We know because we have rules and laws. These rules and laws tell us who must stop and who can go.

Rules and laws make things run smoothly. They also make things safer. If we did not have laws, our communities might be unsafe. When someone breaks a law, he or she is punished. The lawbreaker might have to pay a fine or go to jail or both.

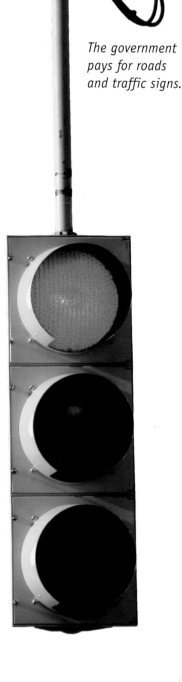

The government pays for roads and traffic signs.

What Do You Think?

Can you imagine a classroom without rules? Now imagine if your whole school had no rules. Do you think your school would be a safe place if there were no rules?

Protect Rights

One of the most important things our government does is protect our rights. Let's pretend that you leave your new bike outside. While you are inside playing, someone steals your bike. You are mad because you know this is not fair. That bike was your property! What can you do?

You can go to the police. They will try to find your bike. They will also try to find the person who stole it. Our country has laws against stealing. These laws protect your *property rights.*

You also have *individual rights.* These are things like your right to share your opinion or your right to belong to the religion of your choice. Our laws protect these important rights, too.

In some countries, people are not allowed to attend any church they want.

The Bill of Rights

Long before Kentucky became a state, our country's leaders wrote a Constitution for the whole nation. It is called the U.S. Constitution.

After it was written and approved, many people thought something needed to be added. They wanted a clear list of the rights belonging to every American. Ten changes, or **amendments**, were added to the Constitution. This list of amendments is called the Bill of Rights.

1st Amendment
Freedom of religion: You can worship as you wish, or not at all. The government cannot choose one religion for the whole country.

Freedom of speech: You can express your opinion about any subject without being arrested. You can even criticize the government. But what you say can't cause danger or harm to others.

Freedom of the press: The government cannot tell people what they can or cannot print in newspapers or books.

Freedom of assembly: You have the right to join and meet with any group. However, you cannot commit crimes with the group.

2nd Amendment:
Right to bear arms: You can own guns to protect yourself and to participate in other legal activities.

3rd Amendment:
Right to not have soldiers in your home during peacetime: In the past, kings had made people feed and house soldiers not only during wars but in times of peace.

4th Amendment:
Freedom from improper search and seizure: You have a right to **privacy.** But if the police have a reason to think you have something illegal in your home, they can get a search warrant and search your home.

5th, 6th, and 7th Amendments:
These have to do with rights people have if they commit crimes. They include the right to a speedy trial and a trial by a jury.

8th Amendment:
No cruel or unusual punishment is allowed.

9th Amendment:
People have other rights not named in the Bill of Rights.

10th Amendment:
A great deal of power will remain with the states. The people did not want the federal government to have all the power.

What Do You Think

Does freedom of speech mean you can write **graffiti** on public property? Can you tell lies that harm others? How can we use our freedoms so they don't hurt anyone else?

KEEP OUT!

With Rights Come Responsibilities

Having rights means we also have responsibilities. A *responsibility* is a duty, or something a person should do. Adults have a responsibility to take part in government. This is what "government by the people" means. Here are some ways we can take part in government:

Right	Responsibility
You can vote when you are 18 years old.	You should learn about the candidates and issues.
You get to help make the laws.	You must obey the laws.
You have the right to meet with any group you choose as long as the group doesn't hurt others.	You should respect those same rights in other people.

You Can Make a Difference

There are lots of things people can do to be good citizens. One of the first steps is to learn how government works. You are doing that right now!

Here are some other things you can do:

- Settle conflicts by using the laws and other peaceful means.
- Obey all of your family and school rules.
- Tell the truth.
- Be polite and helpful.
- Help keep your home and yard clean.
- Never litter or hurt someone else's property.
- Volunteer to help in your community.

Voting is one way to change things you do not like.

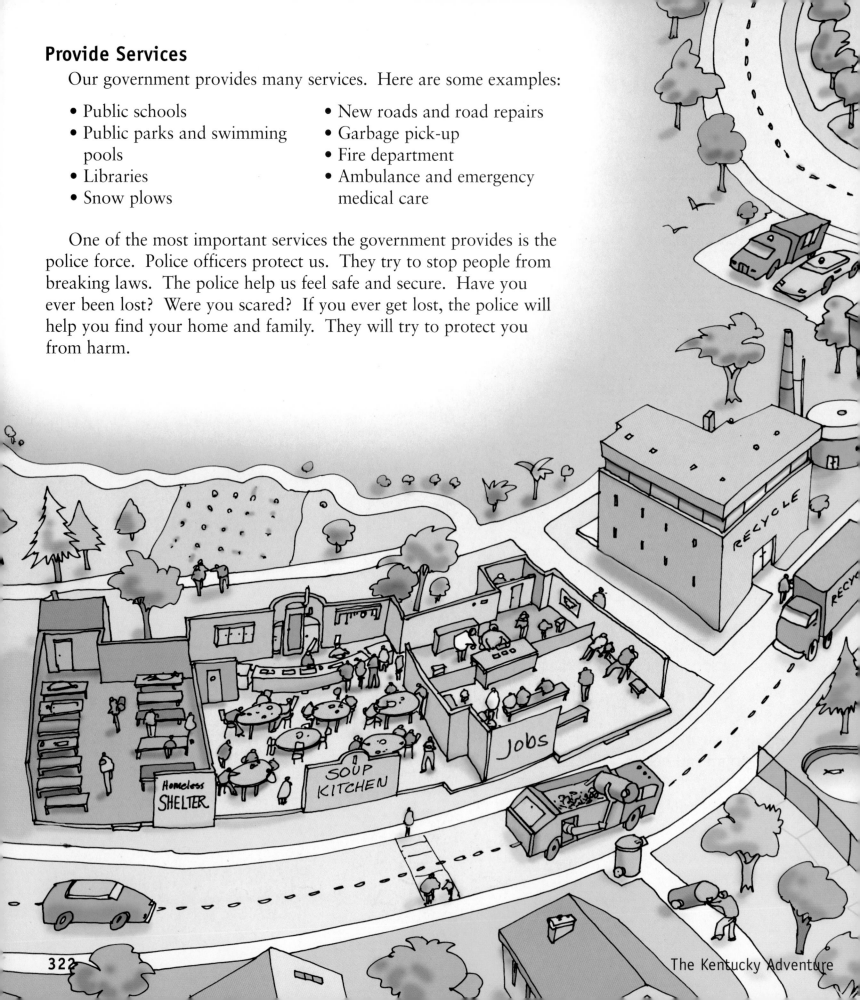

Provide Services

Our government provides many services. Here are some examples:

- Public schools
- Public parks and swimming pools
- Libraries
- Snow plows
- New roads and road repairs
- Garbage pick-up
- Fire department
- Ambulance and emergency medical care

One of the most important services the government provides is the police force. Police officers protect us. They try to stop people from breaking laws. The police help us feel safe and secure. Have you ever been lost? Were you scared? If you ever get lost, the police will help you find your home and family. They will try to protect you from harm.

POLICE

School

SCHOOL

LIBRARY

HEALTH CARE

WATER

Activity

Government Services in Our Town

How many public services can you find in this town? How does the government pay for these services? Cover up one service. What would happen to the town without it? Do you have any of these services near you?

Taxes Pay for Services

How do governments pay for the services they provide? They get money from taxes. A tax is money citizens pay to the government. Taxes are a way of sharing the cost of things we all want.

Taxes pay for fixing roads and for buying books for everyone to share at the public library. If you go to a public school, the buildings, teachers' salaries, and even the lights in your classroom are paid for by taxpayers.

There are many kinds of taxes, but here are the main ones:

Sales Tax

When you buy something at the store, you pay sales tax. The sales tax in Kentucky is 6 percent. That means for every dollar you spend, you must pay an extra six cents in tax. The money from the sales tax goes to the state government.

Property Tax

If you own land, a home, or a building, you pay property tax. If you rent your home, the landlord uses part of your rent to pay property tax.

Income Tax

People and businesses pay taxes on the money they earn. This is called *income* tax. Your parents pay income tax every year. They pay federal income tax to the U.S. government. They also pay state income tax to Kentucky.

Tariff

A *tariff* is a tax on goods coming from another country.

What Do You Think ?

Do you think taxes are fair? How should people be taxed? Should everyone pay the same amount? Should people who earn more pay more?

① MEMORY MASTER

1. What are property rights?
2. Name two services the government provides.
3. How much is the sales tax in Kentucky?
4. What is income tax? Who receives it?

Kentucky's State Government

The people of Kentucky have their own constitution and government. The government of Kentucky is organized a lot like the national government, but some things are very different.

Democracy and the Kentucky Constitution

Kentucky's current constitution is more than 100 years old. While the delegates were writing it, they thought about how to make the best government. They wanted a democracy that would protect life, liberty, and happiness. A ***democracy*** is a government in which power is in the hands of the people—not a king. In a democracy, people have ***liberty,*** or freedom.

Kentucky's constitution protects our lives, our liberty, and our happiness in many ways. For example, how would you feel if soldiers or the police could search your home any time they wanted to?

The Kentucky constitution states, "The people shall be secure in their persons, houses, papers and possessions, from unreasonable search and seizure . . ." That means the police cannot search your home without permission from you or a judge. In this way, the constitution protects our happiness.

WORDS TO UNDERSTAND

balance of power
bill
democracy
executive branch
General Assembly
judicial branch
jury
legislative branch
legislator
liberty
pardon
representative
supreme court
veto

The state constitution helps protect our happiness.

The Kentucky Constitution

Section 1

Rights of life, liberty, worship, pursuit of safety and happiness, free speech, acquiring and protecting property, peaceable assembly, redress of grievances, bearing arms.

All men are, by nature, free and equal, and have certain inherent and inalienable rights, among which may be reckoned:

First: The right of enjoying and defending their lives and liberties.

Second: The right of worshipping Almighty God according to the dictates of their consciences.

Third: The right of seeking and pursuing their safety and happiness.

Fourth: The right of freely communicating their thoughts and opinions.

Fifth: The right of acquiring and protecting property.

Sixth: The right of assembling together in a peaceable manner for their common good, and of applying to those invested with the power of government for redress of grievances or other proper purposes, by petition, address or remonstrance.

Seventh: The right to bear arms in defense of themselves and of the State, subject to the power of the General Assembly to enact laws to prevent persons from carrying concealed weapons.

What Do You Think

The state constitution states that all men have "The right of enjoying and defending their lives and liberties". What does it mean to enjoy life? What does it mean to defend your liberties, or freedom? Which amendments provide for life, liberty, and happiness? How?

Activity

Democracy

What is democracy? How does it work in everyday life? Write the letters of the word "democracy" down the left margin of a piece of paper. Next to each letter, write an idea that begins with that letter that shows what democracy means.

Here's an example: E—Elections give us a way to vote for new leaders. C—Certain rights can't be taken away by the government.

Levels of Government

Kentucky has three levels of government. Local government leaders make decisions that affect towns, cities, and counties. State government leaders make decisions that affect the state. The national government makes decisions for the entire country. Each level provides different services. Look at this chart to see what some of them are.

Level	Place	What It Provides
Local	cities and counties	police, firefighters, city parks, county roads and bridges, water, sewers, garbage pick-up
State	Kentucky	state land and resources, state roads, driver's licenses
National	United States	military, printing money, relations with other countries

Kentucky Representatives

In the United States, every person does not vote to make a law. Instead, voters elect people, called representatives, to serve in the government. These *representatives* make the laws.

In Kentucky, we elect representatives to serve in the U.S. Congress in Washington, D.C. Do you know who Kentucky's two U.S. senators are? Kentucky also has six members of the U.S. House of Representatives. Can you name the person who represents your district? If you can't, you can go to www.congress.org to find out.

Branches of Government

Both the federal government and the state government of Kentucky are divided into three branches. Each branch has the same amount of power the other two branches have. This keeps power equal. It is sometimes called *balance of power.* Balance of power prevents any branch from gaining too much control over our government. The three branches of government are:

- The *executive branch,* which carries out the laws.
- The *legislative branch,* which writes the laws.
- The *judicial branch,* which decides what laws mean.

State Executive Branch

The executive branch carries out the laws. The leader of the state executive branch is the governor. The governor is elected by the people of Kentucky and serves a term of four years.

The governor:

- Makes sure state laws are carried out.
- Suggests actions for the General Assembly to take.
- Signs *bills* into law. The governor can also *veto* a bill, but the General Assembly can veto the governor's veto.
- Calls special sessions of the General Assembly when needed.
- Commands the state National Guard.
- *Pardons,* or excuses, criminals from punishments.

State Legislative Branch

The people of Kentucky elect representatives to serve in the legislative branch of our state government. In Kentucky, it is called the *General Assembly.* It has two houses: the senate and the house of representatives. The 100 members of the house of representatives serve two-year terms. The 38 members of the senate serve four-year terms. These 138 members of the General Assembly are also called *legislators.*

The state legislature holds one regular session every year. When it meets, legislators vote on bills that can become laws. Our lawmakers also decide how much the state will spend on education and other state programs.

Working for the Executive Branch

Most people who work for the executive branch are not elected. State police and park rangers work for this branch. Other workers repair roads or bridges. Some collect taxes, and others work in health and education.

How a Bill Becomes a Law in Kentucky

The rules that govern Kentucky are called laws. This chart shows how laws are made in Kentucky.

1. **PRESENT A NEW IDEA.** Anyone can do this. Even a child can give a legislator an idea for a new law.

2. **RESEARCH THE IDEA.** Legislators and their staffs research the idea. Will it be fair to all? Who will it help? Will it hurt anyone? How much will it cost? Is it against the state constitution?

3. **WRITE THE IDEA INTO A BILL.** The legislator writes the idea down. Now it is called a bill. Other senators or representatives usually help the legislator write the bill.

4. **INTRODUCE THE BILL.** The legislator introduces the bill to the General Assembly at the next session.

5. **HOLD PUBLIC HEARINGS.** The legislator arranges for meetings across the state where citizens can say what they think about the bill.

6. **DEBATE THE BILL.** One house of the legislature discusses the bill in public and then votes on it. If it passes, it goes to the other house for the same process.

7. **GOVERNOR SIGNS THE BILL INTO LAW.** If the bill passes both houses of the legislature, it goes to the governor. If the governor likes the bill, he or she signs it, and the bill becomes law. If the governor does not like the bill, he or she can veto it. The legislature can override the veto with a majority vote. Then the bill becomes law even though the governor does not like it.

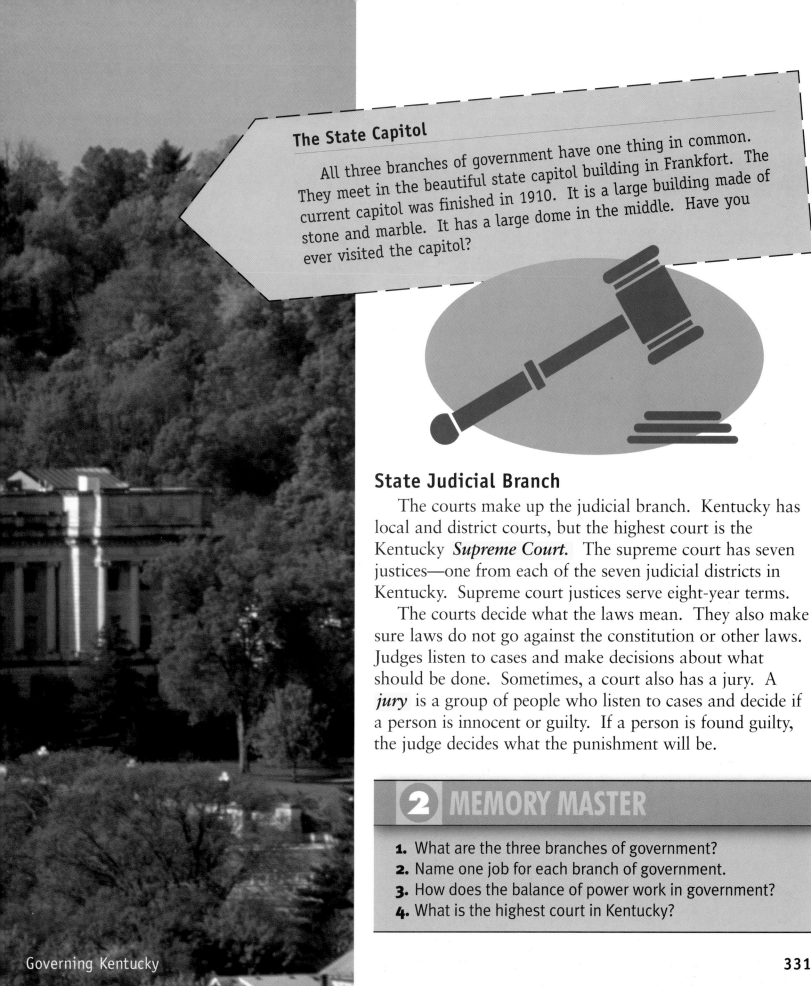

The State Capitol

All three branches of government have one thing in common. They meet in the beautiful state capitol building in Frankfort. The current capitol was finished in 1910. It is a large building made of stone and marble. It has a large dome in the middle. Have you ever visited the capitol?

State Judicial Branch

The courts make up the judicial branch. Kentucky has local and district courts, but the highest court is the Kentucky **Supreme Court.** The supreme court has seven justices—one from each of the seven judicial districts in Kentucky. Supreme court justices serve eight-year terms.

The courts decide what the laws mean. They also make sure laws do not go against the constitution or other laws. Judges listen to cases and make decisions about what should be done. Sometimes, a court also has a jury. A **jury** is a group of people who listen to cases and decide if a person is innocent or guilty. If a person is found guilty, the judge decides what the punishment will be.

2 MEMORY MASTER

1. What are the three branches of government?
2. Name one job for each branch of government.
3. How does the balance of power work in government?
4. What is the highest court in Kentucky?

WORDS TO UNDERSTAND

local
sewage

This is the old county courthouse in Lexington.

Local Government

Both our country and our state have governments. Did you know your county and city have governments, too? County and city government is called local government. *Local* means it is nearby.

Different places have different needs. In some parts of our state, there are very large cities. The streets are crowded and busy. In other parts of the state, farms spread over the land. There are fewer people living there. Local government leaders make rules and laws that fit the people in their community.

County Government

One type of local government is county government. Kentucky is divided into 120 counties. Citizens elect the people who run the county government.

Kentucky Counties and County Seats

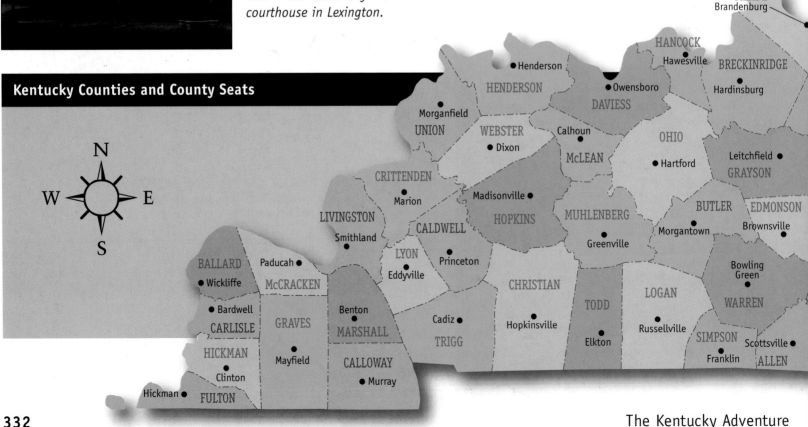

Each county has a county seat. That is the town or city where the county government has offices. In the county seat, there is a county courthouse. Judges and juries hear cases at the county courthouse. Birth, deaths, and marriages are recorded there. If your family owns property, a map of your property is stored in your courthouse or another county building. What is the county seat of your county?

Activity

Counties

The entire state of Kentucky used to be one county. Today, our state has 120 counties. If we had fewer counties, there would be fewer county governments. That would save Kentuckians a lot of money. Do you think Kentucky should combine counties so there are fewer? Why or why not? On an outline map of our state, draw lines to make new counties. Try to make only 60 counties. That would be half the number we have today.

Water treatment is a service provided by city or county government.

City or Town Government

Another kind of local government even closer to home is city or town government. A mayor or city manager is in charge of the departments that provide services for the people in each city. Do you know the name of the citizen who heads your local government?

Cities and towns have rules about what kinds of buildings can be built in different areas. Laws often keep houses separate from businesses. They make sure schools are in safe places. There are city laws about speed limits, too. When people break these laws, they have to go to city court.

Most local governments provide clean water, remove garbage, maintain *sewage* systems, and provide fire and police protection. If you play football, soccer, or softball in a city league, you are using a city service.

In some parts of Kentucky, both cities and counties provide local services. If you live in one of these places, you are served by both the county and the city governments.

③ MEMORY MASTER

1. Name two types of local government.
2. How many counties are in Kentucky?
3. What is a county seat?
4. Who is the head of the city or town government?

Chapter 12 Review

What's the Point?

The purpose of government is to accomplish common goals and establish and maintain order. Government also provides services and protects rights. The government is divided into three levels: local, state, and national. The state and national governments are divided again into three branches: legislative, executive, and judicial. Kentucky's state government has a General Assembly that makes laws. Local government takes care of cities or towns.

Becoming Better Readers: Levels of Government Bookmark

The three levels of government are local, state, and national. To organize the responsibilities of each level, make a bookmark. Cut a bookmark shape from a plain piece of paper. Draw lines to make three sections, and label them "Local", "State", and "National". Use the text from "Levels of Government" on page 327 to fill in the information. Add any designs you would like. Now you have a study aid and a new bookmark!

Activity

Comparing Rules and Laws

What is the difference between a rule and a law? Your school has rules to keep it safe and orderly. Like your school, the government has laws to keep our country safe and orderly. What would your school be like without rules? What would your town be like without laws? Look at the two lists below. Match each school rule with the law that is like it.

School Rules

1. ___ Students should not cheat or copy other students' work.
2. ___ Students should not hit or hurt other students.
3. ___ Students should not take things that belong to other students.
4. ___ Students should wait patiently for their turn.
5. ___ Students should not run in the halls.
6. ___ Students should be courteous and respectful to teachers.

Laws

A. Drivers must obey traffic signs and wait to go until it is their turn.
B. It is against the law for someone to say they wrote something if someone else wrote it.
C. People in courts must be courteous and respectful to judges.
D. Drivers must obey speed limits.
E. It is against the law to steal.
F. It is against the law to hit, abuse, or hurt another person.

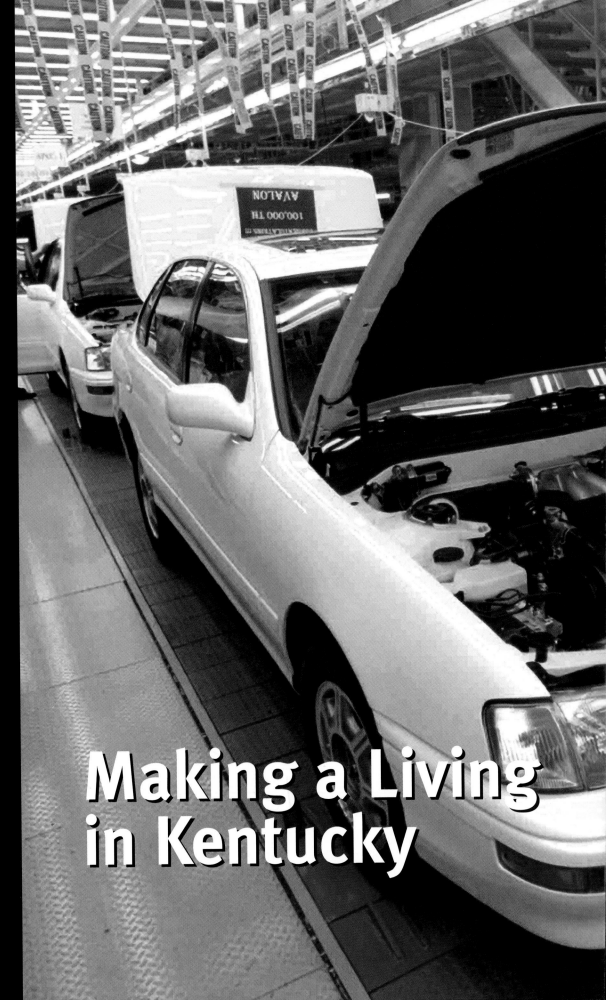

*"Man came around
Askin' for the rent
Man came around
Askin' for the rent
Well, I looked into the drawer
But the money's all been spent"*

—Bob Dylan *"Money Blues"*

Making a Living in Kentucky

Money is very important. People need it to pay for the things they need and want. Most of the money in Kentucky comes from selling goods that are made here. Selling Kentucky goods to people hundreds or thousands of miles away brings millions of dollars into our state. That money helps our businesses to grow. It also makes our state stronger.

A worker at the Toyota plant in Georgetown puts the final touches on a brand-new Avalon.

Goods and Services

People have needs. They also have wants. They need food, clothing, and shelter. They want things, like cars, books, toys, and bicycles. These things are called goods.

People also need help from other people. They need medical care from doctors and dentists. They need education from teachers. They may want help fixing their washing machines or broken windows. These are called *services*.

All products and services have something in common—they all cost money. *Economics* is the study of how people make, transport, buy, and sell goods and services. It is also the study of how people earn and use money.

Economic Systems

An economic system is a way of producing and selling the goods and services people need and want. Different countries use different systems, but all economic systems answer three basic questions:

- What goods and services should be produced?
- How will goods and services be produced?
- Who will buy goods and services?

Does a doctor provide a good or a service?

The Free Enterprise System

The United States has an economic system known as *free enterprise,* or a *market economy.* A market is any place where goods and services are bought and sold. In a market economy, people are free to make, sell, and buy goods and services. Economic choices are made by buyers and sellers, not by the government.

Buyers are also called *consumers.* Consumers buy goods made by *producers,* or sellers. Sellers are people who own the factories and companies that produce goods and services. Sellers decide how much to produce and what prices to charge. They decide where to do business. They decide who they want to help them.

Business owners hire people, called *employees,* to work for them. Employees earn a wage or a *salary.* Many adults in the United States are employees. They use their wages or salaries to buy goods and services.

How a Business Makes a Profit

How do business owners make money? Making money seems easy, but it isn't. When you go to a restaurant, you pay for your food. The restaurant has to pay its employees, buy the food it serves you, and pay for the building. After paying all of those expenses, the amount left over is called a *profit.* A business cannot survive if it does not earn a profit. Let's look at an example.

Expenses: $6
A pizza store pays for flour, tomatoes, cheese, toppings, and a box for a pizza. It also pays the employee to make the pizza. These are expenses.

Price: $9
The pizza store sells the pizza for more than it costs to make it.

Price – Expenses = Profit
$9 – $6 = $3
Profit is the money the business has left after all expenses are paid.

The early explorers traded blankets, weapons, and clothing for goods the Native Americans had. If you were an explorer, what would you offer for trade? What Native American goods would you want in return?

Money

Have you ever traded something with a friend? If you trade your carrots for your friend's apple, then you are bartering.

Today, we use money to buy what we need, but that was not always so. Before people invented money, they traded, or bartered. *Bartering* means exchanging goods you have for goods you want.

Later, banks in towns and cities printed a form of paper money. Then state governments printed real money, but other states sometimes did not value it. The federal government then printed paper money and made coins that could be used in every state.

Banks Provide a Service

Saving money is as important as earning it. Long ago, some people did not trust banks. They hid money in fruit jars, mattresses, or holes they dug in their yards. Today, we have banks that are safe places to keep money. A savings account in a bank is safe today because the federal government *insures* the money. That means if the bank has to close, the government will pay you back your savings.

Banks also help people manage their money. They loan money to people so they can buy expensive items, such as cars and homes.

Interest

Banks pay a small amount of money, called *interest,* on the money put into savings accounts. Some banks also pay interest on money in checking accounts.

You have read that a business needs to make a profit in order to survive. How do banks make a profit? When you put money into a savings or checking account, the money doesn't stay there. The bank loans your money to other people. Those people pay interest to the bank on the money they borrow. That is one way the bank earns a profit.

Each depositor insured to $100,000

FDIC

FEDERAL DEPOSIT INSURANCE CORPORATION

If you see these letters at the bank, your money is protected.

Money makes trading easier. It makes borrowing and saving easier, too.

Cash, Checks, and Cards

Many people do not like to carry a lot of cash. Today, *debit cards* are an easy way for adults to pay for things without cash. Here's how a debit card works: First, a debit card holder puts money in the bank. Then, when the card holder is ready to pay for a purchase, he or she swipes the debit card through the card machine. The card machine is connected to a computer. That computer is connected to the bank. The bank takes the money from the shopper's account and puts it in the store's account. It is very fast!

Shoppers can also pay with checks. Writing a check is another way of spending the money you put in the bank.

Credit cards, on the other hand, are a way to buy now and pay later. A credit card company pays for the things you buy. Then it sends you a bill that shows how much money you owe. The bill also includes a *fee* the company charges for loaning you the money. That means people end up paying more for things they buy with credit cards.

Have you ever seen someone pay for a purchase with a debit card?

What Do You Think

How do you feel about credit cards? Is it a good idea to buy things now and pay for them later? Why or why not?

Activity

What Does It Cost to Live?

How much does it cost to pay for the basic things a family needs? Pretend you have a job and earn $2,000 a month. You have to pay for all of the things listed below. Ask an adult how much each costs.

Income tax	$_____	Electricity	$_____
Housing	$_____	Gasoline	$_____
Car payment	$_____	Fun money	$_____
Food	$_____		

Now, add up all these expenses. How much money do you have left over after you pay all your bills? If you wanted a new TV that costs $500, how would you get it? Could you spend less money on something else? What other expenses should you think about?

Trade-offs and Opportunity Costs

Each time you buy something, you have to make a choice. Sometimes you have to make a trade-off. A ***trade-off*** is choosing not to buy one thing so you will have enough money to buy something else.

Pretend you have $10 to spend. You want to buy a book and a box of colored markers. But you don't have enough money for both. Which would you choose? What trade-off would you make?

Let's say you bought the book instead of the markers. You feel happy because you really wanted the book. Now pretend that the day after you buy the book, your teacher assigns a poster project. You want to make a nice-looking poster, but you need good markers. You already spent your money on the book, so you have to use your old, dried-up markers.

Before you made your choice, you tried to figure out the right thing to do. You wanted to make the best choice. But sometimes things change so the best choice doesn't seem like the best choice anymore. The lost chance to do something after you have done something else is called an ***opportunity cost.***

Business owners have to make choices, too. Sometimes those choices don't turn out to be the best ones. If that happens, business owners lose money instead of earning it. For example, the land used for raising horses cannot be used to grow crops or build houses. If a horse breeder could sell his land for a lot of money, he might be losing money by keeping it to raise horses. It might be an opportunity cost.

1 MEMORY MASTER

1. What is economics? How does it affect you?
2. What kind of economic system do we have in the United States?
3. Name two ways to spend money without spending cash.
4. What is it called when you miss your chance to buy something because you already bought something else?

WORDS TO UNDERSTAND

advertising
capital resource
competition
distribution
human resource
labor
limited resource
natural resource
productive resource
scarcity
specialization
supply and demand
transporting

Producing Goods and Services

Before a company can produce goods or services, three things must come together. These things are called productive resources. *Productive resources* are natural resources, capital resources, and human resources.

Natural Resources

Natural resources are things found in nature. Natural resources include plants and minerals, such as coal. Other examples of natural resources are sand, animals, fish, water, trees, fruits, and vegetables.

If you are making lemonade, you use lemons and water. If you are making tires, then you need rubber. Lemons, water, and rubber all come from the land, so they are natural resources.

Can you spot the three types of productive resources in the bicycle factory?

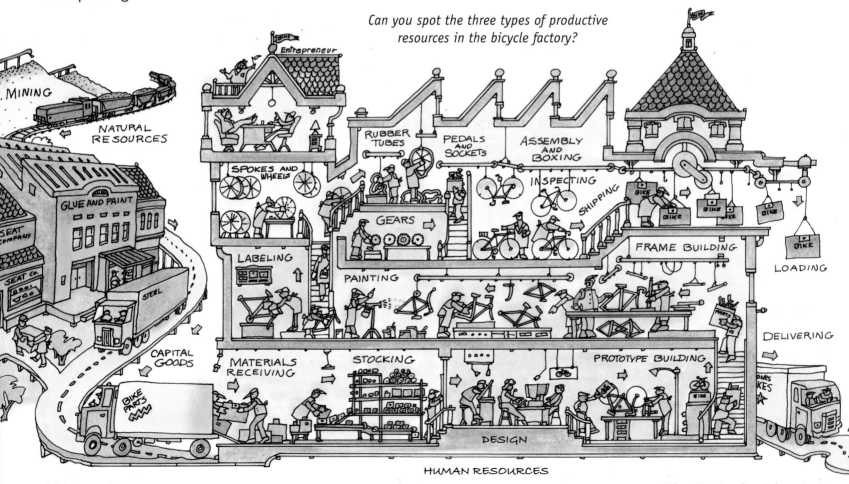

MINING

NATURAL RESOURCES

GLUE AND PAINT

SEAT COMPANY

SEAT Co.

STEEL

CAPITAL GOODS

BIKE PARTS

MATERIALS RECEIVING

STOCKING

DESIGN

PROTOTYPE BUILDING

HUMAN RESOURCES

Entrepreneur

SPOKES AND WHEELS

RUBBER TUBES

PEDALS AND SOCKETS

ASSEMBLY AND BOXING

INSPECTING

SHIPPING

GEARS

LABELING

PAINTING

FRAME BUILDING

LOADING

DELIVERING

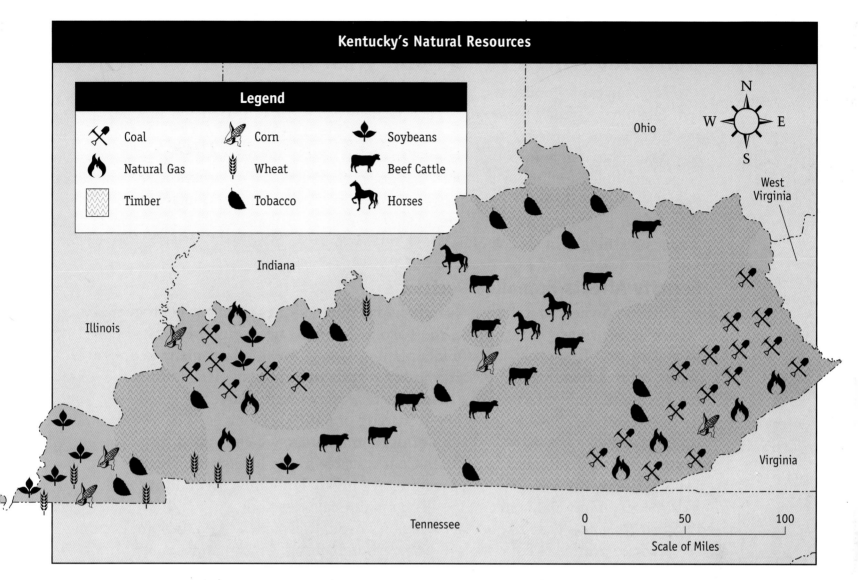

Kentucky's Natural Resources

Legend

- Coal
- Natural Gas
- Timber
- Corn
- Wheat
- Tobacco
- Soybeans
- Beef Cattle
- Horses

Capital Resources

When you buy something and use it to make something else, you are using a *capital resource.* A pizza oven is a capital resource. The tools used to make bicycles are capital resources, too. Most companies use capital resources to produce goods or provide services. A car is a capital resource to a pizza delivery person. If delivery people did not have cars, they could not deliver pizzas.

Human Resources

Goods and services cannot be produced without labor. *Labor* is the work employees do. The workers in a bicycle factory all help the company make and sell bicycles. Workers are sometimes called *human resources.* We depend on people to work as miners, teachers, farmers, and doctors. What other kinds of work do people do?

Making a Living in Kentucky

Scarcity and Productive Resources

Have you ever wondered why you can't have everything you want? One reason is that Earth has **limited resources.** That means we can run out of them. Limited resources is one of the reasons people have economic systems. If we did not keep track of making, buying, and selling, we might run out of some resources.

An example of a limited resource is coal. Earth creates coal over thousands of years. People cannot make more coal. When people want more than existing productive resources are able to provide, the productive resources become scarce. *Scarcity* is when something is in short supply.

Scarcity Affects Economic Decisions

Business owners in Kentucky's land regions think about scarcity when they make economic decisions. For example, the Toyota Company needs hundreds of employees to make cars. Toyota chose to build a plant in Georgetown, where many people live. Workers are a resource that is scarce in some parts of Kentucky. It did not make sense for Toyota to build a factory in a place where workers were scarce.

Businesses also have to think about scarcity of natural resources. For example, central Kentucky has acres and acres of open grasslands, which is good for raising horses. But the region has little coal. Coal is scarce in the Bluegrass. The Eastern Coal Field has many tons of coal, but large areas of grassy land are scarce. In the eastern hills, people mine coal, while in the Bluegrass, people raise horses.

Businesses also have to consider a region's capital resources when they are deciding what to produce. For example, underground wiring is a capital resource. If a region has no underground wires or cable, it would be difficult to run a cable television company in that area. In each region of Kentucky, human, natural, and capital resources help people choose what to produce.

What Do You Think❔

Do you think coal will ever become scarce?

Distributing Goods and Services

Distribution of natural resources and finished goods is very important to business. *Distribution* means giving out or delivering. Without distribution, sellers would not be able to get their products to buyers. Business would almost stop. Distribution includes packaging, *advertising, transporting,* and storing goods.

Can you think of something you buy that comes from far away? Have you ever read the sticker on bananas to see where they come from? Most bananas have to cross an ocean to get to the United States. Coffee is another thing that comes from far away. How do you think these things get to your home? Moving goods is part of distribution.

Packaging and Advertising

Businesses use advertising to tell people about their products. If buyers do not know about a product, they will not buy it. Advertisers run commercials on the radio and TV. They also place ads on the Internet and in newspapers and magazines. You can even see ads on buses and signs on the roads. We see and hear advertising everywhere.

Part of advertising is using packaging that interests people. Think about some of your favorite foods. What kinds of packages do these foods come in? Sometimes, people buy things just because they like the packaging. Being a wise consumer means understanding how and why sellers use advertising.

Transporting and Storing

To transport something means to move it. Many goods are transported in and out of Kentucky on our roads. The Ohio, Kentucky, and Mississippi Rivers are also used to ship goods from place to place. And every day, freight trains and airplanes bring goods into Kentucky and take natural resources, farm products, and manufactured goods out.

Where do all these things go? Most of the time, goods are sent to warehouses. The goods are stored there until the businesses who bought them are ready to use them.

What Do You Think ?

Have you ever bought something because the commercials made it seem exciting? Was the item you bought as good as it looked on TV? Why or why not? Do you think buyers should believe everything advertisements say?

Linking the Past to the Present

Some of the major highways in Kentucky began as simple country roads. Over the years, the government spent millions of dollars to build better roads and highways. How would Kentuckians send and receive goods and services without these roadways?

Consuming Goods and Services

Anyone who spends money on goods or services is a consumer. What kinds of things do you buy with your money? Most people want to spend their money wisely. They compare different brands, prices, and stores. Consumers want to make sure the things they buy are really what they want.

Competition

In our market economy, there are many buyers and sellers. Buyers have many choices. Each company tries to get buyers to choose its product over another company's product. This is called *competition.*

Here's how competition works: Let's say there is an ice cream shop in your town. The ice cream is good, but the prices are high. The workers at the counter are not very nice to customers. They don't treat them well or give them what they want. Last week, another ice cream shop opened in the same area. It has lower prices and better flavors. The workers try to keep customers happy. Which store would you choose?

If the old store does not try to compete with the new one, it will lose customers. What can it do? It can lower its prices. It can try to make better ice cream. It can train its workers to be more helpful to customers. Maybe it can offer something the new store doesn't offer, like a new flavor of ice cream.

Competition can lower the prices of things we want to buy. When companies know buyers have choices, they try to make better shoes, toys, or food. We get better goods and better customer service.

$1.50

$1.25

Activity

Competition in Your Community

What are some companies that compete in your community? Choose a type of business. You might choose toy stores, bike stores, restaurants, or something else. In the yellow pages of the telephone book, look up the type of business you chose. How many different companies that sell the same product or service can you find? What do these companies do to get customers to choose them?

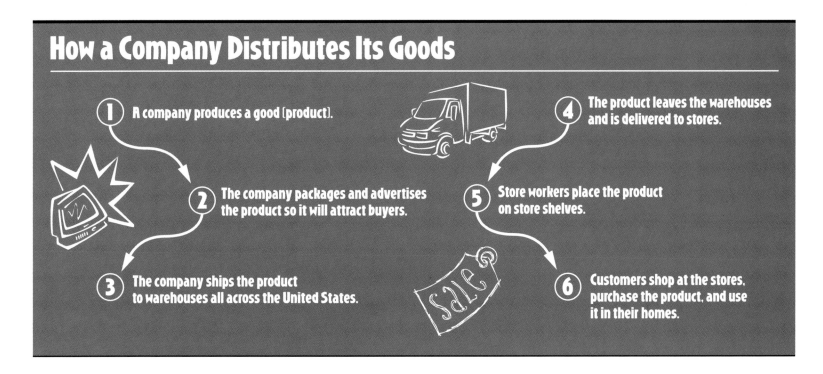

How a Company Distributes Its Goods

1. A company produces a good (product).

2. The company packages and advertises the product so it will attract buyers.

3. The company ships the product to warehouses all across the United States.

4. The product leaves the warehouses and is delivered to stores.

5. Store workers place the product on store shelves.

6. Customers shop at the stores, purchase the product, and use it in their homes.

Supply and Demand

How do owners decide what prices to charge for goods and services? Prices depend on many things.

The price of a product often depends on the cost of the materials to make it. For example, the price of a pair of athletic shoes might depend on the cost of leather and rubber. The price can also depend on the number of shoes the company makes. Still another thing that affects price is how much people want the product.

If the shoes are popular and lots of people want them, the shoe company can charge more for them. But what happens if a company makes a lot of shoes and no one buys them? The company may drop the price, so more people will buy them.

Sometimes, only one company makes a certain product. If buyers want that product or service, they have to pay whatever price the company charges. All these things are parts of the rule of **supply and demand.**

The price of a good often depends on how much people want it.

Specialization

People and countries are more specialized today than they were in the past. For example, there are many different kinds of farmers. Some are dairy farmers. Some are horse farmers. Many farmers only grow one kind of crop. These are examples of *specialization.* When people specialize, they develop special skills and strengths in certain areas.

Countries and regions specialize, too. For example, coffee needs special growing conditions that we don't have in the United States. Countries that have these growing conditions specialize in growing coffee. They grow more than they need, and then they trade the extra for things they do not grow. Countries that specialize usually sell or trade everything they don't use.

Market Connections

Tobacco is one of Kentucky's specialties.

Markets in every region are connected with markets in other regions. For example, oranges are grown in Florida and California, but they are not grown in Kentucky. The orange farmers in Florida

The Kentucky Adventure

sell orange juice to regions that do not grow oranges. In the same way, people in Florida want items made only in Kentucky. They might want to buy Kentucky bourbon or a Toyota Camry.

Kentucky specializes in producing coal, thoroughbred horses, bourbon, tobacco, and cars. Our state then sells these goods all over the world. Kentuckians also buy things that other places specialize in producing. We buy potatoes from the West, silver from the Southwest, corn from the Midwest, cotton and citrus fruit from the South, and fish and seafood from the East.

What Do You Think?

What are your favorite Kentucky products?

Activity

How Many Markets Does It Take?

Have you ever watched a house being built? People who work in many different markets have to work together to build one house. How does each of the following people help build a home?

A truck driver	A boot maker
A hardware store clerk	A plumber
An architect	An electrician
A carpet installer	A refrigerator salesman

Can you think of other people and other markets that are needed to build a house?

2 MEMORY MASTER

1. What are the three kinds of productive resources?
2. What is scarcity?
3. How does competition make prices higher or lower?
4. What do countries that specialize do with the goods they don't use?

WORDS TO UNDERSTAND

hub
legume
tourism

What Do Kentuckians Do?

Not long ago, most people in Kentucky earned their living by farming. Towns grew up near farms. Other jobs, like running a store or a bank, depended on farming, too.

Today, most people in Kentucky work in manufacturing and service industries. Some work in offices; others work in factories. Some repair cars, and others build homes. In some areas of eastern and western Kentucky, people still work in mining. The things people do for a living in Kentucky tell much about our culture.

Activity

Reading a Pie Chart

What do people in Kentucky do for a living? The pie chart to the right shows common jobs in our state. Use the pie chart to answer the following questions:

1. Which kind of job do most Kentuckians do?
2. What kind of job do the fewest Kentuckians do?
3. What percent of the employees in Kentucky work in Agriculture/Mining?
4. Do more people work in the Arts or in Construction?
5. Which kind of job on the chart would you like to have someday?

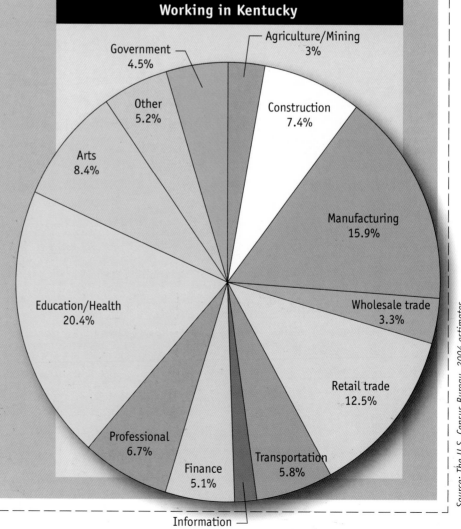

Working in Kentucky

- Government 4.5%
- Agriculture/Mining 3%
- Other 5.2%
- Construction 7.4%
- Arts 8.4%
- Manufacturing 15.9%
- Education/Health 20.4%
- Wholesale trade 3.3%
- Retail trade 12.5%
- Professional 6.7%
- Finance 5.1%
- Transportation 5.8%
- Information 1.8%

Source: The U.S. Census Bureau, 2004 estimates

Tourism

People travel from all over the world to visit Kentucky. They come to watch University of Kentucky basketball games, bet on horse races, or fish in our many rivers and streams. They also come to explore caves or play golf. Some people come to visit abandoned coal mines, Civil War sites, or Shaker homes. Others camp in state parks, attend festivals, or shop at antique sales. All these things are part of **tourism.**

People who visit places away from their homes are called tourists. You can even be a tourist in your own state. Tourists spend money on food, gas, hotels, and activities. All these things earn money for our businesses and workers. Tourism employs thousands of people and makes millions of dollars for the state.

Every year, thousands of people attend the Lincoln Days Festival in Hodgenville.

Activity

Visiting Kentucky

The Internet makes it easy to visit Kentucky with a computer. The Kentucky Department of Tourism has information on many things to do here. Check out its website at http://kentuckytourism.com. Search the site for things to see and do in our state.

1. Make a list of five places you would like to visit in Kentucky. Write down which cities or towns they are in or near.
2. Draw a map of Kentucky.
3. On your map, write the names of the places you want to visit.
4. On a piece of paper, list at least two reasons you want to visit each place you chose.

One of the activities at Kentucky Derby time is the Great Balloon Race.

What Do Kentuckians Make?

You have learned about some of Kentucky's specialties. Do you know what other kinds of products and services come from Kentucky? Some of them may surprise you.

What Do You Think?

Would you like to work for one of these businesses when you grow up? Which one? Why?

Kentucky Fried Chicken (KFC)

Harland Sanders was born to a coal mining family. When his father died, his mother went to work. Harland had to learn to cook for his family. When he opened his first restaurant 75 years ago in Corbin, people came from miles around to eat his secret-recipe fried chicken. Today, people eat more than a billion KFC chicken dinners every year! Harland's recipe is so secret that half of it is locked in one safe, and the other half lies in a separate safe. The company's headquarters are in Louisville.

Duncan Hines

Duncan Hines was born in Bowling Green in 1880. Today, store shelves are lined with Duncan Hines cake and pancake mixes, frosting, jelly, pickles, mushrooms, ice cream toppings, steak sauce, ketchup, chili sauce, and bread. Duncan Hines is one of the most famous brand names in America.

United Parcel Service (UPS)

UPS is the world's largest package delivery company. Each day, UPS delivers millions of packages. One of the most important services UPS provides is overnight delivery. The major **hub** for UPS's Next Day Air Operation is in Louisville. That means every UPS package that goes from shipper to receiver in one day makes a stop in Louisville.

Jif

Did you know that peanuts are not really nuts? They're *legumes* and related to peas. In the United States, the average person eats seven pounds of peanuts and peanut products every year!

The Jif peanut butter plant in Lexington is the largest peanut butter factory in the world. If you spread all the peanut butter made each year in Lexington on a football field, it would make a layer 55 feet thick! It takes more than 1,000 peanuts to make one jar of Jif peanut butter.

Laura's Lean Beef

In 1985, Laura Freeman founded Laura's Lean Beef Company on her family's farm in Winchester. Today, Laura's Lean Beef is a company formed of over 750 family farmers. All these farmers raise leaner breeds of cattle and follow special rules for raising healthy animals. Laura's Lean Beef is sent to more than 4,700 grocery stores in 44 states.

LAURA'S LEAN BEEF®
CATTLE RAISED WITHOUT ANTIBIOTICS, NO GROWTH HORMONES ADDED.

Chevrolet Corvette

Have you ever seen a Corvette? It is one of the most popular sport cars ever made. The company that makes Corvettes is called General Motors (GM). GM built their Corvette assembly plant in Bowling Green in 1981. For more than 25 years, every Corvette GM has produced has been built right here in Kentucky.

Jim Beam

Jacob Beam distilled his first batch of Kentucky whiskey from corn, rye, and barley malt over 200 years ago. During those 200 years, Jim Beam Brands has produced more than 10 million barrels of its genuine Kentucky bourbon. Today, the company lives on under the name of Jacob's great-grandson, Jim. Jim Beam Brands is still based in Clermont.

Papa John's Pizza

Over 20 years ago, a high school student named John Schnatter turned a closet in the back of his dad's tavern into a little kitchen. John sold his car, bought used restaurant equipment, and began selling pizzas. Customers loved the pizza so much that John was able to expand. That was the beginning of Papa John's Pizza. Today, there are nearly 3,000 Papa John's Pizza stores. Based in Louisville, it is the third largest pizza company in the world.

Toyota

In Georgetown, thousands of Toyotas roll off the assembly line each year. One of the cars made in Kentucky, the Camry, is the best-selling car in America. Toyota says the workers in Georgetown are the world's finest automobile builders.

3 MEMORY MASTER

1. How did most Kentuckians earn a living in the past?
2. What kinds of jobs do most Kentuckians have?
3. Name two important products that come from Kentucky.
4. How does tourism bring money to Kentucky?

Chapter **13** Review

What's the Point?

Economics is the study of how people use money for goods and services. The United States operates in a free market system. Banks help people manage money. Cash, checks, credit cards, and debit cards can be used to buy goods and services. To provide goods and services, companies use productive resources. Supply and demand help drive prices. Scarcity occurs when there is a limited supply. Our country, region, and state all specialize. We depend on other countries to specialize in the goods and services we don't have. There are many successful businesses in Kentucky.

Becoming Better Readers: Study a Business

Do you want to study business when you get older? Understanding economics really helps. Pick a business that you admire. It could be one in your town, far away, or an online business. Read all you can about this business. Find out where it is located, when it got started, what it sells, and how it advertises. Look in newspapers, magazines, or online, or ask people you know what they think of this business. What makes this company successful? What businesses compete with this one? What could it do better?

Our Amazing Geography: Where to Build a Business

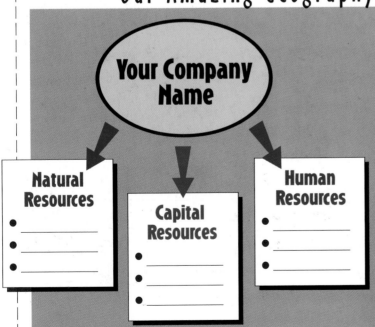

Where would you put a new business in Kentucky? Before you can choose the best place to build your company, you have to decide what you are going to sell. Is it a good or a service? After you have chosen your good or service, choose a name for your company.

As you think about where to build your business, think about natural features, like rivers and natural resources. Also think about where human features, like cities and farms, are located. Think about the productive resources each location has to offer. Now, copy the "Your Company Name" diagram onto your own paper. Fill it in with information from your new, exciting business!

Activity

How Did It Get from There to Here?

Look around you. What products do you see? How did they get to your classroom or home? Think about the many goods you used in the last 24 hours. Most of them had to be produced, advertised, distributed, and consumed. Make a list of ten items. Then pick one from your list. Make a diagram for it like the one on page 349. Use actual facts in your diagram. If you don't know anything about the product, learn about it by reading labels, asking an adult, looking it up online, or researching it at the store.

Activity

How Are We Connected?

Our market economy is made up of buyers and sellers satisfying their needs and wants by using productive resources to make, buy, and sell goods and services. These activities are made easier by having a money system.

Read the story below. Then draw a picture to show the people and businesses in the story. Use arrows (---\>) to connect people and businesses. Each time a money exchange occurs, draw a dollar sign ($) on the arrow. Label these arrows with an "R" for resources, "G" for goods, and "S" for services.

Maria Lopez owns Burger Haven, a restaurant. She hires Jeff Larsen to work as a chef. Jeff uses some of his income to buy new diving equipment from Diver Down. The owner of Diver Down uses the money he receives from Jeff and other customers to pay his employee, Ms. Waters. Ms. Waters uses some of her income to take her family to a concert at Symphony Hall and to dinner at the Corner Café.

Mrs. Lopez also uses some of the income earned from her customers to buy new ovens from Ovens Unlimited. Business has been good for Ovens Unlimited. The owners decide to build a second factory.

Questions:
- What are the businesses in this community?
- What goods and services did the businesses sell?
- What goods and services did the businesses buy?
- Who are the buyers of the businesses' goods and services?
- What did the buyers sell to earn income?
- In each exchange, what is exchanged in addition to the resource, good, or service?
- If Mrs. Lopez closes her restaurant, how might this affect consumers and the other businesses in the community?
- How are the businesses and people in the story dependent on one another?

Pacific Ocean

★ Olympia

Washington

★ Salem

Oregon

★ Helena

Montana

North Dakota

★ Bismarck

★ Boise

Idaho

Wyoming

South Dakota

Pierre ★

Sacramento ★

★ Carson City

Nevada

Salt Lake City ★

Utah

Cheyenne ★

Nebraska

Lincoln ★

Denver ★

Colorado

Topeka

California

Kansas

★ Santa Fe

Arizona

New Mexico

★ Phoenix

Oklahoma

★ Oklahoma City

0   500 Miles

Alaska

0   100 Miles

Hawaii

Texas

Austin ★

MEXICO

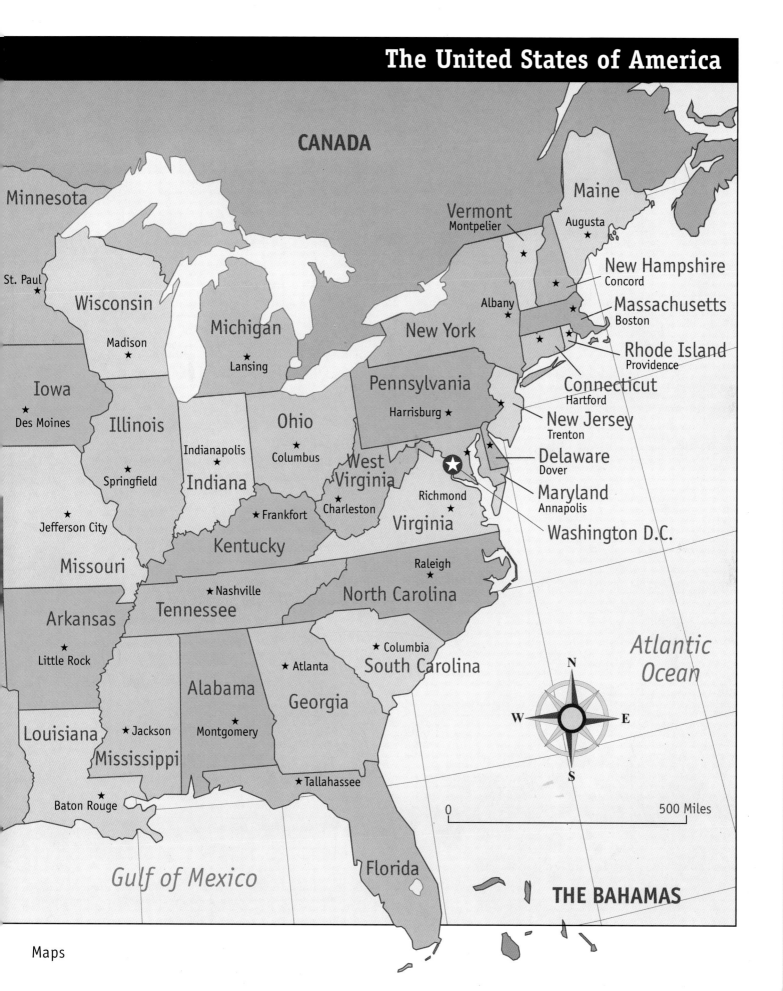

The United States of America

CANADA

Minnesota

Wisconsin

St. Paul ★

Madison ★

Iowa

Des Moines ★

Illinois

Springfield ★

Jefferson City ★

Missouri

Arkansas

Little Rock ★

Louisiana

Baton Rouge ★

Michigan

Lansing ★

Indiana

Indianapolis ★

Frankfort ★

Kentucky

Nashville ★

Tennessee

Mississippi

Jackson ★

Alabama

Montgomery ★

Ohio

Columbus ★

West Virginia

Charleston ★

Virginia

Richmond ★

North Carolina

Raleigh ★

Columbia ★
South Carolina

Atlanta ★

Georgia

Tallahassee ★

Florida

Gulf of Mexico

Vermont
Montpelier

Maine

Augusta ★

New Hampshire
Concord

New York

Albany ★

Pennsylvania

Harrisburg ★

Massachusetts
Boston

Rhode Island
Providence

Connecticut
Hartford

New Jersey
Trenton

Delaware
Dover

Maryland
Annapolis

Washington D.C.

Atlantic
Ocean

N

W   E

S

500 Miles

0

THE BAHAMAS

Glossary

The definitions listed here are for the **Words to Understand** as they are used in this textbook. The number in parenthesis following each word indicates the chapter in which the word first appears.

A

abolish (7): to get rid of; to end

abolitionist (8): a person who worked to end slavery

Academy Award (11): an important award for people who work in the movie industry

accuse (6): to blame

adapt (3): to change

adventurous (5): having to do with exciting activities

advertising (13): making people aware of a good or service

aging (6): to remain undisturbed for a long period of time

aircraft (11): a machine that is able to sustain flight

Allied Powers (11): the countries of the Soviet Union, France, England, and the United States during World War I

ally (7): a friend or supporter

ambassador (7): a person who represents his or her country in a foreign country

amend (10): to change

amendment (12): a change

ammunition (6): bullets, cannonballs, and other weaponry supplies

antebellum (8): before the war

Appalachian Regional Commission (ARC) (11): a government program organized to make improvements in Appalachia

apprentice (7): a student of a master

archaeologist (4): a scientist who studies artifacts to learn how people lived in the past

archaic (4): old

artifact (1): something people made or used in the past

astronaut (11): a scientist who studies and explores outer space

atlatl (4): a tool used to throw a spear farther and faster

attorney general (10): the highest-ranking attorney in the state

awl (4): a pointed tool used for making holes

Axis Powers (11): the countries of Germany, Italy, and Japan during World War I

B

balance of power (12): having equal authority

ballot (10): a document used to vote

barge (7): a large platform used for moving goods and passengers on water

barter (13): to trade

bill (12): a proposed law

black lung (10): a disease caused by breathing coal dust

Black Patch Wars (10): a series of attacks on farmers who refused to join cooperatives

bondage (8): the state of having no freedom

boom (10): a period of great increase

border state (9): a state that wanted to keep slavery but did not want to leave the Union

boundary (6): something that shows a border

boycott (6): to protest by not buying something

broad form deed (10): a document that gave permission to coal companies to take coal from beneath privately owned land

C

canal (8): a man-made waterway

capital resource (13): something used to make something else

card (5): to brush and smooth wool

cash crop (2): a crop grown for the purpose of selling

character (1): the moral qualities of a person

charred (6): burned or darkened by fire

cholera (8): a deadly disease spread through unclean water

Chunkey (4): a game of skill played by ancient people

Civil Rights Movement (11): the efforts of people to end unfair treatment

civil war (9): a war between two regions of one country

climate (2): the pattern of weather over a long period of time

coal tipple (10): a machine used for unloading coal cars

colony (5): a settlement owned and governed by a distant country

committee (7): a group of people working together for a specific purpose

commonwealth (1): a state set up for the common good of all people

competition (13): the practice of working against others to succeed

compromise (6): an agreement between two parties in which neither party gets its way entirely

conductor (8): a person who helped slaves escape on the Underground Railroad

Confederacy (9): the states that broke away from the Union before the Civil War; the South

constitution (7): a document that organizes government and outlines basic laws

consumer (13): a person who pays for goods or services

cooperative (10): an organization of farmers who worked together to get higher prices for crops

corruption (10): dishonesty

council (4): a group of leaders

county seat (3): the town or city where the county government has its office

cradleboard (4): a board used by Native American women to strap their babies onto their backs

credit card (13): a bankcard that allows a consumer to pay for a purchase over time

creditor (8): a person who loans something

cribbing (10): wood framing built inside a mine to support the mine's roof

criticize (7): to speak against; to find fault with

culture (1): the ways and traditions of a group of people

D

Day Law (10): a Kentucky law that segregated schools

debate (9): a formal argument

debit card (13): a bankcard used to withdraw or spend money from a bank account

debt (9): something owed

debtor (8): a person who borrows

declare (6): to state

deed (6): a document that proves ownership of land

deep-shaft mining (10): a method of mining in which miners dig down deep into the ground

degree (2): a unit of measure for circles and angles

delegate (6): a representative

democracy (12): a government in which power is in the hands of the people

Democrat (8): a member of a political party that believes government should support the common man

depression (10): a time when many people can't make enough money to take care of their needs

desegregate (11): to end segregation

dissenting (10): disagreeing

distillery (6): a business that makes alcoholic beverages

distribution (13): the process of delivering

diversity (11): the state of being different

document preservation (1): the act of taking care of records or official papers

duel (7): a formal fight

E

economic panic (8): a time when there is very little money

economics (13): the study of how people use, make, transport, buy, and sell goods and services and how people use money

editor (11): a person who corrects, revises, or adapts a work

elector (7): a person who represents a group of people in the voting process

electric-generating plant (3): a place where electricity is created

elevation (2): the height of a place in relation to the level of the ocean

Emancipation Proclamation (9): Abraham Lincoln's order that was meant to free slaves in the southern states

employee (13): a person who works for a wage or salary

enslaved (6): to be owned by someone; to have no freedom

epidemic (8): a time when many people have the same disease

equator (2): the latitude line that runs east and west around the middle of Earth

erosion (6): the washing away of something

etching (11): a picture made by cutting or carving

European (5): a person who lives in or comes from Europe

evidence (1): something that offers proof

exact location (2): the specific position of a place

executive branch (12): the branch of government that carries out the laws

F

facility (10): a building used for a specific purpose

fee (13): a small amount of money charged for a specific reason

feud (10): an argument that continues for a long time

flax (5): a fibrous plant used to make cloth

floodwall (3): a wall built along a shore or bank to protect an area from flooding

free enterprise (13): an economic system in which people are free to make, sell, and buy goods and services

free state (8): a state that did not allow slavery

Freedmen's Bureau (9): an organization that helped freed blacks and poor whites

G

General Assembly (12): the state legislature

generate (3): to make or create

generator (3): a machine that makes electricity

genetics (11): the study of the development of human beings

geography (2): the study of the land, water, plants, animals, and people of a place

geologist (3): a scientist who studies soil and rocks to see how Earth formed and continues to change

glacier (4): a frozen river; a moving sheet of ice

graffiti (12): words or drawings on public property

grid (2): a pattern of regularly spaced lines, usually forming squares

H

harbor (2): a protected portion of a body of water

hardtack (9): a hard, cracker-like biscuit made from flour and water

hemisphere (2): half of Earth

hemp (7): a plant from which rope and cloth are made

hide (4): the skin of an animal

historian (1): a person who studies or writes about history

historic (4): the period during which written records were kept

homespun (5): handmade cloth

honor guard (9): a soldier assigned to carry a casket

hub (13): a center of activity

human feature (2): something that is built or made by people

human resource (13): people

human system (3): a group of people working together

humid (2): a high level of water in the air

hunter-gatherer (4): an ancient person who gathered or hunted for food

I

Ice Age (4): a period during which Earth was very cold and frozen

immigrant (8): a person who has moved from another place

impressment (7): the practice of forcing American soldiers to join the British navy

income (12): money received

independence (6): the state of being self-reliant

individual right (12): that which is just, legal, or proper to which a person is entitled

insure (13): to protect

interest (13): a small amount of money either paid or charged by a bank

intersection (12): a place where roads meet or cross

invade (6): to enter with force

irrigate (3): to supply water to

J

jockey (7): a person who rides a racehorse during a horse race

judicial branch (12): the branch of government that decides what the laws mean

jury (12): a group of people who listen to a case and decide guilt or innocence

K

karst (3): a type of limestone that dissolves easily

Kentucky Education Reform Act (KERA) (11): a law that improved Kentucky's education system

Kentucky Resolutions (7): a statement, written by Thomas Jefferson and adopted by the Kentucky legislature, that explained why the Sedition Act was wrong

Know-Nothing (8): a member of a political group that believed people who were different were dangerous

Ku Klux Klan (9): a group that committed acts of violence against blacks

L

labor (13): the work employees provide

labor union (10): a group of workers who organize to improve working conditions

laborer (9): a person who performs physical work

land company claim (6): a piece of land given to a worker by a land company

landmark (7): something that marks or shows a certain place

latitude (2): a line running east and west used to describe location on Earth

legacy (10): something handed down from one generation to the next

legal (7): not against the law

legend (4): a story that tells about the past

legislative branch (12): the branch of government that makes the laws

legislator (12): one of Kentucky's 138 elected lawmakers

legislature (7): the Kentucky General Assembly and the U.S. Congress

legume (13): a pod or seed from the pea family used for food

levee (3): a high mound of earth or concrete built in a long strip alongside a river or stream

liberty (12): freedom

limestone (3): a soft, white rock that forms from sediment

limited resource (13): something Earth can run out of

literary critic (11): a person who reads and reviews works of literature

local (12): nearby; close

lock (8): a closed-off section of a waterway in which the water level can be raised or lowered

long hunter (5): a hunter who stayed in the wilderness for long periods of time

longitude (2): a line running north and south used to describe location on Earth

loom (5): a machine used to weave fabric

loudspeaker (10): a machine used to increase volume so large crowds of people are able to hear

Louisiana Purchase (7): a large piece of land purchased from France by the United States

Loyalist (6): a colonist loyal to England

lye (5): a liquid, made from ashes, that is used for cleaning

lynch (10): to kill violently

M

maize (4): the Native American word for corn

mandolin (11): a small, pear-shaped instrument resembling a guitar

man-made (3): created or produced by people

market economy (13): an economic system in which people are free to make, sell, and buy goods and services

memorial (11): something that honors or celebrates people or events

military claim (6): a piece of land given to a soldier by the government

militia (5): army; military

missionary (7): a person who travels and teaches religious beliefs

Missouri Compromise (8): Henry Clay's plan to admit one slave state and one free state into the United States so the votes for and against slavery in Congress would remain equal

moonbow (3): a rainbow created by the light of the moon, appears only at night

mountaintop removal (3): a method of mining in which large amounts of earth are removed; strip mining

N

nation (4): a group of people who live and work together

native (1): coming from or belonging to a place

natural feature (2): something that occurs naturally on Earth

natural resource (13): something found in nature

neutral (9): not joined with either side

New Deal (10): an economic recovery program designed to end the Great Depression

night rider (10): a member of a secret group that terrorized people

Nobel Prize (11): an award for an effort or discovery that promotes world peace

O-P

opportunity cost (13): the lost chance to do something after doing something else

oral history (1): history that is not written down but is passed on through word of mouth

paleo (4): very old

pardon (8): to excuse from punishment

Patriot (6): a colonist who wanted freedom from England

pension (9): money paid to a person after retirement

permanent (5): lasting; not temporary

petition (7): to ask

plaza (4): an open area surrounded by homes or other buildings

poet laureate (11): the most-honored poet

point of view (1): the way a person or group sees something

political party (8): an organization of people with similar political views

politician (6): a leader or someone who works in government

pollution (3): harmful or unclean things in the environment

population (7): the number of people in an area

port (3): a place on a shore where boats pick up or deliver goods

portrait (7): a painted or photographed likeness of someone

pound (5): a British dollar

poverty (11): the state of being poor

prairie (2): a wide, grassy area with few trees

precipitation (2): water in the form of rain, sleet, snow, or hail

predict (5): to foretell the future

prehistoric (4): before recorded history

prejudice (1): a judgment of a person or group before the person or group is known

press aid (11): an employee assigned to work with the media

primary source (1): something that was made, said, written, or used at an event when it happened

prime meridian (2): the longitude line that runs vertically between the North and South Poles and through Greenwich, England

privacy (12): the state of being private

Proclamation of 1763 (5): a law against settling west of the Appalachian Mountains

producer (13): someone who makes a good

productive resource (13): something used to produce something else

profit (13): the money left after expenses are paid

Prohibition (10): the practice of outlawing the production, sale, and use of alcoholic beverages

property right (12): that which is just, legal, or proper to which a property owner is entitled

protest (11): to object

R

racism (11): the belief that races have different qualities that make them better or worse than other races

ratify (7): to approve or accept

reclaim (3): to restore

reclamation fee (3): money paid by mining companies to restore damaged land

Reconstruction (9): a plan to rebuild the South after the Civil War

reenactment (9): the repetition of an event that happened earlier

reform (11): to change for the better

region (2): a group of places that have something in common

relative location (2): the position of a place in relation to another place

repeater (10): a person who illegally votes more than once in an election

replica (6): a copy

representative (12): a person who represents another person or group

responsibility (12): a duty; something a person should do

restrict (7): to limit

revenuer (10): a tax collector

revolution (6): a time of change

right of control (6): legal power over something

rival (5): a person or group to fight against; an enemy

S

sacrifice (9): to give up something of value

salary (13): money paid to an employee

sapling (4): a young tree

scalp (5): to remove the skin and hair from a person's head

scarcity (13): a short supply

scatter tag (10): a round, metal disk used to identify the company that mined the coal

scrip (10): a form of payment used by mine companies; good only at the company store

secede (9): to break away

secondary source (1): something made, said, written, or used by someone who was not at an event when it happened

sediment (3): tiny bits of dirt and sand carried in water

Sedition Act (7): a law that outlawed criticism of government leaders

segregate (10): to separate by race

segregation (11): the state of being separated by race

service (13): work that people do for other people

sewer (7): a tunnel or channel that carries waste

sharecropper (9): a farmer who farmed land owned by someone else

shear (5): to cut

silversmith (7): a person who makes things out of silver

sit-in (11): a method of protesting in which people sit peacefully in public places and refuse to leave

slave (6): a person owned by another person

slave owner (6): a person who owned one or more slaves

slave state (8): a state that allowed slavery

smallpox (5): a disease similar to measles

Spanish Conspiracy (6): James Wilkinson's plan to make Kentucky a Spanish colony

specialization (13): the act of becoming skilled in a specific area

spiritual (7): a song of faith

squatter (6): a settler who lived on the land and worked it for many years without owning it

statehood convention (7): a meeting in which delegates discussed becoming a state

states' rights (7): the belief that states should have more power than the national government

station (6): a settlement of cabins surrounded by a stockade; or (8) a hiding place on the Underground Railroad

stereotype (1): a label, based on opinion, used to describe people

still (6): a machine used to make alcoholic beverages

stockade (5): a wall built for protection

strike (10): an organized attempt to improve a situation by refusing to work

strikebreaker (10): a worker who refused to strike

strip mining (3): a method of mining in which large amounts of earth are removed

stroke (11): a brain injury caused by a moving blood clot

suffrage (10): the right to vote

supply and demand (13): an economic rule that describes how prices are affected both by the quantity of a good or service and the level of interest consumers have in it

supreme court (12): the highest court

surplus (7): extra; more than needed

surrender (6): to admit defeat

survey (5): to measure and set boundaries on land

suspension (9): the condition of hanging

swindle (9): to cheat

symbol (1): something that represents something else

synagogue (7): a meetinghouse for people of the Jewish faith

T

tannery (7): a building where animal hides are made into leather

tariff (12): a tax on goods from another place

tavern (7): a saloon

tax (6): money given to the government by the citizens

technology (3): the use of man-made things, such as machines, tools, or electricity

telegraph (9): a communication system using a series of clicks sent over a wire

terrorist (11): a person who tries to scare others into doing what he or she wants

till (4): to break up or turn soil

toll (7): a usage fee

tornado (2): a powerful, funnel-shaped wind storm

tornado warning (11): a weather indicator that means a tornado might occur

tornado watch (11): a weather indicator that means a tornado has been spotted

tourism (13): the practice of traveling for pleasure

trade-off (13): the act of sacrificing something for something better

transporting (13): moving something from one place to another

treason (6): the act of turning against one's country

treasurer (10): a person who manages an organization's money

treaty (5): an agreement between two groups

trespass (5): to enter without permission

trial (6): a meeting held in a courtroom to decide a person's guilt or innocence

tribe (4): a group of people who live together and have something, such as language or family, in common

turbine (3): a spinning machine part that generates electricity

turnpike (8): a road that connects towns or rivers

U-V-W

unalienable (6): unable to be taken away or removed

Underground Railroad (8): a secret escape system for enslaved blacks

Union (9): the northern states that remained together during the Civil War; the North

veto (12): to not approve; to turn away

wattle and daub (4): a building material made of lashed-together poles and mud

Whig (8): a member of a political party that believed in a strong national government

wigwam (4): a Native American home made of wooden poles covered with bark

Index

Acknowledgments

Writing a textbook for fourth graders in the Commonwealth of Kentucky has been a wonderful experience for someone accustomed to teaching and writing for college students. Fourth graders seem to have a love of history in their DNA, and I have enjoyed this process more than I ever imagined. Writing for this age group has also helped make me a better teacher and writer. I sincerely hope the students who use this book will benefit from it as much as I have.

My students at the University of Kentucky were the first to hear the notes on which this book is based, and their comments and suggestions helped me decide what needed to be included and what could be deleted. I have also had the privilege of working with Kentucky teachers in various programs throughout the state, and that experience helped define this book.

The staff at Gibbs Smith, Publisher has been first rate. My thanks goes to Alan Connell for his amazing design and layout and to Janis Hansen for her tireless photo research. I was especially lucky to have as my editor Valerie Thursby Hatch, whose experience, tenacity, and good advice were much appreciated.

As always, my family deserves special thanks. My wife, Leslie, tolerated the time I spent on this book with her usual good humor and patience. Seeing my oldest son, Alex, suffer through an outdated fourth grade text several years ago convinced me I should try to offer a new version. This book is lovingly dedicated to him and to my youngest son, Drew, whose day in the fourth grade, and in studying Kentucky history, is fast approaching.

Credits

The following abbreviations were used for sources from which several images were obtained:

AJ - Adam Jones/www.adamjonesphoto.com
AP - AP/Wide World Photos
Corbis - Bettemann/Corbis
GR - Gary Rasmussen
Granger - The Granger Collection, New York
GSPA - Gibbs Smith, Publisher Archives
JB - Jon Burton
KHS - Kentucky Historical Society
KT - Courtesy: KentuckyTourism.com
LOC - Library of Congress Prints and Photographs Division
NA - Neal Anderson
NWPA - North Wind Picture Archives
PTG - PhotosToGo.com
SS - ShutterStock.com
UKL - University of Kentucky Libraries

All other photos are in the public domain, from the Gibbs Smith, Publisher archives, or from photos.com. Other illustrations are from the Gibbs Smith, Publisher archives or were obtained from clipart.com.

Cover Image: Adam Jones. **Prelims:** SS/Robert C. Tussey III. **Chapter One:** 2-3 Contemplative Images, Photographer Chuck Summers, 4 AP, 6 Nicole Beutler, 7 (top) AJ, 8 Nicole Beutler, 9 KHS, 10 The Paducah Sun, 11 (left) LOC, (right) AP, 12 NWPA, 13 JB, 14 Shauna Kawasaki, 15 iStockPhoto.com/Bonnie Jacobs, 17 Jane Cochran. **Chapter Two:** 18-19 NASA, 20 AJ, 21 AJ, 26 Valerie Hatch (bottom) CumberlandSeaRay.com (right), 27 (first and third) SS/Robert C. Tussey III, (second) SS/Melissa Tuttle, (bottom) SS/Mark Bonham, 28 PTG/Ewing Galloway, 30 (center) SS/Donald Mallalieu, (right) SS/Natalia Bratslavsky, 31 (left) SS/David Alexander Liu, (right) SS/Chee-Onn Leong, 32 (left to right) SS/Dimitrii Sherman, SS/Jeff Kinsey, SS/Allen Furmanski, 33 SS/Cameron Cross, 34 (left to right) SS/Joe Mamer, SS/Danis Derics, NOAA Photo Library, 35 (left) SS/Brian Kelly, (right) SS/Tony Campbell, 36 (left) SS/Eric Patterson, (right) SS/Michael Byrne, 37 SS/Cristi Bastian, 38 (left to right) SS/Michael Ledray, SS/Jerry Horn, SS/Laurin Rinder, 39 (left) SS/Susan Adams, (right) SS/Darlene Tompkins, 41 Sarah Hatch. **Chapter Three:** 42-43 Melissa Farlow/National Geographic Image Collection, 44 SS/Rosemarie Colombraro, 45 KT, 46 AP, 47 JB, 48 (top) Land Between The Lakes, (bottom) KHS, 49 AP, 52 Tom Till, 53 (top) AJ, (bottom) Mike Martin, 54 JB, 55 SS/Ivars Zoinerovics, 56 SS/Steven Good, 57 (top) KHS, (bottom) SS/Rhonda L. Hamm, 58 AJ, 59 AP, 60 SS/Lisa F. Young, 61 (top) AJ, (bottom) AP, 62-63 SS/Melissa Tuttle, 64 AJ, (left) LOC, 65 National Park Service, 66 SS/Joseph Geronimo, 67 SS/Jodi Hutchison, 69 (top left) SS/Pokrovskaya Elana Alekseevna, (center left) AJ, (bottom left) SS/Holly Kuchera, (top right) SS/William Spangler, (center right) SS/Sylvaine Thomas, (bottom right) KT, 71 (top) SS/Charles Shapiro, (bottom) SS/John Vanhara, 72 SS/Jason A Wright, 73 Digital Library System: US Fish & Wildlife Service. **Chapter Four:** 76-77 National Park Service, 78 JB, 79 (top) GR, (right) Ron & Jean Lukesh, 80 Washington Department of Tourism, 82 GR, 83 GR, 84 SS/Krzysztof Nieciecki, 86-87 Painting by Martin Pate, Newnan, GA, 87 GR, 89 Tara Prindle, Native Tech, 91 (top) NWPA, (bottom) Granger, 93 Photos by Suzanne Chapelle, Courtesy of the Irvine Nature Center, 94 NA, 96 GR, 97 SS/Jason A. Wright, 98 iStockPhoto.com/Norman Eder, 99 SS/GJS, 100 GR, 101 (top) LOC, (bottom) Tara Prindle, Native Tech. **Chapter Five:** 104-105 NWPA, 108 NWPA, 110 LOC, 111 LOC, 113 NWPA, 114 NWPA, 116 SS/Robert C. Tussey III, 117 AJ, 119 Photography Collection, Miriam and Ira D. Wallach Division of Art, Prints and Photographs, The New York Public Library, Astor, Lenox and Tilden Foundations, 120-121 NA, 123 Granger, 124 KHS, 125 LOC, 126 West Virginia State Archives, 129 GR, 131 (bottom) SS/Laura Stone, (right) NW, 132 iStockPhoto.com/Yvette Sandham, 133 Kindra Clineff, 134 NW, 135 (bottom) Courtesy: Kim LeMmon. **Chapter Six:** 138-139 NWPA, 143 National Archives, 144 NWPA, 145 (top) Jean Crossman/Courtesy of the Amherst History Museum, Amherst Massachusettes, (bottom) NWPA, 146 National Archives, 147 United States Capitol Historical Society, 148 Smithsonian Museum, 149 LOC, 150-151 Print Collection, Miriam and Ira D. Wallach Division of Art, Prints and Photographs, The New York Public Library, Astor, Lenox and Tilden Foundations, 152 Granger, 154 KHS, 155 LOC, 157 (top) LOC, (bottom) KHS, 158 LOC, 161 LOC, 163 KHS, 164 Corbis, 165 LOC, 166 AJ, (right) LOC, 167 University of Louisville Special Collections. **Chapter Seven:** 170-171 NWPA, 172 KT, 175 The Kentucky State Seal is reproduced with permission from the Kentucky Secretary of State, 176 LOC, 177 (top) KHS, (bottom) PTG/Jim Schewabel, 178 KHS, 182 KHS, 183 (left) KHS, (right) Museum Purchase, 1956.12.1: The Speed Art Museum, 187 West Virginia State Archives, 188-189 Granger, 190-191 LOC, 193 LOC, 194-195 NA, 196 Corbis, 197 NWPA, 199 Gift of Rowland D. and Elanor B. Miller, Mr. and Mrs. Owsley Brown II, Steve Wilson and Laura Lee Brown and John S. Speed, 2000.4.1: Collection of the Speed Art Museum, Louisville, Kentucky. **Chapter Eight:** 200-201 Corbis, 202 LOC, 203 Corbis, 204 KHS, 205 KHS, 206 Corbis, 207 LOC, 208 LOC, 209 Granger, 210 LOC, 211 SS/Weygan Randolph Mayes, 212-213 Painting "Westward Travelers at Miller's Landing, 1843" by Gary R. Lucy. Courtesy of the Gary R. Lucy Gallery, Inc. Washington, MO - www.garylucy.com, 214 (top) C&O Canal Museum, 215 KHS, 216 (top) LOC, 216-217 SS/Robert C. Tussey III, 217 (top) LOC, 218 LOC, 219 (top) LOC, 220 NWPA, 222 LOC, 223 LOC, 224 General Research & Reference Division, Schomburg Center for Research in Black Culture, The New York Public Library, Astor, Lenox and Tilden Foundations. **Chapter Nine:** 226-227 John Paul Strain Gallery, 228 JB, 229 LOC, 230 Granger, 231 LOC, 232 KHS, 236 (left) LOC, 237 (top) LOC, (bottom) Harpers Weekly, 238-239 LOC, 239 NWPA, 241 (bottom) LOC, (right) KHS, 242 NA, 244 LOC, (left) Susan Myers, 247 (top) AJ, (bottom) LOC, 248 (left) KHS/Philadelphia Commercial Museum Collection, (center, right) LOC, 249 LOC, 250 Granger, 251 LOC, 252 iStockPhotos.com/Stan Rohrer. **Chapter Ten:** 254-255 KHS, 265-257 KHS, 260 KHS, 261 (top) PTG/Ewing Galloway, (bottom) KHS, 262 (top) Corbis, (left) LOC, 263 (top) Corbis, (bottom) LOC, 264 LOC, 265 LOC, 266 KHS, 267 UKL, 268 LOC, 269 (left) LOC, (right) Corbis, 270 National Archives, 271 (top) KHS, (bottom) UKL, 272 UKL, 273 LOC, 275 (left) LOC, (right) KHS, 276 LOC, 277 KHS/Kentucky Geological Survey Photographs, 278 UKL, 279 The Filson Historical Society, 280 (bottom) UKL, 281 (bottom) UKL, 282 UKL, 283 LOC, 284 UKL, 285 SS/A.S. Zain, 286 Keeneland Library, 287 (bottom) Corbis, 288 National Archives, 289 LOC, 290 LOC. **Chapter Eleven:** 292-293 Louise Kelly-Parkansky, 294 National Archives, 295 (left) LOC, (right) Granger, 296 SS/Nicholas R. Elleremann, (left) AJ, 297 SS/Rhonda L. Hamm, 299 SS/June Marie Sobrito, 300 LOC, 301 LOC, 302 LOC, 303 Louisville Courier Journal and Times, 304 (top) KHS, (bottom) LOC, 305 LOC, 307 Scripps Howard Photo Service, Provided by NewsCom.com, 308 ZUMA Press, Provided by NewsCom.com, 309 ZUMA Press, Provided by NewsCom.com, 310 ZUMA Press, Provided by NewsCom.com, 311 ZUMA Press, Provided by NewsCom.com, 312 (left) Corbis, (right) Truman Presidential Museum & Library, 314 AP. **Chapter Twelve:** 316-317 AJ, 319 (top) SS/Robert J. Beyers II, (bottom), JB, 320-321 JB, 322-323 JB, 327 White House/Susan Sterner, 328 (bottom) National Park Service Digital Image Archives, 329 NA, 330-331 AJ, 332 ShutterPoint.com/David Kosmider, 334 SS/Lisa F. Young. **Chapter Thirteen:** 336-337 AP, 338 SS/GeoM, 340 GR, 342 SS/Stephen Cobum, 343 (top) SS/Edyta Pawlowsak, (bottom) SS/Johnny Lye, 344 JB, 346 LOC, 349 SS/Tiburon Studios, 350 SS/Sarah Cates, 353 AJ, 354 Jif, 355 (top left, clockwise) Laura's Lean Beef, AJ, Janis J. Hansen, SS/Steve Quincey.